CLASSICAL CIVND
ANCIENSH
SECOI

CLASSICAL CIVILISATION AND ANCIENT HISTORY IN BRITISH SECONDARY EDUCATION

ARLENE HOLMES-HENDERSON
AND EDITH HALL

LIVERPOOL UNIVERSITY PRESS

First published 2025 by
Liverpool University Press
4 Cambridge Street
Liverpool
L69 7ZU

Copyright © 2025 Arlene Holmes-Henderson and Edith Hall

Arlene Holmes-Henderson and Edith Hall have asserted the right to be identified as the authors of this book in accordance with the Copyright, Designs and Patents Act 1988.

This book is published under a Creative Commons Attribution-Non-commercial Non-derivative 4.0 International licence (CC BY-NC-ND 4.0), https://creativecommons.org/licenses/by-nc-nd/4.0/. The work is supported by the Arts and Humanities Research Council [grant number AH/V006592/1]. It is made open access with the support of UKRI. This licence allows you to share, copy, distribute and transmit the work for personal and non-commercial use provided author and publisher attribution is clearly stated. This licence does not cover any third party material in the book.

Attribution should include the following information: Holmes-Henderson. A. and Hall. E. 2025. *Classical Civilisation and Ancient History in British Secondary Education.* Liverpool: Liverpool University Press.

https://www.liverpooluniversitypress.co.uk/doi/book/10.3828/9781800856080

Further details about Creative Commons licences are available at https://creativecommons.org/licenses/

All rights reserved. No part of this book may be reproduced, stored in a retrieval system, or transmitted, in any form or by any means, electronic, mechanical, photocopying, recording, or otherwise, without the prior written permission of the publisher.

British Library Cataloguing-in-Publication data
A British Library CIP record is available

ISBN 978-1-80085-608-0 paperback
ISBN 978-1-80085-564-9 epdf
ISBN 978-1-83624-985-6 ePub

Typeset by Carnegie Book Production, Lancaster
Printed and bound by CPI Group (UK) Ltd, Croydon CR0 4YY

This book is dedicated to every teacher who has ever excited a pupil about the worlds inhabited by people who spoke Ancient Greek and Latin and their fascinating Ancient Near Eastern, Mediterranean and Black Sea neighbours.

Epigraph

The Greek and Roman authors have not become any less illuminating, stimulating, beguiling or enriching to the human spirit; and their themes still concern us. Love, death, fighting and politics have not been abolished, nor have the social scientists revealed once and for all the nature and destiny of humanity. No new means has been discovered of understanding western civilization without some study of the Greeks and Romans. Plato and Aristotle have not ceased to interest contemporary philosophers, and the relics of Greek artists and craftsmen have not ceased to astonish and enchant anyone who has bothered to look at them.

(John Sharwood Smith)

Contents

Acknowledgements		ix
About the Authors		xiii
List of Images		xv
Preface		xix
1	The Classical World in Translation: A Proud British Tradition	1
2	Reinvigorating Classical Civilisation Education in the 20th Century	33
3	Ancient History Education: Past and Present	61
4	Voices of Experience	81
5	Advocacy for State School Classics Education	109
6	Getting Started	161
7	Next Steps for Classics Education in Policy and Practice	173
Glossary		181
Appendix I: Guide to Resources		187
Appendix II: Questionnaire		195
Appendix III: OCR GCSE and A Level Content		201
Appendix IV: Regional Variations		205
Consolidated Bibliography		219
Index		233

Acknowledgements

So many individuals and institutions have helped us on this exciting journey that it seems invidious to single any out: we thank everyone who has run, spoken at or attended an event, shared information or engaged with the *Advocating Classics Education* (ACE) project online or in person. Henry Stead's quiet support has been consistent throughout. Caroline Latham spent many hours in archives and libraries locating and copying crucial documents illustrating the planning and examining of our subjects historically. Peter Swallow (now MP) has been a stalwart supporter of every aspect of the project from its inception and spent years as its hyper-efficient webmaster, tasks now taken over by Rory McInnes-Gibbons.

Our inspirational cover image was designed by Milo Palmer, then a year 8 student at Cranbrook School in Kent, after winning our nationwide competition. We cannot thank all of the more than two thousand respondents to our online survey individually, but our gratitude is profound. The distribution and collation of the questionnaires was skilfully administered by Edith's daughter Sarah Poynder, who also transcribed interviews, while her younger daughter Georgia Poynder designed our logo. We thank all the questionnaire respondents, whose observations feature in Chapter 5, especially Gemma Adams, Caron Downes, Matthew Gee, Christina Goopta, Francesca Grilli, Jo Hobbs, Laura Jenkinson, Catharine Jessop, Cheryl Juckes, Anna Karsten, Rachel Kirby, Helen Mars, Adam Mason, Nigel McFarlane, David Midgley, Becky Milne, Alex Rooke, Sian Squire, Hilary Stark and Penny Whitworth. Ben Andrews, Emma Bridges, Peter Wright, Penelope Murray and Oswyn Murray gave freely of their time and allowed us to record extended interviews.

Students and Early Career Academics who volunteered in all sorts of capacities, including the organisation of events, included Samuel Agbamu, Marcus Bell, Kitty Cooke, Caroline Latham, Nimisha Patel and Bella Watts. Our energetic patrons are Emma Bridges, Paul Cartledge, Natalie Haynes,

Charlotte Higgins, Malcolm Schofield and Greg Woolf. Amongst our fellow academics and teachers in partner institutions, those who have distinguished themselves for commitment include Susan Deacy, Matthew Fox, Jon Hesk, Phillip Horky, Peter Kruschwitz and Rosie Wyles.

Of the many others who have participated in this journey and offered invaluable support, we owe particular thanks to Eddie Barnett, Simon Beasley, Ed Bragg, Andrew Christie, James Corke-Webster, Stephen Dobson, Paul Found, Maria Haley, Chris Howard, Steven Hunt, Steven Mastin, Anna McOmish, Athina Mitropoulos, Mai Musié, Alex Orgee, Ken Pickering, Nina Rinke, Emma Stafford and Christopher Stray. Edith's husband Richard Poynder did not complain when she personally and frequently subsidised ACE merchandise and numerous other personal expenses out of the family finances.

The project has received advice and support from learned societies and professional organisations across the Classics landscape. We are particularly grateful to the Anglo-Hellenic League, the Classical Association, the Classical Association of Northern Ireland, the Classical Association of Scotland, Classics for All, the Classics Development Group, the Council of University Classical Departments, Euroclassica, the Institute for Classical Studies, the Society for the Promotion of Hellenic Studies, the Society for the Promotion of Roman Studies and the Women's Classical Committee.

The project has received funding from the Arts and Humanities Research Council, the Classical Association, Durham University, King's College London, the Society for the Promotion of Hellenic Studies and an anonymous donor. Without their support, we simply could not have advocated for Classics on a national scale. We remain extremely grateful.

Our achievements are the result of collaborative activities with like-minded people in a range of local, regional, national and international organisations. Without their input, we simply could not have achieved such a significant impact. From the beginning, we felt supported by the Association for Citizenship Teaching, the Cambridge School Classics Project, the Historical Association, the National Association for the Teaching of Drama, the National Association of Teaching of English, the National Association for Teachers of Religious Education and the Schools History Project. Examination boards Cambridge International, Eduqas, the International Baccalaureate, OCR and SQA all cooperated generously with our work.

Museum collaborators were absolutely vital in extending the reach of our work into communities. The British Museum, the Cambridge Museum of Classical Archaeology, the Durham Oriental Museum, the Great North Museum: Hancock and the Liverpool World Museum all generously contributed expertise. Videographers Half Cut Productions in Liverpool, Alan Fentiman in Gateshead and especially Mike Taylor at BigFaceArt in London helped us share our campaign with members of the public.

Finally, Clare Litt at Liverpool University Press supported the project enthusiastically from the moment we first approached her, and the two anonymous readers provided abundant generous and constructive criticism which has improved the volume enormously.

About the Authors

Arlene Holmes-Henderson

Arlene Holmes-Henderson is Professor of Classics Education and Public Policy at Durham University. She previously held positions at the University of Oxford, University of Sussex and King's College London. A former high-school teacher, Arlene investigates the learning and teaching of classical subjects in schools, universities and communities. As an expert in Classics outreach and knowledge exchange, she engages diverse stakeholders to explore ways to widen access to the study of the classical world. Her books include *Forward with Classics* (with Hunt and Musié, Bloomsbury, 2018), *Expanding Classics: Practitioner Perspectives from Museums and Schools* (Routledge, 2022), *Classics in Action* (with Jessica Dixon, Hodder 2024) and *Curriculum in a Changing World* (with Gerry Czerniawski, Sharon Jones, Richard Poutney, Victoria-Marie Pugh and Weiping Yang, Troubador 2024). Working at the intersection of research, policy and practice in both Classics and Education, Arlene collaborates closely with policymakers, school leaders, teachers, exam professionals, museum curators and educators in the UK and around the world to create better learning opportunities for young people. In 2023 she was awarded an MBE for Services to Education and in 2024 she was elected a member of Academia Europaea. In December 2024 she launched the Durham Centre for Classics Education Research and EngagementS (CERES), the first centre of its kind worldwide.[1]

Edith Hall

After teaching at the Universities of Cambridge, Reading, Oxford, Royal Holloway University of London and King's College London, with temporary appointments at Swarthmore College, Northwestern University, Leiden University and Gresham College, in 2021 Edith returned as Professor of

Classics to Durham University, where she had previously held the Leverhulme Chair in Greek Cultural History (2001–2006). She has published more than 35 books on the ancient Greek and Roman worlds and their continued presence in modernity, the most recent being *Epic of the Earth: Reading Homer's "Iliad" in the Fight for a Dying World* (Yale University Press, 2025). She regularly broadcasts on BBC radio, acts as consultant to professional theatre companies and speaks at state schools and Sixth Form colleges. She is the recipient of a Goodwin Award of Merit for *Adventures with Iphigenia in Tauris* (OUP, 2013), the Erasmus Medal of the European Academy, Honorary Citizenship of Palermo for *Introducing the Ancient Greeks* (Penguin, 2015) and *Aristotle's Way* (Penguin, 2017) and Honorary Doctorates from the Universities of Athens and Durham. She is a Fellow of the British Academy and winner of the 2023 UK Classical Association Prize.

Note

[1] https://www.durham.ac.uk/research/institutes-and-centres/durham-centre-for-classics-education-research-and-engagements/

List of Images

0.1	Discussants at event held on 27 November 2015 at King's College London to plan an intervention in the teaching of classical subjects. Photograph by Henry Stead.	xx
0.2	Logo designed by Georgia Poynder for the *Advocating Classics Education* initiative.	xxi
1.1	Frontispiece and title page to the third edition of the English translation of William Camden's *Britannia* (1753). Hall's private collection.	4
1.2	Frontispiece and title page to the English version of Francis Pomey's *The Pantheon* (1694). Hall's private collection.	7
1.3	Cover of William Stead's *Stories from Ancient Rome* (1901). Hall's private collection.	14
1.4	'The Age of Pericles', pediment by Edwin Roscoe Mullins for the Harris Museum in Preston. Photograph by Bruce Lamberton. Public Domain.	18
1.5	Stained glass window by Henry Holiday in the Harris Museum in Preston. Photograph by Edith Hall.	19
1.6	Walter Crane, 'Numa and the Nymph', illustration to F.J. Gould, *The Children's Plutarch: Tales of the Romans* (1910). Hall's private collection.	25
2.1	Christopher Stray and Edith Hall. Photograph by Jaś Elsner.	34
2.2	Photograph of Dora Pym in 1918. Photographer unknown. Hall's private collection.	39
2.3	Frontispiece and Title Page to Dora Pym's *Readings from the Literature of Ancient Greece* (1924). Hall's private collection.	40
2.4	A performance of Aristophanes' *Peace* by girls at Brierton Hill Technical High School for Girls, Hartlepool, in 1967. Photograph held at Hartlepool Museum, reproduced with the permission of its curator.	42

2.5	Photograph of John Sharwood Smith. Public Domain.	50
2.6	E.V. Rieu's bestselling translation of *The Odyssey*. Hall's private collection.	53
3.1	Cover of Moses Finley, *Ancient Slavery and Modern Ideology* (1980). Hall's private collection.	63
3.2	Drawing by Marion Cox of the inscribed statue of Udjahorresnet in the Vatican Museum, reproduced from Maria Brosius, *The Persian Empire from Cyrus II to Artaxerxes I* (*Lactor* 16), revised edition (Brosius, 2023).	65
3.3	Oswyn Murray in 2024. Photograph by Richard Poynder, reproduced with his permission.	67
3.4	Photograph of Boris Johnson outside parliament on 14 May 2007. Photographer David Sandison.	71
4.1	Photograph of Emma Bridges by Edith Hall.	94
4.2	Photograph of Peter Wright in York beside the Statue of Constantine in 2023. Reproduced with his permission.	98
4.3	Photograph of Shirley Barlow with Edith Hall in 2020, taken by Sarah Poynder and reproduced with her permission.	100
4.4	Photograph of Penny Murray in 2024 by Richard Poynder, reproduced with his permission.	102
5.1	Caroline Bristow, Arlene Holmes-Henderson, Edith Hall and Mai Musié at an outreach event at KCL on 17 June 2016. Photograph by Steven Hunt.	110
5.2	The Teachers' Panel at the official launch of ACE, KCL 1 July 2017. Photograph by Edith Hall.	110
5.3	Peter Swallow MP. Photograph reproduced with his permission.	111
5.4	Samuel Agbamu at Leeds University event. Photograph by Edith Hall.	112
5.5	Bella Watts. Photograph reproduced with her permission.	113
5.6	Nimisha Patel. Photograph reproduced with her permission.	113
5.8	Caroline Latham. Photograph reproduced with her permission.	114
5.7	Kitty Cooke. Photograph reproduced with her permission.	114
5.9	Sarah Poynder. Photograph reproduced with her permission.	115
5.10	Paul Cartledge. Photograph: public domain.	115
5.11	Natalie Haynes speaks at Redborne Upper School in Bedfordshire. Photograph by Edith Hall.	116

5.12	Charlotte Higgins at the Exeter University Event. Photograph by Arlene Holmes-Henderson.	117
5.13	Professor Greg Woolf, Leon Levy Director of the Institute for the Study of the Ancient World at NYU. Photograph by Genevieve Shiffrar.	118
5.14	Paul Found in action. Photograph by Edith Hall.	119
5.15	Attendees at Bristol University ACE event at Roman Baths. Photograph by Arlene Holmes-Henderson.	121
5.16	Marcus Bell leads the hoplite phalanx at Exeter. Photograph by Arlene Holmes-Henderson.	123
5.17	Students in the masks they had created in Belfast. Photograph by Arlene Holmes-Henderson.	124
5.18	Legio XX in Belfast. Photograph by Arlene Holmes-Henderson.	125
5.19	ACE at a Parliamentary Education Committee meeting. Photograph by Sarah Poynder.	125
5.20	Chris Pelling and Edith Hall at Swansea. Photograph by Maria Oikonomou.	127
5.21	Some of the Swansea attendees. Photograph by Edith Hall.	128
5.22	Reading planning meeting. Photograph by Amy Smith.	129
5.23	Tony Keen, Kathryn Tempest, Arlene Holmes-Henderson, Edith Hall and Andrew Wallace-Hadrill at Roehampton. Photograph by Susan Deacy.	130
5.24	Teachers' workshop at Warwick. Photograph by Arlene Holmes-Henderson.	131
5.25	Michael Scott, Arlene Holmes-Henderson and Paul Grigsby at Warwick. Photograph by Robert O'Toole.	131
5.26	Emma-Jayne Graham and Jess Hughes describing the Votives Project at the Open University. Photograph by Arlene Holmes-Henderson.	132
5.27	Henry Stead organises filming of Emma Bridges at the Open University. Photograph by Arlene Holmes-Henderson.	133
5.28	Edith Hall, Alex Orgee and Arlene Holmes-Henderson at OCR, Cambridge.	136
5.29	Attendees at Team English National Conference. Photograph by Arlene Holmes-Henderson.	138
5.30	Gemma Williams, Paul Grigsby, Edith Hall and Arlene Holmes-Henderson.	139

5.31	Pupils from Beauchamp Academy in Leicester visit the British Museum. Photograph by Lidia Kuvichak.	141
5.32	Teacher Training Summer Course at KCL. Photograph by Mike Taylor.	144
5.33	Emily Pillinger on Sappho and Vergil. Photograph by Michael Taylor.	144
5.34	Poster advertising workshop for teachers.	147
5.35	Filming with Dr Chrissy Partheni at the Liverpool World Museum. Photograph by Peter Swallow.	149
5.36	Front page of an ACE digital sourcebook featuring the Ince Athena designed by Hardeep Dhindsa. Reproduced by kind permission of Becky McLoughlin, graphic artist at Iconicus Design.	149
5.37	Celebrating ACE's move to Durham.	151
5.38	Teachers and students on ACE study visit to Hadrian's Wall. Photograph by Frances McIntosh.	153
5.39	Rory McInnes-Gibbons, Edith Hall and Arlene Holmes-Henderson filming at the Penshaw Monument. Photograph by Alan Fentiman.	154
5.40	Graph showing trends in GCSE and A Level Classical Civilisation uptake (2004–2024).	155
5.41	Graph showing trends in GCSE and A Level Ancient History uptake (2004–2024).	156
6.1	ACE Impact Map (dropped pins represent the locations of schools/colleges, stars represent partner institutions and squares in circles represent summer school participants' institutions).	161
6.2	Logo for Athena's Owls project.	168
7.1	Logo of Durham Centre for Classics Education Research and EngagementS (CERES).	173
IV.1	Graph showing trend in National 4 Classical Studies uptake (2019–2024).	211
IV.2	Graph showing trend in National 5 Classical Studies uptake (2019–2024).	213
IV.3	Graph showing trend in Higher Classical Studies uptake (2019–2024).	215
IV.4	Graph showing trend in Advanced Higher Classical Studies uptake (2019–2024).	217

Preface

This book has three aims. One is to chart the history of teaching the worlds inhabited by the ancient Greeks and Romans in the round, rather than the languages they spoke, in British secondary education. The second is to explain the content of the qualifications available in these subjects today. The third is more interventionist: we hope to enthuse readers and to support those who are currently teaching or studying Classical Civilisation or Ancient History, or who would like to do so. We are convinced that some knowledge of these fascinating past civilisations makes for better informed, critical citizens, more culturally and emotionally literate individuals, better equipped both at work and at leisure, and a happier, more enlightened world.

The concept of this book was born when we, its authors, first met in spring 2015. We shared our frustration with the state of secondary classical education in the United Kingdom. There is a problem: 93% of our teenagers attend state-maintained schools or Sixth Form colleges, where Ancient Greek and Latin qualifications are almost invariably unavailable. There is also a solution: excellent General Certificates in Secondary Education (GCSEs) and Advanced Level qualifications (A Levels) are available in Classical Civilisation and Ancient History. These provide access to the ancient Greek and Roman worlds through a rich variety of sources. These can be taught by teachers qualified in any academic subject and could therefore potentially be provided to every pupil in the land. Teachers of these subjects have often originally trained as teachers of Drama, English, History, Philosophy, Modern Languages or Religion, but others come from such disparate disciplines as Business Studies, Geography and Physics. Yet there are longstanding obstacles to introducing these subjects to educational institutions. Many people – teachers, students and their parents – either simply do not know that these qualifications exist or do not understand what they are.

What is their history and relationship to traditional curricula which stress intensive linguistic training in Latin and Ancient Greek? What is their content? What skills do they confer? And are they enjoyable? Our main aim here is simply to remove the obstacle of lack of awareness and understanding of these qualifications by providing answers to these questions and thereby encourage a nationwide expansion of their availability. But we also hope that the book will prove useful in practical ways to people who would like to see them introduced.

We decided to combine research into the history of these qualifications with a campaign to increase awareness of them and their presence across the education system. We contacted individuals we knew shared our views and invited them to a brainstorming session at King's College London, where Edith was then employed, on 27 November 2015. Participants included Prof. Richard Alston, Dr Pavlos Avlamis, Eddie Barnett, Simon Beasley, Prof. Hugh Bowden, Dr Emma Bridges, Caroline Bristow, Paul Found, Prof. Matthew Fox, Steve Hunt, Dr Aisha Khan-Evans, Prof. Helen King, Dr Mai Musié, Ken Pickering, Prof. Mike Trapp and Dr Henry Stead, with whom Edith was collaborating on an allied project, Classics and Class (C&C), that had documented historical working-class access to the ancient Greeks and Romans [fig. 0.1].[1] There were teachers from a variety of schools and colleges, academics from Higher Education Institutions (HEIs), representatives from Classics charities and assessment professionals from examination boards. We decided to form a collaborative network to share information on our activities across the four nations and to attempt to get funding to kickstart it.

The breakthrough came when in early 2017 Edith was awarded an Arts and Humanities Research Council (AHRC) Leadership grant for nearly £250,000 to fund activities on which she and Arlene could collaborate. The award of this grant was the first serious sign that Britons at the highest institutional level care about Classical Civilisation qualifications, historically seen as the poor relation of the ancient languages.

The project was entitled *Studying Classical Civilisation in Britain: Recording the Past and Fostering the Future*. We chose the abbreviated acronym *ACE*, short for *Advocating Classics Education*, and commissioned a logo from Edith's youngest daughter, Georgia Poynder, then a year 9 student at a comprehensive

0.1 Discussants at event held on 27 November 2015 at King's College London to plan an intervention in the teaching of classical subjects. Photograph by Henry Stead.

school offering no classical subjects at all. We wanted to fuse an ancient Greek image – a green leaf of the vine, Dionysus' plant, to denote antiquity, flourishing and growth – with the metaphor of an 'Ace' in a pack of cards, a symbol of success [fig. 0.2].

The main academic output specified in the AHRC application was this book. Because the documentation is extensive and diverse, the research underlying it has taken years. Chapter 1 offers an overview of the longstanding British enjoyment of the classical worlds through translated texts, performed entertainment and material culture. Chapters 2 and 3 focus on the origins, implementation and continuing development of courses in Classical Civilisation and Ancient History respectively. For these, we consulted parliamentary papers, debates in both the House of Commons and the House of Lords on Hansard, minutes of the meetings of many organisations including the London Association of Classical Teachers, the Joint Association of Classical Teachers and the Classical Association. Edith's former PhD student, Dr Caroline Latham, meticulously trawled through archives of examination boards. Curriculum policy documentation, exam papers and published guides and handbooks for teachers provided illumination, along with seminal publications such as the journals *Didaskalos*, *Hesperiam* and the *Journal of Classics Teaching*.

0.2 Logo designed by Georgia Poynder for the *Advocating Classics Education* initiative.

We circulated a questionnaire amongst diverse people who have taught or studied classical subjects in schools since the late 1960s; the results are presented in Chapter 4, along with parts of transcripts of interviews with some particularly significant participants in the emergence of the qualifications. We also ran a survey via the platform of our project website, to which we had more than two thousand responses, adeptly collated by Sarah Poynder. Multiple-choice questions revealed that many respondents had experienced early encounters with antiquity through books (75%) or at primary school (53%), though family trips to museums (56%) and watching TV/films (36%) provided childhood exposure for some. Unsurprisingly, most respondents chose to study a classical option because they found the subject interesting (77%), but considerable numbers said their choice was also influenced by their liking for the teacher (28%) and/or their achievement of good results in the subject (26%). Asked if classical studies affected life decisions, respondents identified university subject choice (73%) and holiday destinations (60%) as examples.

But the campaigning component of our project entailed setting up partnerships with 15 institutions across the UK's four nations, where colleagues would engage with schools across their region to draw attention to the advantages of Classical Civilisation and Ancient History, and support their introduction across a growing network of diverse educational settings. Saddened by the lack of detailed accounts and photographs of the seminal meetings and events that took place in the 1960s and 1970s at the dawn of the democratisation of Classics education that we describe in Chapters 1 to 3, in Chapter 5 we provide a record of some of the exciting initiatives that took place 'on the ground' all over the four nations during the first years of ACE's activities as it built up a network of grassroots partnerships, in case it is of interest to those who are motivated to help grow such educational opportunities in the future.

Chapter 6 provides practical advice, based on our experience of working with schools intensively over the last decade, to school leaders, teachers, parents and students, on how to boost provision and widen access to the study of classical subjects. Aware of the need to identify solutions to current barriers in schools and society, we provide in Chapter 7, 'Next Steps', a list of ten recommendations which we hope will shape the directions in which future policies move. The four appendices offer a guide to resources available to those interested in learning more about or introducing courses in Classical Civilisation or Ancient History, the questionnaire that we circulated to former and current students and teachers, the contents of the OCR syllabus at GCSE and A Level and an analysis of the variations in the Classics education landscape across the four nations and Ireland respectively.

We are enormously grateful to everyone in the international classics community who has helped us on this deeply collaborative journey. While the entire book has been co-researched and co-authored by both of us, Edith Hall wrote the preliminary drafts of Chapters 1, 2 and 4, while Arlene Holmes-Henderson wrote them for all the other chapters and appendices. Thanks to funding from UK Research and Innovation (UKRI), this work has been made fully Open Access from its original publication date.

Note

[1] See further https://www.classicsandclass.info/.

CHAPTER 1

The Classical World in Translation: A Proud British Tradition

Introduction

In 1977 a Classics teacher named Eira Lewis, who worked at Cathays High School, Cardiff, expressed her surprise at the 'reviving injection' received by her classrooms in the form of the introduction of Classical Studies. Just ten years previously her school had been a Grammar School (i.e. one of the schools in the top tier as defined by the selective tripartite system comprising grammar schools, secondary modern schools and secondary technical schools, brought in after the Education Act 1944). Her teaching had consisted solely of the Latin language, from an almost exclusively linguistic perspective. Yet, in 1967, her school, along with hundreds of others, had begun the process of transformation into a comprehensive. Christopher Stray has documented in invaluable detail the challenges this development presented at the time, using schools in Swansea as a case study.[1] This historic change in secondary education followed the victory of the Labour Party in the 1964 general election and the inauguration of a comprehensive secondary system.

Lewis admitted that she had been apprehensive about what the transformation would mean for Classics education, both in her exclusive and previously girls-only institution and across the national school system. But a decade later her tone is one of delighted surprise. What she calls 'Non-Linguistic Classical Studies' have required her to develop 'fresh concepts of what our subject is'[2] and have proved successful with much larger classes, containing pupils, boys and girls, from across a far wider social spectrum (Cathays is an inner-city school). She describes in rather romantic terms the new model student to whom the ancient world appeals:

> For the young adolescent the appeal can be easily understood. He is often by nature impatient with what he feels is familiar. He has yearnings, he dreams dreams and creates heroes... He is still partly a

child with a love of a good story, unsophisticated enough to enjoy the supernatural, the brutal, the satisfying meting out of justice. He finds pleasure in looking at a world whose shapes and sounds are different from his own and whose very distance makes it both enchanting and comprehensible. Introduced to the older child, Classical Studies has tapped a hitherto unrevealed, or at least, unsatisfied, interest in the ancient world.[3]

She has discovered that the new approach to teaching the ancient world is not 'easier', but it is different, more inclusive and 'does provide far greater variety and does make room for many boys and girls with lively and enquiring minds'; when the course is finished, 'their memory of the Romans is of a people who thought, acted and felt in ways recognisable to the child'.

In due course Eira Lewis retired, and died in 2014, sadly too early for us to ask her for more examples of her experience of teaching Classical Studies to her comprehensive pupils in inner-city Cardiff. She was not the first to have undergone this experience; the new approach had a specific history in curriculum design that went back to the early 1950s, as we shall see in the next chapter. But the praise she bestowed on this new way of studying classical antiquity was far from unprecedented. British people had benefitted from thinking about the fascinating materials comprising Classical Civilisation and Ancient History for a very long time indeed.

'Classics' today often denotes any iconic, archetypal or ideal example of a thing – vintage cars can be 'classics', as can pop songs, novels or recipes. But we understand the term to refer to the cultural output specifically of the inhabitants of the ancient Greek and Roman worlds in interaction with their neighbours in Egypt, Asia, the Black Sea World, the Balkans and across the Roman Empire. This is what the term means in this book and in educational contexts today. 'Classical Civilisation' and 'Ancient History' do not mean just the written texts of the ancient Greeks and Romans, but their entire cultures, including architecture and archaeology; in this we take our cue from the injunction of Gilbert Murray, the famous early 20th-century Regius Professor of Greek at Oxford, that it is ancient Greece, not ancient Greek, that should be the primary object of the Greek scholar's enquiries.[4]

Early Days

The choice of starting point for any history of engagement with antiquity is necessarily arbitrary. In Britain, we could date the acquaintance of people outside narrow academic circles with the ancient Greeks and Romans at least as far back as the portraits of Vergilian and Ovidian women in Geoffrey Chaucer's *The Legend of Good Women* and the classical love stories, mostly derived from Ovid, in John Gower's late 14th-century English-language *Confessio Amantis*. Another landmark was the first printed edition of an English-language version of Aesop's *Fables*, with spectacular woodcuts, by William Caxton in 1484. Many ancient prose writers were already available in the English language by the end of the 16th century: Xenophon's *Oeconomicus*, a book on household management, by 1532; the now neglected Herodian's history of the Roman Empire by 1550; the Stoic philosopher Epictetus by 1567; the Greek historian Polybius by 1568; Demosthenes' orations known as the *Olynthiacs* by 1570; Aelian's works on animals and his miscellany of anecdotes by 1576; half of Appian's Roman history by 1578; and the first two books of Herodotus on the Persian Wars by 1584.

The groundlings of the Elizabethan London theatres were already enthralled by the plays on themes taken from ancient history as soon as the dramatists had read Plutarch's biographies in Sir Thomas North's English translation of Plutarch's *Lives of the Noble Greeks and Romans*, for example in Shakespeare's *Julius Caesar* (1599). But the epochal event that first transformed Britons' picture of their own history, revealing to them that pre-Christian classical civilisation 'belonged' to them as much as to their neighbours on the European continent, occurred in 1610. This was the year of the publication of the English translation of William Camden's spectacular *Britannia*, printed in Latin twenty-four years previously.

Camden was a London schoolmaster, but he had taken four years out to travel and conduct research across the Roman province of Britannia, transcribing and translating Latin inscriptions, surveying monuments and commissioning engravings of coins. The English translation was by another schoolmaster, the prolific classical scholar Philemon Holland.[5] Holland's vivid translations into English of the Roman historians Livy and Suetonius were still being reprinted as standard texts for reading in schools until the 1920s, and have been used as such long thereafter.[6]

Camden's *Britannia* [fig. 1.1] had an incalculable effect not only on the writing of history but also on the national self-image. One of his greatest achievements resulted from his immersion in classical sources. He was the first scholar ever to assemble almost everything that the ancient Greeks and Romans had said about Britain. His stated aim was to 'restore Britain to Antiquity, and Antiquity to Britain'.[7]

Once the Jacobeans had digested Camden's book, they realised that Jesus Christ had been born in the reign of Augustus, whose stepfather Julius Caesar

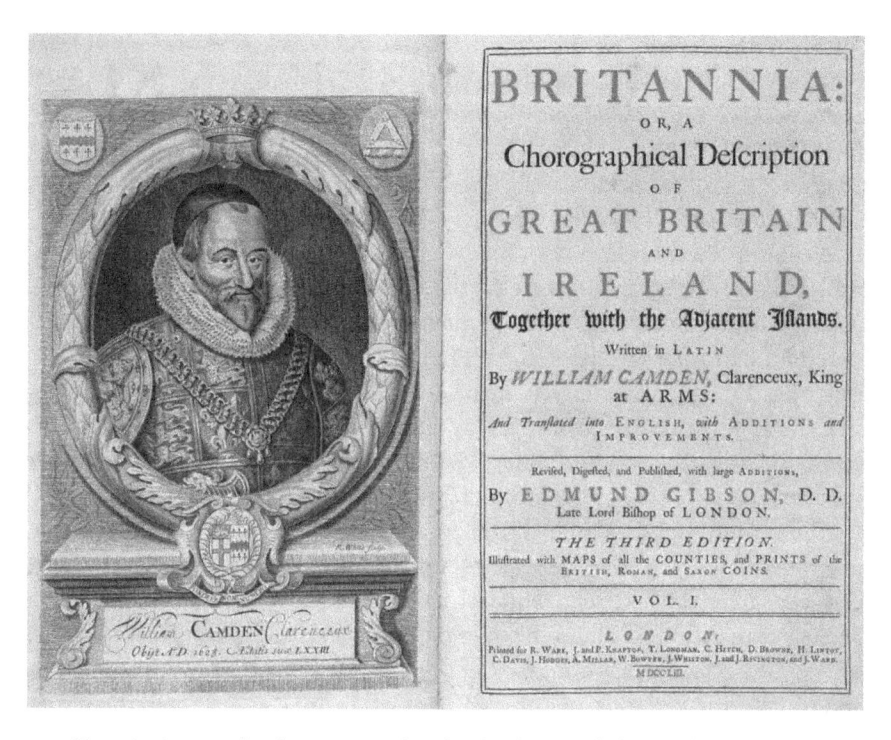

1.1 Frontispiece and title page to the third edition of the English translation of William Camden's *Britannia* (1753). Hall's private collection.

had made earlier Roman incursions into Britain. Already in 1603, when King James came to the throne, he began to project an image of himself as being like the ancient Roman Emperor Augustus, who, after a long period of civil war, brought Rome to peace, unity and an expanding empire.

During the 17th century, English-language translations of the Greek historians, Aristotle's *Politics*, Cicero and Tacitus repeatedly informed the acrimonious political debates between Parliamentarians and Royalists;[8] Lucretius' Epicurean epic *On the Nature of Things* grew in popularity, at a time when Christianity was under unprecedented examination, through John Evelyn's verse translation;[9] plays on classical themes and those which adapted stories from Greek and Roman sources flourished both before the Long Parliament closed the theatres in 1642 (for example, in Ben Jonson's *Catiline his Conspiracy* and *Sejanus his Fall*), and after the Restoration of the Monarchy in 1660. Elkanah Settle's Restoration drama *Cambyses* (1667) could not have been written without the sensational Herodotean account of the deranged Persian monarch's life in book III of his *Histories*, accessed via Barnaby Rich's 1584 English translation.[10]

Greek and Roman works with functional information about practical topics were among the first to be translated. Oppian's useful *Halieutica* ('Fishing Matters') was translated into English in 1722, considerably before Floyer Sydenham and Thomas Taylor first Anglicised most of Plato.[11] More British people seem to have wanted help with catching fish than with philosophical conundrums! Extended excerpts and paraphrases from the ancient treatises and polemics by Lucian, Choricius and Libanius, describing ancient pantomime performances (i.e. serious, balletic realisations of the myths associated with tragedy), began to appear in handbooks on the history of dance at the precise moment when they were needed: that is, the invention of ballet as an elevated, independent art-form at the turn of the 18th century.[12] Or take Artemidorus of Daldis' treatise *On the Interpretation of Dreams*, which so fascinated Sigmund Freud. This manual had been translated into English by 1606 and into Welsh before the end of the 17th century. Presumably this reflected a real interest in Artemidorus' diagnosis of dreams, rather than in his somewhat clunky prose style. Moreover, even the casual reader of Artemidorus in English, consulting him in order to analyse a recent dream, will have picked up a considerable amount of educational information about domestic and civic life in the eastern provinces of the Roman Empire. But the *educational* study of 'classical civilisation' and 'ancient history' in forms that are recognisable ancestors of the secondary-level academic qualifications available in Britain today was not inaugurated until the precise period, sometime after the Restoration, at which 'Classics', broadly defined, was invented as a pedagogical discipline.

The Invention of a Classical Education

There had of course been precursors of the curriculum suggested by the term Classics, notably the list of Christian books supplemented by pagan authors constituting the *Ratio atque Institutio Studiorum Societatis Iesu*. This was designed by Jesuits in Rome in 1599 and exported across the planet by the Society of Jesus' missionaries.[13] But the anti-Jesuit paranoia after the Gunpowder Plot of 1605 had helped to prevent any such systematised set of recommended texts taking hold in the British Isles.

Classics emerged in England (after 1707 'Britain') as a distinct curriculum under that name, comprising the study of the Latin and Greek authors in their original languages with complementary publications relating to 'classical' history, civilisations, myth, geography, artefacts and 'antiquities', between the 1670s and about 1715. This was partly in response to the famous French series of editions *Ad Usum Delphini* originally designed for Louis de France, 'Le Grand Dauphin' (1661–1711), the eldest son of Louis XIV. But, in Britain, the invention of Classics took place in a different social context, where the power of the monarchy had been curtailed by the Bill of Rights in 1689, and the power of the nobility was being challenged by an ambitious mercantile middle class.

It was in 1684 that the term 'the Classics' first occurs meaning ancient authors, certainly including Greek ones, as studied by well-to-do junior males. That year an English translation of Eutropius' epitome of Roman history was published, and its authorship credited by the schoolmaster editor, John Dryden's correspondent Lewis Maidwell (1684), to 'several young gentlemen privately educated in Hatton-Garden'; Hatton Garden was a new residential development off Holborn, with splendid houses.

It is no coincidence that this 1684 translation was published the year after an edition of Eutropius had come out, the work of a young French prodigy, Mademoiselle Anne Le Fèvre, the daughter of a celebrated Protestant academician in Saumur; she is better known by her married name, Madame Dacier.[14] Her Eutropius was one of the early volumes in that Paris-published 'Delphin' series, which was destined to transform educational practice and intellectual life across Europe.[15] The series was not intended for the Dauphin alone. The editor, the Duke of Montausier, recommended to the King that the editions be published so that his subjects could *all* share in the education enjoyed by royalty (illiterate French peasants do not seem to have registered in Montausier's thoughts!); Louis agreed, decreeing that the volumes were all to be published, for the good of the French public and 'all the world'.[16] Eminent intellectuals lavished praise on the initiative. The polymath Gottfried Wilhelm Leibniz saw an opportunity to attack modernising reforms in education, inspired by René Descartes' rationalist philosophy, which emphasised science. Leibniz declared the series would 'revivify the nearly extinguished light of antiquity, and then give the best authors a third life, as after the course of barely one century, contempt for them has revived'.[17] At the Royal Society in London, its first Secretary, Henry Oldenburg, predicted that the series would achieve lasting celebrity, since it reconciled young men, put off by the difficulty of ancient texts, to liberal studies once again.[18]

The books soon arrived in England, to play their role in the invention of traditional 'Classics'. But, importantly, publishers also commissioned translations into English of the Delphin authors, correctly assuming that the

1.2 Frontispiece and title page to the English version of Francis Pomey's *The Pantheon* (1694). Hall's private collection.

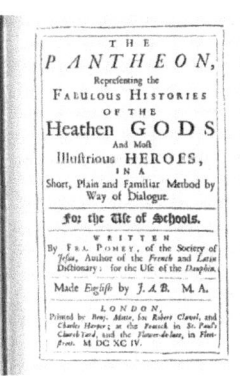

youths reading these texts at school just might want some help in construing them. In 1714, the entrepreneurial Smithfield printer and bookseller John Nicholson, having already profited from several Classics books including a new, expanded 1706 edition of John Potter's popular *Archaeologiae Graecae: or, the Antiquities of Greece*, and synoptic English translations of moral essays by Seneca and Plutarch,[19] published an anonymous translation he had commissioned of Florus, almost certainly inspired by Anne Dacier's renowned 1674 Delphin edition. There were hundreds of other translations of this kind published between about 1705 and the 1740s, often by one or more anonymous and now unidentifiable scholars, some of whom are likely to have been women.[20] The schoolboy's and undergraduate's 'crib' was born. There are far *more* English translations of classical authors than of the Delphin editions or any other untranslated ancient texts in the catalogue of books auctioned in 1729 that had belonged to the prematurely deceased Mr Lusher, of Pembroke College, Oxford.[21]

It was discovered that, by reading in English translation, it was possible to gain a much broader grasp of classical culture. All of Tacitus could be digested in the time it took to read a few chapters in Latin; seven ancient plays could be read in the time it took to construe 70 lines of a Roman comedy or Greek tragedy. The new possibilities that translated classics had introduced directly stimulated a demand for teaching materials that put texts and authors into social or historical context, or explained the religious beliefs underlying them, or visually illustrated the ancient theatres, palaces and marketplaces where ancient life was physically experienced. The new plethora of English translations was instrumental in the invention of studies in Classical Civilisation and Ancient History, which in turn vastly improved the quality of the education offered by ancient texts, whether read in English or in an ancient language.

One of the most famous textbooks was the English edition of the French Jesuit François Pomey's *The Pantheon*, which had gone through no fewer than 32 reprints in London by 1810 [fig. 1.2]. The striking illustrations accompany succinct descriptions of classical gods between a teacher and his inquisitive pupil. Other new books to help in the contextual study of the Classics were already being published in the 1690s. In 1695, Basil Kennet published his *Romanae Antiquae Notitia, or, The Antiquities of Rome*, which, he tells us in the Preface, offered information, 'gather'd from the Classicks and other Writers',[22] on Roman religion, festivals, politics, warfare, education and erudition, 'with copper cuts of the principal buildings' and a fold-out map. This was followed swiftly by John Potter's 1697 *Archaeologiae Graecae: or, the Antiquities of Greece*,[23] and, in 1700, by Pierre Danet's *A Complete Dictionary of the Greek and Roman Antiquities Explaining the Obscure Places in Classic Authors and Ancient Historians*.[24] These new publications, which filtered to the general public via the flourishing second-hand book market, began to have an impact beyond formal educational contexts on a wider readership, including working-class autodidacts and women, who were excluded from access to training in the ancient languages.[25]

The Great Age of English Translation: Realms of Gold

The excitement that reading Classics in translation can evoke was memorably defined by the Greekless Keats in his rightly famous sonnet 'On First Looking into Chapman's Homer' (1816). This is a poem usually brought to the general public's attention when some stunning new astronomical discovery is made, and yet it is actually an expression of the psychological experience of an English-speaking person reading an ancient author in English.[26] Keats has been infected by the personal feeling of the Hertfordshire-born George Chapman that he had actually been inspired by the soul of Homer when he published his English-language *Odyssey* in 1615: in the epistle to the Earl of Somerset with which he introduced it, he promised his patron no less a gift than 'Homer, three thousand yeares dead, now reviv'd'.[27]

It is appropriate to quote the first eight lines of Keats' sonnet, precisely because it is such an intense and intellectually engaged celebration of the very way of accessing the classics that is offered by modern courses in Classical Civilisation, and it can therefore serve as a manifesto for every person about to open an electronic text or a paperback translation of any classical author in the hope that it will 'speak out loud and bold' across the centuries:

> Much have I travell'd in the realms of gold,
> And many goodly states and kingdoms seen;
> Round many western islands have I been
> Which bards in fealty to Apollo hold.
> Oft of one wide expanse had I been told
> That deep-brow'd Homer ruled as his demesne;
> Yet did I never breathe its pure serene
> Till I heard Chapman speak out loud and bold.[28]

But the availability of classical authors in translation had not really taken off until a lifetime after Chapman's Homer. It was in the wake of the first Poet Laureate John Dryden's bestselling translation of Vergil into smooth and sonorous couplets (1697), the publication of which was a national event, that the 18th century soon became the golden age of English versions of Greek and Latin authors. This development was not greeted with universal enthusiasm by the elite, especially when fairground showmen started adapting bits of the *Aeneid* into colloquial English rhyming couplets to entertain audiences at the London fairs.[29] Translations were criticised both by those who had paid large sums to educate their sons in the ancient languages and by prudish Christians who were horrified when the racier passages of Ovid or Martial became accessible in English: a vehement controversy between advocates of reading in translation or the ancient texts themselves is demonstrated in many polemics of this era.[30]

So are altercations between proponents of literal and free translation of classical authors, informed by Dryden's famous 'Preface' to the 1680 translation of Ovid's *Epistles*.[31] The wittiest supporter of paraphrase was Aaron Hill, who wrote in 1709 that he wholeheartedly respects 'the Classics', but that

> Literal Translation *commonly appears* Confin'd, Uneasy, Close *and* Aukward, *like a* Streght-Lac'd Lady *in her* New Made Stays, *but when* the Version *has put on an* Easy Paraphrase, *and the* Fine Lady *is completely* Dres'd, *with* Ribbons, Manteau, *and her* Looser Ornaments, *tho' they are* still *the* same, *they were before, they brightly double* Former Graces, *and become* Adorn'd *with an* Attractive Majesty.[32]

The Delphin series, despite expurgating all passages regarded as too obscene for the young Dauphin, was an important stimulant to these debates and the whole publishing sector.

Pope's translations of Homer's *Iliad* (1715–1720) and *Odyssey* (1725) proved transformative in bringing a canonical ancient author to a much larger audience than ever before; readers now included literate workers and women who had never had the opportunity to learn Greek. Take Esther Easton, a Jedburgh gardener's wife, visited by the poet Robert Burns in 1787. He recorded that she was a very remarkable woman 'for reciting poetry of all kinds ... she can repeat by heart almost everything she has ever read, particularly Pope's "Homer" from end to end ... and, in short, is a woman of very extraordinary abilities'.[33] Pope's Homer captured the childhood imagination of another Scot, Hugh Miller. This stonemason and autodidact grew up to become a world-famous geologist. Even as a boy he saw the *Iliad* as incomparable literature. He wrote in *My Schools and Schoolmasters* (1854) that he had learned early 'that no other writer could cast a javelin with half the force of Homer. The missiles went whizzing athwart his pages; and I could see the momentary gleam of the steel, ere it buried itself deep in brass and bull-hide'.[34]

In his fine study of the reading culture of the British working class, Jonathan Rose has drawn attention to the extraordinary excitement that many individual autodidacts in the 18th to 20th centuries experienced when they began to read certain of the Greek and Latin classics (often Homer) in translation – the thrill of life-changing imaginative discovery. The Labour MP Will Crooks, who grew up in poverty in the East End of Victorian London, was dazzled by a two-penny second-hand *Iliad* (probably Pope's): 'Pictures of romance and beauty I had never dreamed of suddenly opened up before my eyes. I was transported from the East End to an enchanted land.'[35]

Pope's version was crucial in widening access to Homer, not because it was written for poorer people, but because it was such a commercial success that it quickly filtered down to the bustling second-hand book market. As Penelope Wilson has noted, by 1790, Pope's *Iliad* had been through 27 editions, and the *Odyssey* 33.[36] This encouraged dozens of other ventures in translating ancient authors over the 18th and 19th centuries. For Wilson, the defining characteristic of these vernacular classics was their 'commitment to the broadest possible spectrum of "literary" readers; collectively they ensured the continuing awareness and prestige of ancient texts in what was in many ways an aggressively modern world'.[37] In a comparable way to the collateral beneficence of the BBC's 'Third Programme', which aimed to deliver a high-brow cultural experience to a higher class of listener, but was in its early years often accessed by culturally undernourished but engaged poorer listeners, these translations, printed in increasing numbers, reached constituencies that Homer and Vergil had never seen before via market stalls and hawkers' baskets.[38]

Publishing Ventures

If the 18th century was the great age of translation from the classics, the 19th century saw a flood of cheap mass-market publications that gave tens of thousands of Britons access to, amongst other things, accounts of ancient Greek and Roman culture.[39] There are several heroic publishers who contributed to this development. The first was George Miller (1771–1835), a Dunbar philanthropist bent on social reform via mass self-education.[40] In 1795, Miller invested in East Lothian's first printing press at Haddington, a town with a reputation for an educationally advanced population. The region boasted a couple of libraries, but according to Miller they were of no use to the public because the books were written in Hebrew, Greek and Latin.[41]

Miller's *Cheap Tracts*, which abound in classical material, were inexpensively printed pamphlets containing literature chosen for its instructional, moral and literary qualities. There are features on ancient pastimes, Achilles, Alexander the Great, Aesop, Caesar and Pompey, Antigonus, Plato, Socrates and Alcibiades.[42] Miller also bought and sold diverse new and used texts in local auctions, often under the banner of BARGAIN or POPULAR BOOKS. His 'popular books' included Charles Rollin's evergreen *Ancient History*, Ovid's *Metamorphoses* translated by George Sandys (first published in full in 1626), Gibbon's *History of Rome* and James Banister's translations of Pindar's *Odes* (1791).

Also in Scotland, the trailblazing publisher of popular periodicals, William Chambers, who had been raised in Peebles in the Borders, in 1832 wrote the inaugural editorial for his soon-to-be-famous weekly *Chambers's Edinburgh Journal*, often just called *Chambers's Magazine*.[43] When his younger brother Robert, a contributor, agreed to become joint editor, the magazine became a national institution. William defined his 'grand leading principle' as taking 'advantage of the universal appetite for instruction which at present exists'. His imagined reader is 'the poorest labourer in the country' or the schoolboy 'able to purchase with his pocket-money, something permanently useful – something calculated to influence his fate through life.'[44]

William planned to improve the educational quality of reading material that less advantaged children could afford and enjoy:

> I intend to do a great deal for boys .... I was many years the worst scholar in the whole school ... often did I think that mankind had entered into a conspiracy to torment boys with Latin. My distaste of this language drove me from the perusal of every kind of books, and I was near turning out an ignorant blockhead.[45]

Chambers' aversion to Latin, however, by no means extended to classical civilisation. In just the first few months, topics included 'Ancient Pottery'; 'Grecian Monuments'; 'Grecian Philosophers and Christianity compared'; 'Romans'; 'Pompeii and Herculaneum'; 'Athens and Sparta'; and 'A Roman City–Pompeii' (adapted from a Society for the Diffusion of Useful Knowledge publication in the series *Library of Entertaining Knowledge*).[46] Chiming with contemporary taste for antiquarianism and the Pompeii-mania, the renewal of open-air excavations at Herculaneum in 1828, material culture and archaeology predominate, while Greek philosophy takes part in an instructive discussion on Christianity.[47]

But it was the Mancunian John Cassell (1817–1865) who brought education in classical civilisation and ancient history to an unprecedentedly large readership. He ventured into the world of educational publishing, 'for the purpose', as he wrote in May 1851, 'of issuing a series of publications ... calculated to advance the moral and social well-being of the working classes'.[48]

In 1852, Cassell launched his famous *Popular Educator*, which was rich in articles on the ancient world and immediately became the staple reading of autodidacts and their children. They included the future Prime Minister David Lloyd George,[49] and a workhouse boy who later became Oxford Professor of Comparative Philology, Joseph Wright.

Henry Bohn (1796–1884) made an even deeper contribution to the availability of an education in Classics. He pioneered the provision of translated literature to the Victorian mass market, thus proving instrumental in the democratisation of reading. 'Bohn's Classical Library' (established in 1848), consisted of 79 titles,[50] which amounted to 116 volumes, each bound in durable dark-blue cloth boards ingeniously treated to resemble leather, with gilt titles on the spine and embossed with a luxurious pattern. The series was designed to provide what it termed 'literal translations' of Greek and Roman classics. The 1840s–1850s therefore saw a departure from the earlier model of fluent 'Englished' texts. The Classical Library, ran the advertising copy, would 'comprise faithful English translations of the principal Greek and Latin Classics'. These volumes were enticingly cheap (between three and five shillings), but their uniformly ornate aesthetic made them desirable to collect. Their popularity endured several decades. In 1924, Edward Bell (who had taken Bohn's over) was still claiming annual sales of over 100,000 volumes.[51] No library was complete without blocks of Bohn's dappled blue and gold on their shelves. One obituary relates how the British Library had to remove Bohn's books from the reading room because they quickly 'became so mutilated by students who were not content with reading them during the hours at which that institution was open'.[52] We do not know whether readers were smuggling them away, or tearing parts out. But they appealed widely and were abundantly useful.

Classical literature thus began to arrive in many homes of the British middle and working classes.[53] Cheaper than Cassell's National Library were the thin wire-stapled and intentionally ephemeral volumes of W.T. (William Thomas) Stead's 'Masterpiece Library'. Stead (1849–1912) brought out weekly pamphlets.[54] They sold for one penny. And sell they did, 11.5 million copies in a year.[55] His first issue was a Penny Poets version of Thomas Babington Macaulay's *Lays of Ancient Rome* (1895), which sold 200,000 copies in four months. As Lockwood has noted, the 'fairly austere classicism' of Macaulay's *Lays* was a conscious choice by which Stead created the maximum 'clash' between the lofty content and its cheap medium, complete with advertisements for cocoa and tonics for various ailments.[56] But he also published versions of classical works specifically for children.[57]

The 'Books for the Bairns' series launched in March 1896 with *Aesop's Fables*. The son of an under-employed iron foundry worker and later an iron-moulder himself, Joseph Stamper (born in 1886), recalls reading Stead's pamphlets as a child in St Helens, Lancashire. Stamper disliked school. 'Every day I came out … with the feelings of a prisoner released after a long "stretch".'[58] But he was enchanted by the tales from ancient Greece and Rome. He discovered them in Stead's 'Books for the Bairns', which 'had a pink cover and contained selections from the ancient classics: stories from Homer, the writings of Pliny the younger [i.e. the *Epistles*], Aesop's "Fables" [Books for the Bairns Nos. 1 & 26]. I took a strong fancy to Aesop, he was a Greek slave from Samos, in the sixth century BC, and workpeople were only just beginning to be called "wage slaves".'[59]

Of the titles issued between March 1896 and June 1920, ten were from classical sources: *Aesop's Fables* [1]; *Aesop's Fables Pt 2* [26]; *The Labours of Hercules* [27]; *The Story of Perseus and the Gorgon's Head* [30]; *Stories from Ancient Rome* [64] [fig. 1.3]; *Some Fairy Tales of the Ancient Greeks* [99]; *The Quest of the Golden Fleece* [101]; *Stories of the Persian Kings* [152]; *Stories of the Greek Tyrants* [210]; and *The Quest of Orpheus* [235]. *Stories from Ancient Rome* [64], issued in May 1901, was as usual lavishly illustrated, with prints on almost every page. The writing is divided into two thin columns, summarising tales from Vergil's *Aeneid* and Livy's *History of Rome from its Foundation* (*Ab Urbe Condita*).[60]

Stead encouraged other cheap publishing endeavours, lauding the 1901 launch of Grant Richards' 'World's Classics' series: 'A publisher has arisen who has had the courage to attempt to bring out at one shilling books fit to stand on any library shelf containing complete editions of the very best work

1.3 Cover of William Stead's *Stories from Ancient Rome* (1901). Hall's private collection.

to be found in the literature of the world.'[61] Richards was forced to sell his series to OUP, in 1906, because his firm had insufficient capital investment to cope with the demand, and an ambitious move to large central London premises put an intolerable strain on its finances. But before he was rendered bankrupt, Richards had published Pope's *Odyssey* (1903) and Dryden's Vergil, including the *Aeneid, Georgics* and *Eclogues*.[62] The quality of these shilling books is remarkable. They are a rich navy blue octodecimo with gilt titles and gilt patterned spines, somewhat resembling Bohn's duodecimo volumes. Cheap but looking expensive, they were also portable. They could be read out of doors, or on a train, but were small enough to shelve even in a cramped household.

While Richards' 'World's Classics; or, bound books for the million' was pioneering, and its afterlives at OUP (1906 to present) and George Allen (between 1907 and 1912) contributed significantly to educational publishing, Joseph Malaby Dent's 'Everyman's Library', however, launched in 1906, took cheap-reprint publishing and cross-class access to the Greek and Roman

Classics to another level. Everyman's Library printed 1,000 titles in its first 50 years. 46 titles are listed as 'classical' in genre; they include most standard works of Greek and Roman philosophy, poetry and prose, from Marcus Aurelius' *Meditations* (the first classical text released), and the oratory of Demosthenes, the dramatic works of Aeschylus, Sophocles, Euripides and Aristophanes, to the epics of Homer and Vergil. The three-volume Plutarch's *Lives* were sold as 'biography', but his *Moralia* as 'classical'. Josephus (1 volume), Livy (6 volumes) and Tacitus (2 volumes) appear in the 'History' category, alongside the 12-volume Grote's *History of Greece* (1906), which had always been popular amongst working-class readers on account of its pioneering defence of Athenian democracy,[63] the six-volume Gibbon's *Roman Empire* and Charles Merivale's single-volume *History of Rome* (1912).

The classical genre also includes Winifred Margaret Lambart Hutchinson's three-volume *The Muses' Pageant: Myths & Legends of Ancient Greece* (1912, 1914), a 'patchwork' narrative of Greek myths which aimed 'to give a bird's-eye view, so to speak, of the "realms of gold"',[64] and became one of the century's most widely read works on classical mythology. Hutchinson (born 1868), an associate of Newnham College, Cambridge, authored *Aeacus, a Judge of the Underworld* (1901) and *The Golden Porch* (1909, 'a book of Greek fairy tales' for children), *The Sunset of the Heroes: Last Adventures of the Takers of Troy* (1911), *Evergreen Stories* (1920), and *Orpheus and his Lute* (1931); she revised William Melmoth's 18th-century translation of Pliny's *Letters* (1921–1927). In 1909, she edited five books of Cicero's *On the Ends of Good and Evil* (1909).

Material Culture

Since even rudimentary education for children under ten did not become completely compulsory until the Elementary Education Act 1880, even personal study of antiquity in modern translations would have been beyond the reach of the sizeable proportion of the British population who, at least until the late 19th century, had difficulty reading a text of more than a few pages in extent.[65] The way we think about literacy was changed, however, by Richard Hoggart's *The Uses of Literacy* (1957), which includes, under the heading of working-class literacy, activities quite other than the reading of continuous printed texts – the consumption of entertainments and culture via theatre, cinema, radio, television, pictures in magazines and advertisements. Peter Burke has explored a range of ways in which we can use visual culture as a historical source.[66] These scholars would have approved of Sian Lewis' reminder that the slaves of ancient Greece poured their masters' wine from vases decorated with mythical, ritual and domestic scenes; since vase-paintings were 'an open form of communication, available to every gaze', their meanings were construed in the minds of slaves as well as those of free people.[67] Similarly, the meanings of many hundreds of such vases on display in British collections have always been construed in the minds of viewers, whether literate or not.

This was well understood by Henry Brougham, the Whig politician committed to extending education, who had masterminded the foundation of the Society for the Diffusion of Useful Knowledge (SDUK).[68] The publications initiated by the Society offered visual alongside textual education. Charles Knight's cheap weekly *The Penny Magazine* (1832–1845), which was for several years a great success,[69] contained attractive wood-engravings reproduced by steam printing press. This made it extremely popular, especially amongst working families with children.[70] On numerous occasions the cover image depicted a famous work of ancient art such as the Portland Vase,[71] often with a suitable classical text printed after it in translation.[72]

In terms of the visual consumption of ancient Rome, there has been no rival in Britain to the popularity of scenes of destruction of Pompeii, still a newly discovered wonder in the late 18th century. The English painter Joseph Wright, from Derby, visited Italy in the 1770s and in 1775 made a preliminary gouache sketch, now in Derby Museum and Art Gallery, of Vesuvius in the process of erupting. He painted the scene at least 30 further times.[73] Londoners were treated to a cataclysmic visual experience of Pompeii's last hours when, in 1823, John Martin's apocalyptic painting 'The Destruction of Pompeii and Herculaneum' was displayed in the form of a diorama at the Egyptian Hall, Piccadilly.[74] Martin was the most popular painter of his day: railings were used in art galleries to keep admiring crowds at a distance.[75] The Pompeii craze was given its biggest boost by Edward Bulwer's (as Bulwer-Lytton was then known) bestselling novel *The Last Days of Pompeii* (1834), which was reissued in many 19th-century reprints and editions, often with dramatic illustrations. The destruction of Pompeii was a staple of Victorian spectacular entertainments, and of early cinema, as were stories from the classical world in general.[76] Many people without access to an expensive private education have first been introduced to the ancient world through visual media, whether cinema or more recently comic books, television and computer games.[77]

Museums in Britain have long provided an important point of access to classical culture, and they have historically been visited by a wider class cross-section than their equivalents in France, Germany and Italy, where the admission of visitors to the princely galleries was closely monitored.[78]

In Britain there was a sense that art and archaeology somehow belonged to the nation rather than exclusively to wealthy individuals, and free admission was customary. 'These were spaces where, in theory at least, people of all classes were offered the same experience, and permitted to see objects that in the past would have been the preserve of the few. At a time of wild disparities of educational provision, this was already a considerable, if grudging, concession.'[79] Lower-class visitors were drawn to museums out of curiosity; their memoirs often imply that what they saw nurtured an impulse towards self-education.

When Zacharias Conrad von Uffenbach toured the Ashmolean Museum in Oxford in 1710, he was shocked at what he perceived as the vulgarity of the visitors.[80] Ralph Thoresby, whose collection at the Musaeum Thoresbyanum, founded by his father in Leeds in the late 17th century, included Roman British finds, complained bitterly about visiting hordes.[81] A Prussian traveller was surprised in the 1780s that the visitors to the British Museum, founded in 1753, were 'various ... some I believe, of the very lowest classes of the people, of both sexes, for as it is the property of the nation, everyone has the same right ... to see it, that another has'.[82] Museum keepers expressed fears about the uncouth behaviour which they associated with the policy of free admission.[83] In 1815, the museum's Principal Librarian, Joseph Planta, complained to its trustees that 'our popular Visitors ... in the fervour of independence, pride themselves in showing a disdain of order'.[84]

The desire to display objects from classical antiquity, especially after the British Museum acquired Sir William Hamilton's classical collection in 1784, and the Parthenon sculptures from Lord Elgin in 1816, was a motor behind the 19th-century emergence of municipal museums.[85] A typical example is the Harris Museum in Preston. A combination of funds raised by the local people and a large bequest left in the will of lawyer Edmund Harris allowed the Preston Corporation to set up a library, museum and art gallery to honour the memory of Harris' father, the Reverend Robert Harris (1764–1862). The longstanding Headmaster of Preston Grammar School, he was himself the upwardly mobile son of a 'goods carrier' whose success was owed to his aptitude for Classics, spotted in childhood.

The grand neoclassical building to house all three was designed by local architect James Hibbert and eventually opened in 1893. Besides finds illustrating local history including Roman Lancashire, the décor of the building itself was planned by Hibbert to edify his fellow Prestonians: it is a material monument to great artworks and authors of antiquity. The impressive pediment in the tympanum, supported by the six fluted Ionic columns of the imposing portico which faces into the market square, is filled

1.4 'The Age of Pericles', pediment by Edwin Roscoe Mullins for the Harris Museum in Preston. Photograph by Bruce Lamberton. Public Domain.

by a sculpture, the work of Edwin Roscoe Mullins. It is partly inspired by those of the Parthenon and known locally as both 'The Age of Pericles' and 'The School of Athens'. Pericles sits helmeted in the centre of 12 other figures representing philosophers, poets, orators and artists [fig. 1.4]. Around the lantern the epigraph reproduces a sentence from Pericles' 'Funeral Speech' in Thucydides. The sides of the building bear two inscriptions from Marcus Aurelius' Stoic *Meditations*.[86]

Inside, more columns and mosaic floors create a classical aesthetic, enhanced by the plaster casts of famous ancient sculptures – Assyrian (the Nimrud frieze of Ashurnasirpal), Greek (the Parthenon frieze and metopes, along with the frieze from Apollo's temple at Bassae) as well as Florentine art. Most jaw-dropping is the stained-glass window celebrating ancient Greek achievements in philosophy, science, art, literature and equestrianism, exemplified by the cavalrymen riding horses bareback to the Parthenon [fig. 1.5].

The lowest window panel portrays Sappho, Aeschylus, Sophocles, Euripides and Homer, with quotations in ancient Greek from Sappho and the *Iliad*. The middle panel, with its Greek inscription 'The Great Panathenaea', is a vivid rendition of some Parthenon horsemen. The top panel portrays philosophers, artists and scientists, including Aristotle and Pheidias. The mill-workers of

1.5 Stained glass window by Henry Holiday in the Harris Museum in Preston. Photograph by Edith Hall.

Preston could learn a great deal about ancient Greece in a single afternoon at their museum. By Edwardian times the same could be said by the crofters, masons and fisherfolk of Aberdeen, after more prosperous citizens added to their Museum and Art Gallery a new hall to display casts of ancient Greek statues and a reproduction of the entire Parthenon frieze. George Reid's Aberdonian replica of Pheidias' masterpiece was one of hundreds displayed nationally in galleries and educational establishments.[87]

Adult Education

Classical subjects were on the curriculum offered by the most successful of the working men's colleges, founded in the working-class area of Camden in central north-west London in 1854 (and still in operation on Crowndale Road).[88] The curriculum was designed to offer something far more ambitious than vocational instruction. The 1885 prospectus defines the subjects taught as those 'with which it most concerns English citizens to be acquainted'.[89] As one lecturer defined it that year, the college taught many subjects with no vocational or business content, but which he saw as valuable solely 'as elements of a liberal education' which fitted people to be citizens.[90]

The London Working Men's College became nationally famous under its Principal between 1883 and 1899, Sir John Lubbock. He made a speech there in 1887, one of a series entitled 'The Pleasures of Life', which abundantly cites ancient thinkers (Aesop, Aristotle, Cicero, Epictetus, Epicurus, Herodotus, Marcus Aurelius, Plato, Plutarch, Xenophon).[91] In 'The Choice of Books', he drew up a list of the 100 books it was most important for a 'working man' to read.[92] It was leapt upon by readers all over the English-speaking world as a guide to a speedy self-education. Lubbock, who became the first Baron Avebury, came from a privileged banking family and was educated at Eton. He was a reform-minded Liberal MP for Maidstone and subsequently for London University. Although he had not attended university himself, he was a prodigious polymath, specialising in archaeology and biological sciences.[93]

In Lubbock's List, the proportion of classical authors is remarkable: Homer, Hesiod, Marcus Aurelius, Epictetus, Plutarch's *Lives*, Plato's *Apology*, *Crito* and *Phaedo*, Aristotle's *Ethics* and *Politics*, Augustine's *Confessions*, Demosthenes' *On the Crown*, Xenophon's *Memorabilia* and *Anabasis*, Cicero's *On Duties*, *On Friendship* and *On Old Age*, Vergil, Aeschylus' *Prometheus* and *Oresteia*, Sophocles' *Oedipus*, Euripides' *Medea*, Aristophanes' *Knights* and *Clouds*, Herodotus, Thucydides, Tacitus' *Germania*, and Livy. In addition, two famous works on ancient history, Gibbon's *Decline and Fall* and Grote's *History of Greece*, make it onto the list as necessary reading for any educated person, along with the most popular novel then in existence set in antiquity, Bulwer-Lytton's *The Last Days of Pompeii*.[94]

More than a quarter of all the books are classical authors, and with the addition of books entirely addressed to classical antiquity, the proportion is about one third. The classical riches on the self-educator's bookshelf after 1887 can in large measure be attributed to Lubbock's ideal curriculum. Old translations of items on the list were reprinted and marketed as one of 'Sir John Lubbock's Hundred Books', for example Lord Brougham's rendering of Demosthenes' *On the Crown* (1840), intended to convey 'to persons unacquainted with the original some notion of its innumerable and transcendent beauties'.[95] One son of a London policeman recalls his father reading his meticulous way through the entire list not long after it was published.[96]

Thereafter, the Camden WMC's impressive array of courses included Greek literature by Arthur Sidgwick (1840–1920). Sidgwick described teaching a 'little group of tired city clerks, telephone operators, and mechanics in Camden Town'.[97] In his evening class at the WMC he taught Plato's *Republic* and Sophocles' *Oedipus Tyrannus* in the rhyming translation of Gilbert Murray, former pupil of Sidgwick and Regius Professor of Greek at Oxford.[98] He was impressed by his students' response to contact 'with an unknown literature and civilisation', and their 'excitement and zest of discovery'.[99]

An Edwardian Pioneer

Gilbert Murray's translations from the ancient Greek dramatists were performed on the Edwardian London stage and across the nation by amateur dramatic societies, making ancient tragedy and comedy more familiar than ever before.[100] The translations were also a publishing phenomenon, being reprinted many times and read in educational establishments across the land. Many schoolchildren in the first half of the 20th century were introduced to the ancient world by enterprising teachers through Gilbert Murray's translations. But one figure stands out as the immediate ancestor of formal Classical Civilisation and Ancient History courses in Britain and indeed internationally. Frederick James Gould (1855–1938) developed a revolutionary pedagogical approach in the first four decades of the 20th century, his engagement with ancient Greek and Roman history informing his vision of a secular moral education that could use ancient storytelling to transcend nation and religion and to build a more peaceful world.[101]

In *History the Teacher: Education Inspired by Humanity's Story* (1921), Gould defined his concept of education, adducing Pericles' funeral speech and a quotation from Thucydides' version of it, as translated by Benjamin Jowett (Thucydides 2.43.3–4):

> At a great public crisis, Pericles appealed to the Athenians, and, casting about for a strong motive, he found it in history:
> 'The whole earth is the sepulchre of famous men. Not only are they commemorated by columns and inscriptions in their own country,

but in foreign lands there dwells also an unwritten memorial of them, graven not on stone, but in the hearts of men. Make them your examples, and, esteeming courage to be freedom and freedom to be happiness, do not weigh too nicely the perils of war'.[102]

For children between the ages of five and eight, Gould recommends that mythical figures form an introduction to actual history, which he calls 'the Story of Humanity'; an early-years teacher should encourage pupils to enjoy 'good feelings' by hearing how Prometheus brought fire and knowledge of the healing powers of plants:

And suffered the pains which all suffer who mould morality and culture to greater values, and win progress by forethought. Or she [i.e. the teacher] may tell the legend of one-eyed Polyphemus, and the escape of ingenious Ulysses ... Even Plato's cave and its wonderful shadows may be lightly hinted at in a simple picture.[103]

Ancient history, myth and philosophy are all fertile sources for education. But the particular influence Plutarch exerted on Gould lay in more than content: it instilled in him a conviction that stories, often juxtaposed in pairs or thematic groups, and especially stories of exemplary lives, were essential for effective mass pedagogy.

Gould was born in Brighton to self-educated parents; his father was an impoverished jeweller, aspiring opera singer and avid reader of *The Penny Cyclopaedia*. Gould Junior was educated at the Evangelical Free School in the village of Chenies, Buckinghamshire. The teenager was employed as a teacher there.

British education was transformed by the Elementary Education Act 1870. This aimed to put a primary education within reach of every child in England, however poor, under the jurisdiction of eight locally elected school boards. Most boards made education between the ages of 5 and 13 compulsory and free. Many new 'National Schools' were opened, while pre-existing Church Schools were incorporated into the system; this inevitably led to tensions over the role of religion in the curriculum.[104] Gould moved to London in 1879, and hurled himself into the education of some of London's poorest children, including a high proportion of immigrants, Roman Catholics and Jews, at London Board Schools in the East End. There he gained the pedagogical experience that underpinned his vision of a secular education and his many textbooks. He founded the East London Ethical Society in 1890 and began delivering lessons to children before adult audiences, to inform teachers and parents about his methods. Through this practice he developed the first draft of his *Plan for Ethical Teaching*, which was circulated in many thousands of copies and formed the basis of the four volumes of his *Children's Book of Moral Lessons*, the first of which was published in 1899.[105]

Gould proposes that many ideas underlying 'Western Civilisation' were produced by non-Christians such as Socrates, Plato, Marcus Aurelius and Epictetus.[106] In 1899, he published the first volume of *The Children's Book of Moral Lessons*. There are 187 lessons across four volumes. Volume I reveals how extensively Plutarch's *Lives*, in addition to other classical sources, featured in Gould's pedagogical practice. He uses stories about Alexander and Bucephalus, Julius Caesar and Lycurgus to teach self-control; Solon and Croesus, Cincinnatus, Pompey's troops and Marius Curius to teach temperance; Aesop's 'Hare and the Tortoise' to teach perseverance; Demosthenes and the pebbles to teach self-improvement; Thermopylae to teach courage; Cleanthes and Zeno to teach self-reliance; the Spartan Paedaretus, Cincinnatus and Caesar Augustus to teach modesty; Xenocrates in court to teach candour; Mercury and the carpenter, and the Athenian, the ape and the dolphin of the Piraeus to teach truthfulness; Mercury and the mean traveller and the story of Regulus to teach fidelity to promises; the stories of Stilpo, Cleanthes, Ulysses and Archimedes to teach the importance of acquiring knowledge; Pericles and the eclipse as an example of putting theories to the test; and the ancestral geese of Rome to demonstrate the difference between a story and a fact. He concludes with Pheidippides to ponder the nature of true rewards.[107]

Volume II illustrates maternal virtue with Veturia, mother of Coriolanus, and Cornelia, mother of the Gracchi. Respect for fathers is illustrated by Appius' son and Epaminondas. But most of this volume uses myth rather than history. The exemplar of love of siblings is Antigone. Kindness was demonstrated, Gould proposes, by the tears of Achilles for Penthesilea and the benevolence of Hercules towards Prometheus. Helios was an exemplar of magnanimity in lending his golden boat to Hercules, as was Camillus to the schoolboys. Marcellus, Regulus and Manius Curius were exemplars of honour.[108] Volume III, which has a sociological focus, discusses Greek and Roman family loyalty, including that of Themistocles, the importance of the Prometheus story to understanding the impact of fire on human progress, the architecture of Greek and Roman houses, with attractive illustrations of a house in Ionia and one in Athens, the skill of ancient Greek sculptors, and the stories of Pythagoras, Aristotle and Archimedes to illustrate ancient Greek science. Five entire lessons are devoted to Greek and Roman religion and mythology.[109]

The focus of volume IV, in which Gould used Plutarch himself as an exemplary moral hero (see above), is on citizenship and politics, and thus the classical examples are mostly historical. Lack of patriotism and perfidy were demonstrated by Pausanias of Sparta and Timophanes, brother of Timoleon; injustice was exemplified by Trajan's son and Agamemnon in the *Iliad*. Commitment to the common weal is illustrated, as we have seen, by Plutarch and also by the story of Curtius in the Roman forum. Codrus of Athens was a great ancient patriot. The sword of Damocles, Augustus breaking the vases of Pollio and anecdotes about Macedonian and Roman coinage illustrate the correct attitude to wealth. The section on cities includes a long description of ancient Rome, as do the discussions of government and slavery.[110]

Gould moved to Leicester, where he served on the Leicester School Board. Here Plutarch finally received the official recognition from Gould that he was his single most important inspiration. Gould's *The Children's Plutarch* was first published in 1906, a bestselling retelling of Plutarch's *Lives* as a school textbook and for private bedtime reading. *The Children's Plutarch* was originally conceived and designed as a standard textbook for use in all non-private schools at an exciting moment in British educational history. The most striking feature of the book is that it is indexed not according to proper names of ancient heroes, battles and places, but according to moral virtues such as 'Honesty and Honour' and 'Perseverance' or thematic topics such as 'Mother', 'Veracity' and 'Riches and Poverty'. This idiosyncrasy is explained by the 'Code of Regulations for Public Elementary Schools' for 1906, a code which Gould had played a vital role in getting passed through Parliament by persuading Augustine Birrell, Minister of Education, to speak in its favour in the House of Commons on 28 May 1906.

The new code stipulated that 'Moral instruction should form an important part of every elementary school curriculum'.[111] The document said that the subject of this instruction 'should be on such points as courage; truthfulness; cleanliness of mind, body, and speech; the love of fair play; gentleness to the weaker; humanity to animals; temperance; self-denial; love of one's country, and respect for beauty in nature and in art'. Moreover, the teaching 'should be illustrated as vividly as possible by stories, poems, quotations, proverbs, and examples drawn from history and biography'.[112] But there were few textbooks suitable for Moral Instruction classes. Gould's collection of biographical stories from Plutarch, indexed according to virtues, was designed precisely to support this new part of the curriculum.

The publisher was William Swan Sonnenschein, who was enthusiastic about the Plutarch project because it was wholly exceptional amongst the school textbooks for moral and civic instruction produced in this period.

His enthusiasm was connected with the work of his brother Edward Adolf Sonnenschein, a famous Classics Professor at the University of Birmingham, a pioneer in teaching classical literature in translation, and co-founder of the UK Classical Association.[113]

The Children's Plutarch was designed for the top classes at elementary school (10–14-year-olds), after which he says they go direct to 'the wise, manly and entertaining pages of Plutarch himself'.[114] He proudly reports that the plan was adopted wholesale by 30 Local Education Authorities (LEAs), and delivered therein to 3,500 schools; a further 50 Local Education Authorities had used part of the plan.[115] More English children were being edified by stories from ancient history in Edwardian England than ever before. Gould's 1906 retellings of all the *Lives* except Theseus, Cleomenes, Eumenes, Nicias and Poplicola were presented in an attractive book, light and small enough to be held in tiny hands, with excellent illustrations by the world-famous artist Walter Crane [see fig. 1.6]. These begin with the enticing, movement-filled

1.6 Walter Crane, 'Numa and the Nymph', illustration to F.J. Gould, *The Children's Plutarch: Tales of the Romans* (1910). Hall's private collection.

frontispiece depicting Alexander taming Bucephalus. It is not surprising that Gould's *The Children's Plutarch* has proved to have transhistorical stamina. It has been repeatedly reprinted, sometimes partially as either the Greek or the Roman lives, most recently in English in 2012 and even in Slovenian in 2017.[116]

A further set of exemplary tales was published in 1916, under the title *Worth While People*, which shows Gould, as pressure for female suffrage mounted internationally, trying harder to provide exemplary females for girls to emulate. This collection was promoted by the publisher as a sequel to 'the author's already famous *Children's Plutarch*', since 'From Thermopylae to the Panama Canal Mr Gould tells of deeds worth doing. The wide range of his great experience as a successful story-teller has guided him in choosing the essential points of tales of historic figures'.[117] These are the stories Gould told repeatedly as he now travelled intensively, demonstrating his educational methods not only across Britain, but in the USA, Europe and India.[118] Between 1909 and 1923 he gave 900 lessons, in the presence of some 80,000 people, including in 200 towns and villages across England, Scotland, Wales and Northern Ireland.[119] The demonstrations attracted large audiences of interested members of the public as well as teachers, teacher trainers, local governors and parents. During World War I, Gilbert Murray once watched Gould give an example of Moral Teaching on the theme of 'service' and was impressed, saying that the audience 'had laughed again and again during the lesson, and I think tears were in most eyes at the end'.[120]

Gould had met Murray because they were both involved in setting up the League of Nations (the forerunner of the United Nations) after the war, in which Gould's only son, Julian, was killed. He conducted extensive work for the league and secured an interview with the then Minister of Education, the progressive Charles Trevelyan, on how to spread cosmopolitan ideas in English schools.[121]

His increased commitment to the peace movement is evidenced in his 1924 collection *300 Stories to Tell*, which turns to Plutarch's *Moralia* for anecdotes about the Greek piper Canus, the Delian orphan Charila, Diogenes and the statue, the Spartans replying to the letter from Philip of Macedon with the simple one-word message 'if', a saying of Livius Drusus, two sayings of Agesilaus proving his sincerity, the poet Philoxenus' refusal of a life of permanent leisure in Sicily, King Pythes and the gold mine, the eloquent versus the efficient architect at Athens, Dionysius of Syracuse and the confiscated hoard and Apelles and the inferior painter.[122] From Herodotus he takes the story of Leonidas and the original 300 heroes;[123] he includes unsourced stories about Pythagoras,[124] and the deaf old man and the harp-player in classical Athens.[125]

Gould's books were used in schools in all countries where English was spoken; they were also translated for use in India, Sri Lanka (then Ceylon), Brazil, Japan and several European countries including Poland, Spain, France, the then Czechoslovakia, Italy and Norway.[126] His reputation in France is proven by an early biography.[127] Gould was both a visionary and a man of his time. His own position on the British Empire was conflicted; he certainly believed in the export to the rest of the world of European 'Enlightenment' values, yet all his versions of history emphasise the bravery of colonised peoples standing up to occupying powers, not only the barbarians exploited by the Greeks and Romans, but the Americans who defied the British in the War of Independence; he denounces the misbehaviour of rampant self-interested colonialists such as Clive of India.[128] He welcomed the official replacement of the term 'British Empire' with 'The Commonwealth of Nations' and ardently advocated peace. We could still learn a good deal from this remarkable pedagogue's vision of the place of ancient history in a secular education fit for the 21st-century global village.

Conclusion

In the course of this chapter we have seen that accessing, enjoying and studying ancient Roman literature, civilisation and history has a long and proud British backstory extending to the rediscovery of Roman Britain in the late 16th century; ancient Greece, too, achieved a place in education through translations as much as through linguistic training by the turn of the 18th century. The availability of ancient authors in translation sparked new publications explaining the social and historical contexts in which these authors wrote; the opening of public museums, the Pompeii craze, the Parthenon sculptures and adult and autodidactic education fed the increasing appetite for knowledge about classical antiquity. Classical material was admired for its beauty, but also instrumentalised in teaching citizenship values and ethical principles.

On the other side of the Atlantic, Thomas Jefferson, drew from Aristotle the idea of the pursuit of happiness, which he describes as an inalienable right in the *Declaration of Independence*. In *Notes on the State of Virginia* (1782), he defined the one real goal of education as equipping people to defend their freedom, and history, in which he included ancient history, he argued is the subject which makes citizens so equipped.[129] To stay free requires also comparison of constitutions, fearlessness about change and critical, lateral and relativist thinking across time and different cultures.

The ancient Mediterranean world offers an ideal context for the development of these forms of intellectual understanding and skills. Matthew Arnold, who had observed hundreds of schools in France and Germany as well as in Britain as one of Her Majesty's Inspectors, criticised the excessive linguistic emphasis of contemporary Classics teaching in a talk he gave at Eton while advocating the importance of studying the entirety of Graeco-Roman civilisation. He said that a linguistic emphasis destroys the precious facility 'to conceive also that Graeco-Roman world, which is so mighty a factor in our own world, our own life … as a whole of which we can trace the sequence, and the sense, and the connection with ourselves'. He argued that the purpose of education is 'to know himself and the world', and that the value of the study of antiquity 'is that it affords for this purpose an unsurpassed source of light and stimulus'.[130]

As Neville Morley has more recently put it, 'classical antiquity and its legacy still have power in our world, for good or ill'.[131] In the 21st century, we need to educate our future citizens in a way that will equip them to face a world threatened by military conflict, social unrest, economic uncertainty and environmental degradation. Education in Classical Civilisation or Ancient History fits perfectly with the vision of the New Humanism as outlined in 2015 by Hans d'Orville, Special Advisor to the Director-General of UNESCO: 'the promotion of education for all, of a democratic participation of all' and concentration on 'widening and deepening collective efforts in the fields of education, science, culture and access to information'.[132] He called for cosmopolitan education that will strengthen the process of countering 'cultural stereotyping, prejudices and intercultural misunderstandings'.[133]

This new humanist movement stresses the transformative power of education, sciences, culture and communications to develop a truly historical understanding of the way human society has evolved. Education needs to encourage people to participate in the 'conscience of humanity', and the idea that humanity is 'a collective effort that holds governments, civil society, the private sector and human individuals equally responsible to realize its values'. There is an urgent need for high-quality education that not only makes young people employable, 'but also critical citizens of the spaces in which they live'.[134] Exactly this type of high-quality education is represented by the qualifications in Classical Civilisation and Ancient History which form the subject-matter of this book.

Notes

1. Stray (1977) 128–239.
2. Lewis (1977) 29.
3. Lewis (1977) 30.
4. Murray (1889) 13.
5. See Harris (2015).
6. The 1905 editor of Holland's translation of Livy's account of Hannibal in Italy for the series *Blackie's School English Texts* called Holland 'translator-general of the Elizabethan age' and his style 'rich, dignified and sonorous' (Holland (1905) 3, 4); the 1923 editor of Holland's translation of Suetonius' *History of the Twelve Caesars* stated that the edition was not aimed at established scholars but to make Suetonius accessible to 'the non-classical reader', and praises its 'vigour', 'quaintness' and 'charm' (Holland (1923) v).
7. Camden (1610) 'The Author to the Reader'.
8. Norbrook (1999).
9. Evelyn (1656).
10. Rich (1584). On Settle's play and the impact of Herodotus in English translation in this period see Hall (2020).
11. Diaper (1722); Sydenham (1761); Taylor and Sydenham (1804).
12. Hall (2008a).
13. See Cueva, Byrne and Benda (2009); Hall (2021) 36.
14. This book was also printed by a woman, who called herself on the title page 'widow of Antonius Cellier' (Apud viduam Antonii Cellier). Like the Daciers, Antoine Cellier was a Protestant who had converted, and his wife's name seems to have been either Anne or Florence. See Hall (2021) 40 nn.20–21. On Dacier see further Wyles (2016).
15. Shelford (2007).
16. Shelford (2007) 172.
17. In a letter to Huet of 15 April 1673, reproduced in Leibniz (2003) 363, translated by Shelford (2007) 173.
18. Oldenburg (1975) 343–346.
19. Anon. (1702) and (1704).
20. Wyles and Hall (2016) 21–22; Hall (2016).
21. Curll (1729).
22. Kennet (1695) 'Preface', n.p.
23. Potter (1697).
24. Danet (1700).
25. Hall and Stead (2020).
26. Hall (2008b).
27. Chapman (1615), Dedication, n.p.
28. Keats (1817) 89.
29. See Hall (2018).
30. See Coney (1722) 19, 'The most Debauch'd of the *Classics* have been turn'd into our Language with some additional Strokes to their *Original Obscenity*; and appeared in a more loose dress in *England*, than they ever dar'd to in *Rome*'. See further Hall and Stead (2020) 39–41.

[31] Dryden et al. (1680).
[32] Hill (1709) xiv.
[33] Hall and Stead (2020) 4–6.
[34] Hall and Stead (2020) 5.
[35] Haw (1917) 22.
[36] Wilson (2012) 31.
[37] Wilson (2012) 31.
[38] On BBC's Third Programme see Whitehead (1989) and Wrigley (2015) 51–53.
[39] Hall and Stead (2020) 53.
[40] Couper (1914) 8.
[41] Couper (1914) 77.
[42] *The Cheap Magazine*, September 1813, vol. I, no. 9, 407–411. *The Cheap Magazine*, October 1813, vol. I, no. 10, 460. *The Cheap Magazine*, July 1814, vol. II, no. 7, 234–235.
[43] The title was changed in 1854 to *Chambers's Journal of Popular Literature, Science, and Art*, and to *Chambers's Journal* in late 1897.
[44] *Chambers' Magazine* (Saturday 4 February 1832) no. 1, 1.
[45] *Chambers' Magazine* (Saturday 4 February 1832) no. 1, 1.
[46] Clarke (1830–1831).
[47] See further Hall and Stead (2020) 245.
[48] Nowell-Smith (1958) 22.
[49] See pp. 34–35.
[50] Including the *Dictionary of Latin Quotations* (1856) and Bohn's own *The Standard Library Atlas of Classical Geography* (1861).
[51] Quoted in O'Sullivan (2009) 112.
[52] Anon. (1884). See also O'Sullivan (2009) 112.
[53] Altick (1957) 11–12.
[54] On Stead's 'Penny Poets' see Lockwood (2013). On his output as publisher 1890–1903 see Brake (2012).
[55] Whyte (1925) 2, 229; Anon. (1896) 30.
[56] Lockwood (2013) 11.
[57] Lockwood (2013) 8.
[58] Stamper (1960) 100.
[59] Stamper (1960) 162.
[60] Table of Contents for 64: I. Æneas, the father of kings -- II. The twins -- III. Romulus, the founder of Rome -- IV. The Horatii and Curatii -- V. The geese of the capitol -- VI. The story of Coriolanus -- VII. Cæsar's ambition -- VIII. Antony and Cleopatra.
[61] Stead (1901) 545.
[62] Pope (1903); Dryden (1903). Richards also published Gibbon's *Roman Empire*, Vol. I.
[63] Azoulay (2014) 205–206.
[64] Hutchinson (1912) 1.1.
[65] The intellectual elite of course found new ways of disparaging the vastly expanded readership produced by late 19th-century legislation, and the more arcane aspects of early literary Modernism, which was rich in its own form of classicism, were part of their response. See the brilliant study of Carey (1992).
[66] Burke (2001).

[67] Lewis (1998–1999); Hall (2006) 196–206.
[68] For detailed discussions of all the publications of the SDUK, including those on Classics and classical archaeology, see Cavenagh (1929) and Rauch (2001).
[69] Gilbert (1922) 70.
[70] See Bennett (1984).
[71] 'The British Museum: the Portland Vase', no. 31, 29 September (1832) 249–250.
[72] In 1832 alone, see also 'Ancient paintings', no. 24, 18 August, 200; 'Zeuxis', no. 25, 25 August, 207–208; 'The British Museum: the Elgin Marbles', no. 28, 8 September, 228–229; 'The Warwick Vase', no. 29, 15 September, 233; 'Description of the shield of Achilles', no. 33, 22 September, 241–242; 'Tivoli', no. 34, 13 October, 273.
[73] See Nicolson (1968).
[74] Daly (2012) 26; see Pendered (1923) 107 with plate.
[75] See Pendered (1923) 19–41, 186–195; https://www.artfund.org/news/2016/08/03/curator-of-the-month-julie-milne-tyne-and-wear-archives-and-museums.
[76] Michelakis and Wyke (2013).
[77] See e.g. Rollinger (2020), Draycott and Cook (2022, ed.) and below pp. 52, 54, 163.
[78] Waterfield (2015) 3.
[79] Waterfield (2015) 37.
[80] Quarrell and Quarrell (1928) 31.
[81] Waterfield (2015) 23.
[82] Moritz (1795) 68.
[83] Waterfield (2015) 37.
[84] Quoted in Wilson (2002) 67.
[85] Waterfield (2015) 3.
[86] Hartwell and Pevsner (2009) 519–522.
[87] St Clair (1998).
[88] See https://www.wmcollege.ac.uk/.
[89] Lucas (1885) 162.
[90] Lucas (1885) 183.
[91] Lubbock (1887) 1, 8, 15, 28, 30, 32, 36, 40, 42, 44, 47, 56, 64, 95–96, 98.
[92] Lubbock (1887) 65–88.
[93] Hutchinson (1914).
[94] Lubbock (1887) 65–88.
[95] Brougham (1840) 12 and Brougham (1893).
[96] Rolph (1980) 82–85, 95–96, 132.
[97] Sidgwick (1920) 259.
[98] Murray (1911).
[99] Sidgwick (1920) 259.
[100] Hall and Macintosh (2005) 448–504; Hall (2013a) 239–251; Hall and Stead (2020) 146, 193–195, 197, 509.
[101] For a detailed account see Hall (2024).
[102] Gould (1921) 5; Jowett (1881) 122. See also Gould's pamphlet *History: The Supreme Subject in the Instruction of the Young* (London 1918: no publisher) 3: 'By "history" we here mean the story, or tale, or spell, of human love, human order (material, moral, aesthetic, intellectual, social), and human progress, or evolution, realized in individual lives, and in the life of communities'.
[103] Gould (1921) 23–24.
[104] Bérard (1987) 233–234.

[105] Gould (1923) 76–78.
[106] Gould (1890) 35.
[107] Gould (1899) 1–2, 11–13, 14–15, 21, 22, 38–39, 49, 56, 67–68, 96, 98, 100–101, 110, 113–115, 119–121, 130–131, 136, 168, 181–182, 185–189.
[108] Gould (1903) 8–9, 26–27, 37–40, 60–62, 100–101, 183–184, 186.
[109] Gould (1904) 3–5, 53–54, 68–71, 85–86, 99–101, 162–184.
[110] Gould (1907) 1–4, 12, 14–15, 37, 41, 52, 71, 87–88, 92–95, 118, 168–172.
[111] Quoted in Gould (1906a) viii.
[112] Quoted in Gould (1906a) 2 n.1.
[113] See Stray (2006).
[114] Gould (1906b) viii.
[115] Gould (1906a) 326–327.
[116] Gould (2012) and Gould (2017).
[117] Gould (1916) 'Publisher's Note', n.p.
[118] See University of Wisconsin (1913), Gould (1915), Banaji (1918).
[119] Gould (1921) 117.
[120] Hayward and White (1942) 63–64.
[121] Hayward and White (1942) 133–147.
[122] Gould (1924) 8, 20, 25–26, 118, 136, 140, 142, 143, 144–145, 146.
[123] Gould (1924) 32.
[124] Gould (1924) 61.
[125] Gould (1924) 79.
[126] For bibliographical details see Hall (forthcoming a).
[127] Feliciano de Oliveira (1938).
[128] Gould (1925) 35, 37.
[129] Jefferson (1784 [1782]) 271–274.
[130] Arnold (1882) 186; see Rapple (2017) 144–146.
[131] Morley (2018) 130.
[132] d'Orville (2015) 97.
[133] d'Orville (2015) 96.
[134] The words of Crain Soudien (2017) 318, Deputy Vice-Chancellor at the University of Cape Town.

CHAPTER 2

Reinvigorating Classical Civilisation Education in the 20th Century

Introduction

The proud British tradition of reading classical authors in translation, as we saw in the previous chapter, produced encouraging results in schools after the Education Acts of 1870 and 1880; at that time, teaching both ancient historical subjects and ancient literature was introduced in some British state educational institutions. There were always a few heroic teachers who saw the value of teaching children about the ancient world. One enlightened Unitarian Hackney schoolmaster had called as early as 1814 for female education, as well as male, in general knowledge about antiquity.[1] But teachers of traditional and narrowly linguistic Classics within elite educational institutions, a pedagogical tradition with its roots in the early 18th century and analysed in dazzling and dispassionate detail in a pathbreaking monograph by Christopher Stray [fig. 2.1],[2] poured out a continuous flood of arguments in traditional elite Classics' favour. They implicitly, and all too often explicitly, decried any form of education about ancient Greece and Rome that was not dominated by grammatical and syntactical rules.[3]

This chapter focusses on more recent times and specifically on curriculum design and formal qualifications. As late as 1943, the Classical Association persuaded leading figures in Law, Medicine, Engineering, Natural Science, Business and the Professions to attend a symposium and deliver speeches defending the mental 'precision' supposedly conferred by the study of Latin grammar. The last contributor praised the Workers' Education Association courses at Reading University, which delivered talks on Greek Literature, Philosophy, Science and Politics to the general public during the war years, *not* because they were of inherent educational value, but because they had inspired a few participants to start studying the languages.[4] Such conservative voices could not stop the tide of history, however, even if the tide took time to turn. Ancient History became available at A Level in

2.1 Christopher Stray and Edith Hall. Photograph by Jaś Elsner.

1951 in England and Wales. A similar chronology applies to Scotland and Northern Ireland. The real impetus to mass expansion in these subjects, and in particular the reform of the Ancient History syllabus and the emergence – at last – of nationally recognised qualifications in Classical Civilisation, came somewhat afterwards, in the late 1960s and 1970s. Further exciting modifications have occurred in the syllabuses at regular intervals subsequently. It is the heroic struggle for the democratisation of classical education, the rousing developments of more than 50 years ago and the colourful characters and controversies they entailed which will occupy the bulk of this chapter.

A Missed Opportunity: 1921

In hindsight it is astonishing and regrettable how long it took for the benefits of a broad acquaintance with the ancient Greek and Roman worlds, which had been appreciated across a wide cross-section of the British populace for centuries, to be embraced within the modern school curriculum. There was a crucial missed opportunity just over a century ago, at a time when Denmark, for example, had recently extended the study of the ancient world via Danish translations and reproductions of classical art across secondary education.[5] In the UK, the *notional* approval at national governmental level of the teaching of Classical Civilisation and Ancient History to all children can be dated to the *Report of the Committee Appointed by the Prime Minister to Inquire Into the Position of Classics in the Educational System of the United Kingdom*, published in 1921.

The Prime Minister, David Lloyd George, had always been interested in the ancient world. As a youth he had educated himself in classical topics from Cassell's *Popular Educator*. He had encouraged the use of the figure of Caractacus, the ancient Briton who according to Tacitus had resisted Roman imperialism, in the recruitment drive during World War I.[6] His mistress, Frances Stevenson, had studied Classics at Royal Holloway and was a romantic Philhellene; she encouraged his support of the Greeks' claim to territorial gains after the Ottoman Empire was defeated in World War I, a cause which ended in catastrophe for the Greeks at the end of the Graeco-Turkish War (1919–1922).[7] Perhaps just as importantly, Lloyd George was influenced by the Deputy Secretary to the Cabinet at the time, fellow Welshman Thomas Jones (1870–1955), who had a passionate autodidactic appetite for Classics. He had been able to feed this appetite as a young man in the Rhymney Workmen's Institute Library, where he read Greek and Roman authors in English translation.[8]

The man whom Lloyd George appointed to lead the Inquiry was from a very different background, however. Robert Offley Ashburton Crewe-Milnes, the Marquess of Crewe (1858–1945), had been educated in Classics at Harrow School and Trinity College, Cambridge, from where he graduated in 1880; he entered politics and in due course became leader of the Liberals in the House of Lords. He retained his interest in the ancient world, being appointed Fellow of the Society of Antiquaries, and was a published poet. But it was probably his longstanding interest in education that led to his appointment as leader of the inquiry. He had been President of the Board of Education in 1916, served as Chairman of the Governing Body of Imperial College London (1907–1922), and as Chancellor of Sheffield University.

In a document extending to over 300 pages, 285 of them tortuously analyse the history, current status and future prospects of the teaching of Latin (and, to a lesser extent, Greek), almost all in the assumed context of Public Schools and in relation to entrance examinations for Oxbridge. Just 20 pages address other ways of teaching Classics in schools, and these reveal the disappointingly conservative viewpoint of its author.

The report notes that Ancient History is not 'prescribed by any examining body as part of the examination in Classics';[9] some examining bodies do, however, ask for answers to simple historical questions, which are 'casual and incidental', to be answered as they arise in passages set for translation. Crewe-Milnes tentatively suggests that papers on prescribed ancient texts could be supplemented by 'one or two simple questions of a more general character than those arising directly out of the passages set for translation but relevant to the author and period concerned. The inclusion of such questions would have a stimulating effect'.[10] But vastly more words are spent arguing that entrance exams set for candidates even in Modern History in Oxbridge Entrance Exams should be expected to answer questions on Ancient History.[11]

Crewe-Milnes waxes lyrical about the 19th- and early 20th-century archaeological discoveries across the Greek world, in the Roman Forum, Egypt and the Ancient Near East, and in papyrology at Oxyrhynchus. He enthusiastically recommends that a traditional Classics education should be supplemented by visits to museums and material aids such as photographs, lantern slides and maps and, if possible, performances of ancient plays.[12] The report expresses an uncharacteristically adventurous view in saying that such discoveries have prompted 'the realisation that they have something to contribute to the problems of the present day and the permanent life of man'.[13] This observation is developed into an argument which could usefully have supported introducing the study of Classical Civilisation across the entire school sector:

> [W]e are beginning to realise more fully than ever that most of the questions that press upon us at the present day, in politics, sociology and economics, in law and government, in literature and art, and even in science first presented themselves to Greek and Roman thinkers and statesmen. Many of the problems of democracy, of internationalism, of industrialism, to name no others, were known to the ancient world ... because Greece and Rome offer the spectacle of civilisations running their course from start to finish, the study of their history may form the best preparation for that of our own difficulties.[14]

But only the vaguest of suggestions ensue for putting this noble apprehension into practice and it is conceded that it 'is difficult to see what time can be found for the vast subject of Mediterranean history except in its broadest outlines'.[15]

Crewe-Milnes further undermines his own case here by his squeamishness about reading in translation, as if terrified that readers will imagine that he considers it any kind of substitute for a traditional Classics education. Indeed, it is felt to be somehow dangerous. Children with no knowledge of ancient languages must never be taught by a scholar unless he has a good classical training, 'which will save him from being misled by a translation in which the language and style of the original is wholly recast in the mould of modern English'.[16] Moreover, while introducing children to a classical author via a translation may occasionally be allowed, the purpose is only to make 'their task of mastering its grammatical structure easier'.[17] Further caveats follow. Translations must *never* be used simultaneously with the original (no explanation for this ban is supplied!), 'Editions like the Loeb Classics, with the original and the translation on opposite pages, are quite unsuitable for use in form'.[18]

There is a section 'Classical Studies in the New Secondary Schools' (i.e., the more than a thousand new schools, including girls' schools, introduced by the 'Balfour' Education Act 1902, which standardised and upgraded the educational systems of England and Wales). But, astonishingly, these new schools occupy fewer than three pages, or 1% of the entire report; the section is introduced by the daunting statement that the topic 'presents great difficulties'.[19] It is acknowledged that these schools 'contain the vast majority of those boys and girls who pursue a full-time education after the age of 14', that their numbers are increasing exponentially and that '[t]hese young people will play a leading part in every activity of national life in the future'.[20]

A more farsighted educationalist could have responded here that a broad introduction to the ancient world might equip these youngsters to understand issues relevant to citizenship, for which ancient Mediterranean societies provide perfect case-studies. Yet, instead, Crewe-Milnes insists that attempts must be made to make classical *languages* available in these schools. He patronisingly commends parents who want Greek made available to their children in the new schools; some parents, 'especially perhaps those who have come under the influence of such bodies as the Workers' Educational Association, have a real interest in Greek civilisation from certain points of view; more of them are genuinely anxious to get the best possible education for their children, and believe that the best education is that which has been traditional for the "governing classes" in the past'.[21] He even argues, wholly impracticably, that Latin (albeit supplemented by incidental information about ancient history) must be available in the Technical Schools and the Continuation Schools which under the terms of the 1918 and 1921 Education Acts had made part-time school attendance for school-leavers between 14 and 18 compulsory.[22]

Despite acknowledging the perennial 'relevance' of the ancient world to the modern, Crewe-Milnes' inability to see reading ancient authors in translation as anything other than a very poor second-best to training in grammar and syntax can be seen, in retrospect, as preventing the renovation of the teaching of classical subjects at the precise moment when far more children were receiving extended secondary education than ever before. The report regrettably stalled the arrest of innovation for three decades and achieved little more than maintaining the status quo. It consolidated the divisive distinction between narrowly linguistic Classics to be taught in formal examined courses to the future ruling class brought up in socially elite families, and sparsely and unevenly available informal tuition in classical material for all others, who were likely to leave school at the age of 14 anyway.

Winds of Change

It was only in the 1950s that the rigid social stratification of secondary education, even more glaringly obvious in Classics than in other subjects, began to be challenged. But an 'apartheid' system still continued in education, including Classics, between 1951 and the mid-1960s. Despite the high profile of the ancient world in public and popular culture (see below), the 'elite' associations of linguistic Classics and the unfortunate corresponding class-based denigration of the more wide-ranging and colourful types of classical subject-matter became even more entrenched in Britain. Classical languages were offered to pupils in the private sector and, in addition, to those pupils selected competitively by the 11-plus examination to receive their secondary education at a Grammar School or Direct Grant school subsidised by the state (Edith Hall was one of the last to be sent to a Direct Grant school under this system in Nottinghamshire).

This selective system was consequent upon the 'Butler' Education Act 1944 and the Education Act (Scotland) 1945. These pieces of legislation had also raised the school-leaving age to 15 and led to the replacement, in 1951, of the qualification available to the small minority of children who stayed in education to 16 or beyond. The old School Certificate, established in 1918, was replaced with GCE O Levels at 16 years old and A Levels at 18. These included the option of Ancient History, at that time rarely taught except as part of History qualifications; it now became a separate additional qualification, usually offered alongside Latin and/or Greek in the private sector and in Grammar Schools and Direct Grant Schools (see the following chapter).

The vast majority of teenagers, after being told they had 'failed' the 11-plus, attended secondary modern or technical schools; at these, a few were taught by enterprising and committed teachers determined to offer them access to the cultural capital and intellectual stimulus provided by ancient Greece and Rome, engaging with classical culture or history through translation and material culture. Some of the innovative courses and materials developed in the classroom even in the 1950s were of dazzling creativity; many teachers were passionately committed to bringing the intellectual riches of the ancient world to the majority of British children 'left behind' by the selective system.

As early as 1949, Francis Kinchin Smith, who was responsible for the training of Classics teachers at the University of London Institute of Education, had convened a conference under the title 'Classical Background in Emergency Training Colleges and Modern Schools', to bring such committed and visionary teachers together to pool ideas. He raised the issues addressed at this conference with the (conservative, at the time) Classical Association,[23] apparently to little effect. There is a chapter with the title 'Classics in the Secondary Modern School' by Tommy Melluish in a handbook on Classics teaching published by the Incorporated Association of Assistant Masters in Secondary Schools (IAAMSS) in 1954; regrettably, although Melluish even acknowledged how popular general and 'background' classes on the ancient world had proved across the secondary school system, he was committed to the point of obsession to traditional teaching of linguistic Classics and did not feel comfortable with this material.[24]

2.2 Photograph of Dora Pym in 1918. Photographer unknown. Hall's private collection.

But far more adventurous questions were asked at two conferences organised the same year by the enterprising Dora Pym, who had responsibility for the training of Classics teachers at Bristol University [fig. 2.2]. She was a passionate believer in the benefits bestowed by reading the greats of ancient literature in translation and had published with George Harrap two elegant, annotated collections of excerpts for precisely this purpose: *Readings from the Literature of Ancient Rome* (1922) and *Readings from the Literature of Ancient Greece* (1924) [fig. 2.3]. At her Bristol gatherings, the whole place and purpose of Classics in the school curriculum was placed under critical examination. Pym's motives are revealed in a memorandum which she wrote to her Professor: 'The teaching of Classics in all but a few schools is hampered, not as it appears on the surface, only by examination requirements and deep controversy about 'methods', but also by unexamined assumptions as to the place and contribution of the Classics in contemporary schools'.[25]

2.3 Frontispiece and Title Page to Dora Pym's *Readings from the Literature of Ancient Greece* (1924). Hall's private collection.

Some dedicated teachers in secondary modern and even a few technical schools, despite the problems Pym identified, did indeed succeed in introducing their pupils in the 1950s to the ancient Greeks and Romans. But it was not until the requirement for O Level Latin for undergraduate admission was removed from the statutes of Oxford and Cambridge Universities in May 1960 that the Classics community belatedly, and largely motivated by expedience rather than principle, began to focus on the need to change. Hitherto, Public and Grammar Schools and parents had unquestioningly supported compulsory Latin classes because a qualification in Latin was needed to secure a coveted undergraduate place at Oxbridge. Little attempt had been made to develop any other rationale for the educational utility of Latin beyond the oft-repeated but unsubstantiated claim that it fostered greater intellectual precision than studying a modern language. With the removal of the argument that Latin O Level provided part of a ticket to Oxbridge, the future of secondary Classics education suddenly seemed precarious. By 1969, Latin entries at A Level had fallen to less than 2% of the total and Greek to far below even 0.5%.[26] Something, at last, had to change and progressive classicists in both schools and universities sensed that the moment for democratising and enlivening their subject had arrived.

Regrettably, it must be said that there was considerable opposition to change from a sizeable proportion of Classics teachers who much preferred to continue concentrating on Latin. They were reluctant to learn new approaches to antiquity and knew that any form of teaching in translation would make new and different demands on them. They either believed (or, more likely, chose to claim) that radical new methods, such as teaching Greek democracy or the social experiences of Roman women, were inherently inferior. The debate was always dominated by teachers in elite schools, who were those most powerful in the historic associations of Classics teachers, rather than those with experience of exciting new courses on the ground across the spectrum of types of school. Nevertheless, largely thanks to the tenacity and diplomacy of John Sharwood Smith, visionary trainer of Classics teachers at the London Institute of Education, the much more forward-thinking and inclusive Joint Association of Classical Teachers (JACT) emerged in 1962. It brought teachers introducing the ancient world in translation to secondary schools into contact with members of the Classical Association, the Association for the Reform of Latin Teaching and the (most unfortunately named) Orbilian Society (Orbilius was Horace's astringent Latin language teacher, notorious for thrashing his pupils, *Epistles* 2.1.70–71!).

Professor Sharwood Smith is the hero of this tale. A former RAF pilot who had joined up in 1939 and was promoted to Squadron Leader, and wrote a 3-volume memoir about his adventures (sadly for us without containing much information about his days reforming the curriculum), he was the single most important figure in the creation of modern 'Classical Civilisation' qualifications. His obituary by Bob Lister, former comprehensive school teacher and former head of the Classics Postgraduate Certificate in Education at the University of Cambridge, concluded that 'without John's farsighted understanding of classics and the contribution it could make to the school curriculum there would be little, if any, classics in any non-selective state school today'.[27] He was the driving force behind the crucial discussions in the 1960s, in particular by founding the Joint Association of Classical Teachers in 1962. Cambridge Ancient Historian Moses Finley referred to him as 'the presiding genius over the renewal in our time of classical studies in this country'.[28] One of Sharwood Smith's initiatives at this time was the foundation of JACT's journal, *Didaskalos*, which was first published in 1963 and was to run until 1977; it included articles on courses in these subjects as well as language teaching.

Access for All to Qualifications: the CSE

The early issues of *Didaskalos* reveal that at that time, non-linguistic 'foundation courses' designed for children in their first years at secondary school, on themes such as 'The Trojan War' and 'Roman Home Life',[29] were developed at speed. They adopted a 'story-centred' approach which lent itself to team teaching and, importantly, delivery by specialists not in Classics but in, for example, English and even Physics, at schools including St Michael's School in Stevenage and West High School, Leek, Staffs (one of the chief advantages of Classical Civilisation courses today, too, is that they can be – and are – taught with great success by teachers qualified in quite different subjects).[30] A 'foundation course' designed for the first forms at the Llanedryn comprehensive school in Cardiff, 'The Development of Man', was predominantly focussed on classical civilisation.[31] An inspiring, grainy photograph is all that remains of the performance of Aristophanes' *Peace* by girls at Brierton Hill Technical High School for Girls, Hartlepool, in 1967 [fig. 2.4], its unclarity seeming to express the difficulties we have encountered in researching these early educational experiments. Since most children left school at the age of 15 without any qualifications, these initiatives were often their only hope of contact with the ancient world.

But radical change was imminent. JACT's seminal first pamphlet, *Robbins and the Classics*, was published in 1964 in response to the report of the Committee on Higher Education, usually known as the 'Robbins Report', produced for the British government in 1963. The recommendation that universities and the number of young people attending them be expanded immediately resulted from the utopian 'Robbins Principle' that university places 'should be available to all who are qualified for them by ability and attainment', one of the aims being 'to transmit a common culture and common standards of citizenship'.[32]

This was music to the ears of progressive classicists both in Higher Education, especially Professors of Greek T.B.L. Webster (London) and

2.4 A performance of Aristophanes' *Peace* by girls at Brierton Hill Technical High School for Girls, Hartlepool, in 1967. Photograph held at Hartlepool Museum, reproduced with the permission of its curator.

E.R. Dodds (Oxford), as well as to Sharwood Smith. The preface to *Robbins and the Classics*, written in March 1964 by Sharwood Smith and his co-editor C.W. Baty, welcomed the spirit of the Robbins Report, applauding the expansion of the universities and the emergence of comprehensive schools as waves of 'educational democracy'; if Classics teachers perpetuated their previous 'masterly inactivity' in the face of these exciting, democratising waves, they urged, it would be impossible for their subject to survive.[33] The aim of the pamphlet was to 'provoke thought on an urgent topic' and 'promote collaboration between teachers in schools and universities in the discussion and planning of syllabuses designed to meet the challenge'.[34]

Webster's trenchant contribution to the pamphlet argued that it was essential to start taking seriously the teaching of classical literature in translation and ancient art. He pointed to the success of such methods in both Denmark and New Zealand.[35] B.R. Rees, Professor of Greek at University College, Cardiff, candidly wrote that the main obstacle to a bright new future for reformed classical education was no external enemy but 'the innate conservatism of teachers of classics', which did not 'augur well for the chances of a thorough re-appraisal'.[36] He stated that he had proposed the introduction of an O Level course in classical literature in translation several years previously to the Welsh Education Committee. Disappointingly, it had been rejected on the grounds that it would damage linguistic teaching (an erroneous claim, as the availability of broad courses in Classical Civilisation has subsequently been shown to *increase* appetites for classical languages in almost all types of educational context and organisation).[37]

Only some teachers of Classics were inherently conservative, however. Many others were delightedly celebrating the prospect of the rise in the school-leaving age to 16 (this eventually happened in 1973), which would make a fifth year of secondary education compulsory for all; they embraced the introduction of the Certificate of School Education (CSE), which was first examined in 1965. The CSE was the brainchild of the Beloe Committee, which met from 1958 to 1960 under the farsighted leadership of Robert Beloe CBE, Chief Education Officer of Surrey from 1940 to 1959. He had created numerous successful 'bilateral schools' in that county, which were effectively comprehensive schools.

Prior to the introduction of the CSE, 80% of pupils at secondary modern schools were offered no school-leaving exams set by external bodies whatsoever, and so left education without any qualifications that were recognised nationally. Once the leaving age was raised to 16, all children would at last stay at school long enough to be prepared for nationally recognised school-leaving qualifications. Pupils at Independent and Grammar Schools had been sitting O Level exams at 16 and A Levels in academic subjects at 18 since 1951; the CSE was designed to offer vastly more children qualifications in a wider range of subjects, including vocational skills, and controlled course-work assessment as well as examinations. The more enlightened teachers of Classics seized this opportunity and set assiduously to work. They realised that the new school-leaving age and the CSE offered an outstanding opportunity to revitalise their subject, make the ancient Greeks and Romans more relevant to the modern world and offer ways of engaging with their cultural ancestors to vastly more British teenagers.

The result was the foundation document of modern Classical Civilisation courses, *Classics and the Reorganisation of Secondary Schools*, published by JACT in late 1964.[38] The contributors ended their Preface with the rallying cry that Classics 'is not the monopoly of old-established schools; with imaginative reconstruction, the Classics are capable of making a vital contribution to a new "common culture"'.[39] These pioneering teachers did face huge problems, not least that the national organisation of secondary education had become chaotic. They guessed (but could not be sure of the precision of the figure) that 75% of the 148 Local Education Authorities in England and Wales had now departed from the long-established tripartite division of grammar/technical/modern schools; they noted the 'considerable heat and acrimony' these changes were generating.[40]

But they warmly applauded the absolutely crucial proposal for a CSE examination in Classical Studies,[41] and presciently saw the desirability in the future of a course available in the Sixth Form.[42] The East Midlands C.S.E. Regional Examinations Board had already set up Classical Studies Panels and invited teachers to make suggestions for a suitable CSE syllabus and examination, and the result was the inclusion of Classical Studies in the Certificate, the first exams being available in May/June 1965, which makes it an outstanding candidate for the official birth date of Classical Civilisation national qualifications in British schools.

The syllabus was entitled 'Greek and Roman Life and Literature' and its contents are recognisably direct ancestors of components in the Classical Civilisation GCSE today. Of the two papers, the first asked questions on myths, public and domestic life, religion, visual arts, architecture, political institutions, science, theatre and entertainment. The second asked questions on the set books, which were Sophocles' Theban plays, a portion of the *Odyssey*, the first six books of the *Aeneid* and selections from Pliny's letters – all still texts central to Classical Civilisation qualifications.[43] D.J. Morton of the Department of Education at Nottingham University stated at the time,

'If we believe that some encounter with classical civilisation contributes to the cultural development of those who experience it ... then we shall address ourselves to the urgent task of making this encounter more widely available'; what is needed is to attend to this aim 'with vigour, imagination and conviction'. That is all, he rightly insisted, that is needed to make classical scholarship thrive.[44]

One of the most exciting documents in the history of Classical Civilisation courses is the report of what must have been a thrilling working conference held at the University of London Institute of Education's Teachers' Centre in the Easter vacation of 1967. The venue was Beatrice Webb House, Dorking, in Surrey. The desirability of opening access to classical material to every child in the land was reflected in the conference's focus on helping pupils who had just arrived in secondary education develop an interest in the ancient world.

The report begins with a resounding 'Preamble' which lays out five benefits of Classical Studies for pupils aged 11 or 12. (i) Graeco-Roman civilisation can be accessed from several different but complementary perspectives which can include language, but also art, history and philosophy. (ii) 'It is possible to see more clearly the significance of events in a civilisation which can be viewed in perspective'; (iii) Such study encourages pupils to think *comparatively* about their own culture and that of others. (iv) Imaginative contact with such a vivid art and literature offers pupils psychological relief. (v) Since the Graeco-Roman world contributed so much to modernity, knowledge about it 'is necessary to a fuller understanding of our own traditions and civilisation', but is stimulating as well as instructive.[45]

What follows is a joy to read. The suggested course materials, assembled by a group of teachers from Birmingham, Hampshire, Lancashire, Manchester, Middlesex, Nottingham, Sheffield, Warwickshire and Worcestershire, repeatedly stress that these courses must be suitable for including every kind of child from every kind of background and as exciting as possible. There are plans for 'Epic', 'Legend', 'Everyday Life' and 'Mythology'. There are tips on how to include creative sessions, using dramatic enactment, painting and creative writing. There are rich suggestions on visual aids, texts such as Plutarch's *Life of Theseus*, with its fascinating cycle of heroic labours, which are richly illustrated in Athenian vase-painting, and how to decode and remember ancient proper names (e.g. Ceres by handling a Cereal Box). Audio recordings such as Orpheus' lament in Gluck's opera are mentioned.

Later in the same year, in September, a conference devoted to Classical Studies was held at Leeds University: it was the seventh *Didaskalos* conference, but the first to be held north of London. The minutes of this meeting, which survive in typescript in the British Library, reveal a lively, almost rebellious atmosphere in which teachers from every kind of school except Independent Schools, and from as far north as Aberdeen, Glasgow and Ayrshire and as far west as Wales, as well as from Lancashire, London, Hampshire, Staffordshire, Surrey and Yorkshire, pooled their experiences and plans to promote the exciting new qualifications which they all patently welcomed. The chair was taken by Kenneth R. Rowe of Leeds University, an expert on ancient terracottas and animals in art. His opening salvo reported that Leeds was now receiving applications for undergraduate places from children whose only classical education was through Classical Civilisation and that these students were excellent; those who did want to start learning Greek were proving far better at it than those who had prior training in Latin![46]

William Thompson, from the Leeds Department of Education, urged that studying classical material was a necessity 'for *all* pupils, not just for an elite'; moreover, 'the doctrine of the elite' and 'the narrow linguistic approach' were actually the precise 'dangers' inherent in the classical tradition.[47] The teachers shared observations and their sense of excitement at the new CSE in Classical Studies is palpable. Mrs Cecily Hodgson of Yorebridge Grammar School in Leyburn, Yorkshire, reported that the CSE students, after being read an excerpt from Euripides' *Hippolytus*, demanded to read the whole play.[48] There are accounts of teachers of other subjects including Drama, English, Geography and Religious Studies coming on board to deliver the new syllabus, with great success.

Sharwood Smith was on fighting form and shrewdly asked for accounts of disappointments and failures in the northern schools, from which more might be learned than from the successes. The major challenge to which the teachers confessed was that in co-educational establishments, the girls tended to want Greek myth and literature while the boys were fixated on Roman military history![49]

The delirious excitement which this democratisation of classical education engendered at the time is well described in a Department of Education and Science (DES) document published later, in 1977:

> Classical studies can now be found in the early years of sufficient comprehensive schools for it to be necessary to remind ourselves from time to time that of all the forms of classical teaching this is easily the youngest, with barely a decade's growth behind it. During the late sixties the enthusiasm for foundation courses, as they came to be called, was infectious. In particular the universal appeal to the pre-adolescent of many of the myths and legends of Greece so apparent to Kingsley

and others a century or more ago was rediscovered at a time when classics badly needed to enlarge its scope across the extended range of ability in the 'new' comprehensive schools. To purvey this wider interest and appeal the classics teacher has had to attempt to acquire a range of skills and techniques not previously demanded of him when teaching classical languages ... Most difficult of all, he has had to widen the aims of his teaching to include the cognitive, aesthetic, and even social development of his younger pupils and to make far-reaching adjustments ... In this situation some teachers have discovered in themselves surprising versatility and an unsuspected range of skills and resources.[50]

In 1966, the year after Classical Civilisation exams were first taken as part of the CSE by a small number of London and Midland pupils, Sharwood Smith presided over the establishment of JACT's first local branch, the London Association of Classical Teachers. A meeting of nearly 300 Classics teachers was convened, significantly at a comprehensive school. LACT's seminal conferences were to prove crucial for the development of modern Classics courses at different stages of secondary education, its influence spreading far beyond the metropolitan area.[51] Several excellent, detailed and annotated lists of secondary reading were prepared by hardworking teachers, names such as Miss Jean Ashbridge of Banbury School – all that is left of long and dedicated careers at the classroom coal-face.[52]

LACT produced a Working Paper in 1970, *Classical Studies in CSE*, arguing that the success in foundation courses for 11–13 year-olds in many parts of England and Wales led to the pressing need for Classical Studies in the Certificate of Secondary Education now to be made available nationwide[53] and examined by all 15 English, Welsh and Northern Irish School Boards.[54] Experience had shown that this required at least three periods a week for three years, or four to five periods over two years.[55] LACT was refreshingly determined that literature and civilisation, hitherto taught separately, should be taught as a single entity through 'topics', relating Greek drama to classical Athens and Livy to ancient Roman history, for example. This principle has remained at the heart of Classical Civilisation at secondary level, developing skills in asking how art and literature relate to and interact with the social and historical contexts in which they are produced.

The Working Paper provides a model for examination boards, proposing that questions be attempted on three Greek and three Roman topics, in the form of short essays and passages or artefacts from the prescribed materials for comment:

Greek Civilisation
The Anger of Achilles with selections from the *Iliad*.
The Return of Odysseus with selections from the *Odyssey*.
Greek Tragedy: *Oedipus Tyrannus*.
Comedy in Athens: Aristophanes' *Acharnians*.
Persia and the Greeks: selections from Herodotus.
Pericles and Alcibiades: selections from Thucydides and Plutarch.
Trial and death of Socrates: Plato *Apology, Crito* and selections from *Phaedo*.
Life in Classical Greece (material culture).
Development of Greek Sculpture.

Roman Civilisation
Aeneas and the Roman hero: *Aeneid* 2, 6, 12.
Aeneas and Roman Religion: *Aeneid* 2, 4, 6.
Legends of Early Rome: Livy 102.
Hannibal Victorious: Livy 21 and 22.
Roman Lyric poets: Catullus, Horace and Ovid (Michael Grant's *Roman Readings*).[56]
Life and Times of Pliny (*Letters* selections).
Life in Ancient Rome.
Roman Britain.
Roman Architecture.

The Working Paper also provides exemplary and abundant help with the choosing of translations, secondary reading and audiovisual aids on these topics for the proposed nationwide CSE rollout. In addition, a grant was given by the Nuffield Foundation to the Cambridge School Classics Project (CSCP), which from the late 1960s, under the aegis of Martin Forrest, compiled experimental folders of material dealing with topics in Greek civilisation which were tested in 60 diverse schools, affecting 6,000 pupils, and published in 1972.[57] The topics were 'Troy and the Early Greeks', 'Gods of Mount Olympus', 'Greek Religion' and 'Athens, Sparta and Persia'.

'To Enrich Many': the 1970s and 1980s

But what about children who did not leave secondary education at 16? We shall see in the following chapter that JACT introduced its Ancient History A Level in the late 1960s, by which time it had also begun developing

Advanced Level syllabuses in Classical Civilisation, as had individual teachers such as Mr A.F.J. Brown at Colchester Royal Grammar School;[58] the first teenagers to be offered courses at A Level in Classical Civilisation for one northern board sat their exams in 1970, the specifications and teaching materials having been made available in 1968.[59] Some other boards followed suit, drawing extensively on the materials that had been developed for teaching Classical Civilisation by Martin Forrest for the CSCP.[60] For various reasons, the introduction of the JACT's own Classical Civilisation A Level was delayed until the late 1970s, but then went quickly from strength to strength, especially after the publication of the indispensable sourcebook *The World of Athens: An Introduction to Classical Athenian Culture* (1984).

Teachers of both Classical Civilisation and Ancient History were assisted by visits to their schools from the small handful of academics who were enlightened enough to see that the future lay in these courses, notably Pat Easterling (then a Lecturer at Cambridge University and Fellow of Newnham College), but were mightily assisted by the (still today) indispensable London Association of Classical Teachers – Original Records (LACTORS), collected and annotated translated texts on themes such as *The Athenian Empire* (No. 1, 1968) and *Inscriptions of the Roman Empire* (No. 4, 1971). These have become a widely known and respected range of translated texts, still widely in use in Sixth Forms and in university courses, as will be discussed more fully in the following chapter.

Astonishingly, the Department of Education and Science seems to have failed to register the extent to which JACT, under the leadership of Sharwood Smith [fig. 2.5], had hit the ground running. The DES pamphlet *Classics in the Curriculum* (1971) does make the case 'for offering to the majority of secondary pupils some knowledge of Greece and Rome as the source of much of the culture that they have inherited'.[61] The pamphlet recommends a foundation course in Classical Civilisation to be taken for at least two years by all pupils in the early years of secondary education and strongly advocates making examined courses in Ancient History more widely available in the Sixth Form. Yet, bafflingly, it still limits its discussion of examined syllabuses in 'Classical Literature in Translation' or 'Greek and Roman Civilisation' to a single sentence, merely noting that they are now available, without even specifying from which boards.[62]

But the situation was to change again in the 1970s with the ending of the Direct Grant system, the abolition of most selective Grammar Schools and the vast increase in comprehensive schools. These eventualities all stemmed from 'Circular 10/65', the government circular to Local Education Authorities authorised by Labour politician Anthony Crosland in 1965, when he was Secretary of State for Education. From this point onwards, availability of classical languages outside the fee-paying sector, already exiguous, had begun to become almost non-existent. Muriel Telford proposed in her presidential address to the JACT Annual General Meeting in 1971 that 'How do we save Classics?' and 'What future is there for Classics in a comprehensive school?' were the wrong questions; she suggested, instead, that they needed to ask, 'What are the needs of children; how and what do we teach?'[63] She movingly describes watching children compare Leek market place to the Athenian agora and the amount others had learned from Classics. She urged teachers not to 'defend' Classics but to 'attack with it', not 'to secure further privileges for the few ... but to enrich many. And in doing so you'll save Classics incidentally'.[64]

2.5 Photograph of John Sharwood Smith. Public Domain.

A proportion of comprehensive schools and Sixth Form colleges now saw Classical Civilisation and Ancient History as exciting subjects for pupils of *all* abilities and backgrounds. Some of the modern universities, especially Kent, Leeds, Liverpool and Warwick, were now offering degrees in classical subjects without an emphasis on the ancient languages. A Levels in Classical Civilisation or Ancient History were warmly welcomed by admissions tutors at such institutions, as they are today not only in the case of applications for places in all classical subjects, but across all the disciplines available at all UK universities.

In 1977, the DES commissioned a report as one of the HMI series *Matters for Discussion* (no. 2), entitled *Classics in Comprehensive Schools*.[65] It was authored by 'some members of HM Inspectorate of schools'. It was based on an enquiry conducted between 1973 and 1974 into 309 comprehensive schools and Sixth Form colleges and published 'as a means of highlighting some of the problems of resources, organisation and teaching style which need to be solved if classics is to make the contribution which many believe it should make to the curriculum'.[66] The authors express their hope that their findings would 'promote debate at all levels so that they can be given due weight when educational developments are being assessed or planned', but ruefully add that nothing they say 'is to be construed as implying Government commitment to the provision of additional resources'.[67]

The report praises the 'much greater diversity of classics courses' that 'has thus emerged, catering for a much more varied population of pupils and selecting from a much wider range of objectives'.[68] At this time, when there was still a substantial number of examination boards, there was indeed considerable diversity in the delivery of classical education. Latin seemed to be dying in the state sector despite the best efforts of laudable initiatives, especially the Cambridge School Classics Project, but more children were studying classical antiquity than ever before. The report writers noted that Ancient History or a combined course called 'Ancient History and Literature' was available in some educational establishments to both O Level and A Level, as was Classical Civilisation, which went under several other names including 'Classical Studies'; they complimented the Classical Civilisation A Level offered by the Southern Universities Joint Board, praising its freshness and imaginative combination of topics, and noted the marked growth in popularity of all these courses.[69]

They also observe the perennial popularity of the Roman Britain option and express delighted surprise at how evidently Greek myth, in one outstanding example the myth of Daedalus, Theseus, the Minotaur and the Cretan labyrinth, stimulated a wide cross-section of pupils to artistic creativity and artworks of which they were all clearly proud.[70] They are pleased that the CSE course was proving to be an excellent training in discovery, analysis and interpretation of empirical data: moreover, 'pupils are being introduced ... to a world of ideas which would otherwise be quite outside their experience'.[71] At A Level, they are impressed at the opportunities provided to pupils by the stimulus of a completely new topic, since both Ancient History and Classical Civilisation have 'the advantage, particularly valuable in the sixth form college' that they are 'not directly dependent upon a foundation laid below the sixth form' (part of the appeal of Classical Civilisation courses today similarly results from students' ability to study the subject from scratch at either GCSE or A Level).[72] They conclude with approval that Classics courses are at last 'making a substantial contribution to the general education of a majority of pupils'.[73]

One problem that this 1977 report did not address was the two-tier system of examination at the age of 16. O Levels were still regarded as more academically demanding than CSEs, a divisive situation which badly needed tackling. GCSEs were introduced in September 1986 and the first examinations were sat in 1987, replacing both CSE and O Level qualifications. JACT was quick off the mark here, issuing a leaflet in 1986 announcing with some pride that teaching had now begun on the 'much heralded' JACT Classical Civilisation GCSE. The bureau in charge would oversee the syllabuses of all Examining Groups under the supervision of the Secretary, Miss Jenny Gibbon. But the bureau would draw on the experience of several of the Examining Groups in England and Wales: the London East Anglia Group, Midland Examining Group, Northern Examining Association, Southern Examining Group and Welsh Joint Education Committee (Cyd-Bwyllgor Addysg Cymru). There was a choice of no fewer than 15 Classical Civilisation syllabuses to choose from![74] Some included only Greek and some only Roman material. Some required coursework on additional topics and some required that coursework be tied to the examined topics. They all required both short-answer questions on gobbets and longer answers. The focus was to be resoundingly thematic and to approach ancient societies in the round: Literature in Translation would no longer be available as a qualification, and literature was not allowed to make up more than 75% of the syllabus.[75]

Public Access to Classics

The 1977 report *Classics in Comprehensive Schools* noted an increasing realisation that the ancient world belonged to everyone and that no single avenue of approach to it was inherently superior to any other. Publishers, authors and makers of film, theatre and programmes for the new medium of television had discovered that the general public had a huge appetite for the ancient Greeks and Romans. Take E.V. Rieu's novelistic prose translation of the *Odyssey*, the founding volume of the Penguin Classics series. It was first published for just one shilling and sixpence in 1946 (early copies were misdated 1945). [fig. 2.6] By 1964 it had sold over two million copies, which was a staggering feat; sales now exceed three million. Until the publication of D.H. Lawrence's *Lady Chatterley's Lover*, Rieu's *Odyssey* actually reigned supreme as the bestselling paperback in the UK, whereas only two of the versions of the epic poem available for the whole of the two inter-war decades had achieved sales of even three thousand copies. But Rieu's translation has been repeatedly republished; it has been recorded as an audiobook; it has been abridged for children; it has been illustrated with lithographs by Elisabeth Frink; it has been excerpted and interspersed with passages from more recent authors; it has been revised by his son Christopher Rieu and reissued; it is still in print at Penguin.[76] The irony is that Penguin were initially anxious about the financial viability of the project. But later the editor-in-chief,

2.6 E.V. Rieu's bestselling translation of *The Odyssey*. Hall's private collection.

William Emrys Williams, downplayed Homer's role by observing that Rieu had 'made a good book better'![77]

Another bestseller was Aubrey de Sélincourt's 1954 paperback Penguin Herodotus, a pacey, natural-sounding translation. As superbly revised and annotated by John Marincola (2003), it is still the translation of choice in many schools and universities. It had been a game-changer. Before 1954, anyone requiring any literary merit in a Herodotus translation, rather than a schoolroom crib, was faced with a dismal choice. The explicit aim of J. Enoch Powell's 1949 version was to imitate the language of the authorised Bible, resulting in ersatz Jacobean with none of Herodotus' lexical finesse. The Oxford high churchman George Rawlinson, who lent noisy Homeric and Old Testament resonances to his grandiloquent Herodotus, published in 1856–1880, before presenting it to Gladstone, produced prose both archaising and prudish: Herodotus' famous discussion of the genitals of Indian camels was of course omitted. Other versions were available, all by academic gentlemen, but they were dull and stilted (G.C. Macaulay, 1914) or dull and inaccurate (A.D. Godley, 1920). These translators universally assumed that Herodotus, who wrote in an eastern Greek dialect, must already have sounded quaint and old-fashioned to his allegedly more sophisticated mainland Greek audience. When the breezy and dynamic (as well as impressively accurate) de Sélincourt came on the market, Herodotus seemed fresh, up-to-date, funny, exciting – and therefore almost unrecognisable.[78]

Classical scholars, affronted that a freelance writer (albeit a former school teacher and an acknowledged expert on poetry and the history of exploration) was translating one of their canonical historians, accused him of making Herodotus sound journalistic and slick. But the yachtsman living quietly on the Isle of Wight had exactly the kind of real-life experience which equipped him to put excitement and verve into the story of war between superpowers: having survived Gallipoli and joined the Royal Flying Corps, he had been shot down by flying ace Werner Voss and ended World War I incarcerated in a POW camp.

So revolutionary did de Sélincourt's idiomatic version of Herodotus seem that the Greek scholar Hugh Lloyd-Jones sneered at its style, complaining that de Sélincourt had rendered Herodotus 'into flat, functional modern prose, about as distinguished as that of Agatha Christie'.[79] Had he been able to read Christie, of course, Herodotus would probably not have regarded the comparison as an insult, since she was wonderfully in control of structure and slid gracefully between description, narration and dialogue. But the comparison was certainly intended as an insult. Lloyd-Jones was horrified to discover that Herodotus had the potential to appeal to a wide public as interested in a good read as in studying the minutiae of ancient history.

Dozens of post-war films lent an excitement and glamour to classical antiquity that fed the public appetite for classical education of a vivid and accessible kind; reciprocally, better education in classical subject-matter amongst the general public makes creative artists more likely to reimagine classical antiquity for commercial purposes. 1950s blockbusters included Mervyn LeRoy *Quo Vadis* (1951), for which Peter Ustinov's unforgettable performance as Nero won the Golden Globe Award for Best Supporting Actor; Robert Rossen's *Alexander the Great* (1956) starred Richard Burton; *Ben-Hur* (1959), directed by William Wyler, was at the time the second-largest grossing film of all time (after *Gone with the Wind*); Stanley Kubrick's *Spartacus* was the highest grossing film of 1960; Rudolph Maté's *The Three Hundred Spartans* (1962) brought the battle of Thermopylae to millions; Joseph L. Mankiewicz's *Cleopatra* (1963) won four Academy Awards and is one of the most watched films of all time; Ray Harryhausen's astounding special effects in Don Chaffey's *Jason and the Argonauts* (1963) thrilled generations of children, including Edith Hall, being constantly replayed on television in the 1970s, like all those mentioned here.[80]

British radio and television producers realised what a draw were ancient Greece and Rome, a phenomenon which has begun to be researched as socio-historically important in its own right, despite such media often being regarded as ephemeral and trivialising by conservative classicists at the time.[81] The 1976 BBC serial *I, Claudius*, which adapted Robert Graves' 1934 novel *I, Claudius* and its 1935 sequel *Claudius the God*, regularly attracted audiences of nearly three million. It was in the late 1960s and 1970s that ancient Greek tragedy was also revived in an unprecedented number of productions, and was made into internationally successful films by Michael Cacoyannis, beginning with his award-winning *Electra* in 1962. The British public appetite for classical civilisation could never be sated, and more enlightened educationalists began to see links between 'popular' culture and the way that Classics was taught in schools,[82] supplying lists of suitable programmes for children to watch and ways in which to discuss them.

Conclusion

The original idea for this book can be traced to Edith Hall's personal introduction to the JACT Classical Civilisation A Level, which she first taught to teenagers in the mid-1980s. She had herself studied Latin, Greek and English Literature at A Level, and a four-year undergraduate course in Classics and Modern Languages at Oxford; she was now back at Oxford researching for her doctoral thesis in ancient Greek literature, specifically the representation of ethnic difference in Athenian tragedy. But despite her long years immersed in ancient Greek and Latin texts, and her training in papyrology, ancient metre and textual and literary criticism, she found the content of the Classical Civilisation A Level to be a revelation.

It was intellectually demanding and she needed to work hard in order to prepare teaching materials. Her grasp of the socio-economic background to ancient literature was wholly inadequate; she had never studied slavery, the social position of women, the workings of Athenian democracy or Augustan material culture. She learned much from the brilliant collections of sources in the Classical Civilisation textbook *The World of Athens* (first edition, 1984) and the LACTORS, such as *The Culture of Athens* (no. 12, 1984).[83] Hall was proud that her first A Level student achieved top marks and is now thrilled that the book resulting from her doctoral thesis, *Inventing the Barbarian*

(1989), is one of the inspirations behind an optional component of the current OCR A Level in Classical Civilisation (for the contents of which see Appendix III), 'The Invention of the Barbarian'.

The experience had a direct impact on her own research, leading her to draw connections between Athenian literature, topography, geopolitics, economics and society in ways she had not encountered before. It helped alleviate her sense that the skills and values she had absorbed via a traditional Classics education sat uneasily with her own commitment to the problems of the real world and to social progress, a sense she found best expressed by the poet Louis MacNeice when he ironically pondered the relationship between the ancient languages and social privilege in his autobiographical poem *Autumn Journal* (1938):

> Which things being so, as we said when we studied
> The classics, I ought to be glad
> That I studied the classics at Marlborough and Merton,
> Not everyone here having had
> The privilege of learning a language
> That is incontrovertibly dead,
> And of carting a toy-box of hall-marked marmoreal phrases
> Around in his head.[84]

It also convinced her, as she watched Latin and Greek increasingly retreat into the private sector, that the future of classical education at secondary level, for the more than 90% of the nation's children in state education, undoubtedly lay in the brilliant subjects Classical Civilisation and Ancient History, respectively invented and reformed in the heady days of educational democratisation in the 1960s and 1970s.

Summer 2025 marks the official 60th anniversary of Classical Civilisation's institutional recognition as an academic subject in those first CSE examinations sat in 1965. It is a subject that emerged from the grassroots, with experiments in numerous different Local Education Authorities and by diverse regional examination boards, and its evolution reflected in the new courses offered in Higher Education by the 'Robbins' universities. It is an exciting story of 'bottom-up' initiative and growth in centres widely dispersed, initially across England and Wales. As we shall see in the following chapter, the democratisation of education about the ancient Greeks and Romans took a very different trajectory in the case of Ancient History, where the decisive although equally progressive changes filtered down from action taken at a much more elite, and far more centralised, level.

Notes

1. Morell (1814).
2. Stray (1998).
3. E.g., amongst numerous others, Bruce (1818), Clark (1855), Jones (1866).
4. Livingston (1943).
5. See Funder, Kristensen and Nørskov (2019), especially Chapter 2, 'Classical Antiquity in the Danish Classroom'.
6. Hall and Stead (2020) 254–268.
7. Markovich (2018) 139–140.
8. Hall and Stead (2020) 59–60.
9. Crewe-Milnes (1921) 88.
10. Crewe-Milnes (1921) 88–89.
11. Crewe-Milnes (1921) 104–105.
12. Crewe-Milnes (1921) 163–167.
13. Crewe-Milnes (1921) 140–141.
14. Crewe-Milnes (1921) 156.
15. Crewe-Milnes (1921) 158.
16. Crewe-Milnes (1921) 160.
17. Crewe-Milnes (1921) 161.
18. Crewe-Milnes (1921) 162. On the history of the Loeb Classical Library from its early days, see Horsley (2011).
19. Crewe-Milnes (1921) 169.
20. Crewe-Milnes (1921) 169.
21. Crewe-Milnes (1921) 123.
22. Crewe-Milnes (1921) 260–261.
23. CA Council Minutes, 2 July 1949.
24. IAAMSS (1954) 128–152.
25. Forrest (2003) 43–44.
26. Geen (1974) 135–136.
27. Lister (2007a).
28. In Finley's foreword to Easterling and Muir (1985).
29. LACT (1970b); for a discussion of the 'golden era in the teaching of classical studies foundation courses', for the design of which Martin Forrest at the Cambridge School Classics Project must take much of the credit, see Lister (2007b) 42–48.
30. Lawton (1970); Geen (1974) 169 n. 176; Hunt (2018a).
31. *Humanities for the Young School Leaver* (1967) 5.
32. Robbins (1963) 8, 7.
33. JACT (1964a) 3.
34. JACT (1964a) 3.
35. Webster (1964).
36. Rees in JACT (1964a) 31.
37. Rees in JACT (1964a) 32.
38. JACT (1964b).
39. JACT (1964b) 3–4.
40. JACT (1964b) 5.
41. JACT (1964b) 12.

[42] Morton (1964a).
[43] Morton (1964b) 39.
[44] Morton (1964b) 41–42.
[45] Planning Classical Studies (1967) 1.
[46] Leeds Conference (1967) 2.
[47] Leeds Conference (1967) 2.
[48] Leeds Conference (1967) 6.
[49] Leeds Conference (1967) 7–8.
[50] DES (1977) 48.
[51] Forrest (2003) 55–56.
[52] Ashbridge and Hubbard (1968).
[53] LACT (1970a).
[54] Associated Lancashire Schools Examining Board; East Anglian Examinations Board; East Midland Regional Examinations Board; Metropolitan Regional Examination Board; Middlesex Regional Examination Board; Northern Ireland Schools Examination Council; North Regional Examinations Board; North West Regional Examinations Board; South-East Regional Examinations Board; South Western Examinations Board; Southern Regional Examination Board; Welsh Joint Education Committee (WJEC); West Midlands Regional Examination Board; West Yorkshire and Lindsey Regional Examining Board; Yorkshire Regional Examinations Board.
[55] LACT (1970a) 4.
[56] Grant (1958).
[57] DES (1971) 9.
[58] Geen (1974) 136.
[59] See Kenneth Rowe's intervention in Leeds Conference (1967) 11.
[60] Hunt (2013) 27.
[61] DES (1971) 2.
[62] DES (1971) 19.
[63] Telford (1971) 3.
[64] Telford (1971) 7.
[65] DES (1977).
[66] DES (1977) iii.
[67] DES (1977) iii.
[68] DES (1977) 3–4.
[69] DES (1977) 42.
[70] DES (1977) 50–51; 53.
[71] DES (1977) 54.
[72] DES (1977) 54.
[73] DES (1977) 59.
[74] JACT (1986) 4.
[75] JACT (1986) 5.
[76] Bell (2004) 41; Hall (2008c) 23.
[77] Blok (2002); Hall (2008c) 23.
[78] Hall (2013b).
[79] Lloyd-Jones (1991) 53.
[80] Theodorakopoulos (2010); Elley (2014); Pomeroy (2017).
[81] See e.g. Hobden and Wrigley (2019); Potter and Gardner (2022).

[82] See e.g. the remarks of L.A. Moritz, Professor of Latin at University College, Cardiff, in JACT (1964a) 26–27: 'The widespread interest in the ancient world manifested by, for example, the large sales of Penguin Classics ... should provide our greatest encouragement'.
[83] Sabben-Clare and Warman (1978).
[84] MacNeice (1979) 125.

CHAPTER 3

Ancient History Education: Past and Present

Introduction

Ninety years ago, Ancient History was taught as part of the History curriculum in secondary schools. All History teachers were expected to teach about great men such as Archimedes and Julius Caesar, according to the Board of Education's *Handbook of Suggestions for Teachers* (1937): 'The important thing ... is to concentrate on those parts of the world's story from which modern civilisation can trace a direct descent, i.e. Palestine, Greece and Rome'.[1] In this 600-page tome, which covers every area of the school curriculum from nursery to the senior phase, the value of Ancient History in the school curriculum was justified thus: 'rightly taught in biography and story and picture, the pupil may learn to recognise what we owe to Greece and Rome: the feeling for beauty and the beginnings of scientific thought and method, on the one hand, the spread of law and order, on the other; and how the fusion of the two made western civilisation, as we know it, possible'.[2]

Ancient History was limited not just to the senior phase. Rather, it is described as an important part of the History curriculum in junior schools: 'The younger the children, the stronger should be the romantic element in the narrative'. These topics were highlighted for inclusion in the junior school History curriculum: 'The Siege of Troy' and the stories 'of Leonidas, Socrates and Alexander, Horatius and Hannibal', as well as the *Odyssey* and 'stories from Herodotus [and] Plutarch'. It was noted that experience had clarified that children 'can often feel a deeper and a more personal interest in the story of Leonidas at Thermopylae, of Regulus returning to captivity at Carthage ... than in the incidents of more recent centuries'.[3]

The introduction of A Levels in 1951 saw Ancient History diverge from History as a separate subject, as from Latin and Greek. It was taught almost exclusively in Grammar Schools and fee-paying schools.[4] It was seen as a suitable third subject to complement the Latin and Greek languages, but was, intellectually speaking, alarmingly stagnant.

A Level Ancient History

The syllabuses were focussed on 'Great Men' narratives, military and narrowly political history and the location of places on maps.[5] With the support of Moses Finley (then Reader in Ancient Social and Economic History at Cambridge) and Peter Brunt (Camden Professor of Ancient History at Oxford), Sharwood Smith organised two conferences on the teaching of Ancient History in the mid-1960s. These followed the publication in 1962 by the Classical Association of *Re-Appraisal: Some New Thoughts on the Teaching of Classics*. At the JACT conference in London in March 1964,[6] schoolteachers and academics reviewed the Ancient History qualifications available and decided that change was necessary. The second conference (in January 1965) had the explicit aim of developing a JACT A Level syllabus in Ancient History; it was attended by delegates from examination boards and addressed by a lecturer from the University of Sydney, with experience of the success enjoyed by more thematically conceived Ancient History in Australian schools.[7]

Finley (Chair of the JACT Ancient History Committee until 1971, when Brunt took over) was a charismatic American scholar who had left the USA after appearing in 1954 before the United States Senate Subcommittee on Internal Security, which believed that he was associated with the Communist Party of the USA. The McCarthyite pressure drove him to migrate to Britain. As University Lecturer and then Reader at the University of Cambridge from 1955, he had already revolutionised the teaching of Ancient History there,[8] introducing a far more sociologically and anthropologically inflected approach,[9] with celebrated courses on, for example, ancient slavery (based on research which came to fruition in his pioneering *Ancient Slavery and Modern Ideology* in 1980 [fig. 3.1]) and Greek and Roman political theory. The success of his initiatives, as well as his luminous publications, notably his 'little masterpiece' *The World of Odysseus* (first published in the UK in 1956),[10] won him the post of Master of Darwin College in 1976 and the Professorship of Ancient History in 1979.

Finley proposed a completely new approach, which still underlies Ancient History A Level today, involving comparison and analysis of original sources, cultural phenomena such as theatrical entertainment, religion and crowd behaviour, conscious discussion of parallels with, and differences from,

3.1 Cover of Moses Finley, *Ancient Slavery and Modern Ideology* (1980). Hall's private collection.

modern problems and the more in-depth study of much shorter chronological periods.[11] His famous broadside against the Ancient History A Level syllabus appeared in the 1965 edition of *Didaskalos*, the JACT journal, challenging (a) the qualification's requirement for students to learn strings of events and (b) its perceived 'value' as merely providing a background to the study of Greek and Roman literature.

Echoing the discontentment expressed by practising Ancient History teacher F.H. Sparrow, who in the same edition of *Didaskalos* called for greater focus on 'topics such as literature, art, architecture, economics and science which are regular features of most modern history papers',[12] Finley suggested a greater diversity of ancient authors as prescribed sources for students of Ancient History: in addition to Tacitus and Thucydides, Horace and Aristophanes should be prescribed reading. This would allow Ancient History students to cultivate skills similar to those of Modern History students and stimulate wider and deeper discussion between teachers and students.

Both Sparrow and Finley decried the narrow thematic focus of the Ancient History A Level (with the 1963 University of London summer exam papers a particular focus for Sparrow's vitriol). Sparrow concluded that the syllabus in its current form was both overloaded and discouraging to the candidate. Finley adopted a solutions-oriented approach: it should be about more than chronology, military tactics and constitutional matters. It 'should serve to enrich the students' understandings of society, politics, culture in terms of, and in the interests of, their own experience and ultimately of the situations they will face in our society'.[13] He cautioned that students in the 20th century should refrain from speculating too much on the psychological motivations of the Greeks and Romans. They had, after all, been dead for more than two thousand years. Finally, he urged a review of the lengthy timespans for each paper (Outlines of Greek History, Outlines of Roman History and Greek and Roman History). The focus, he maintained, should be on shorter periods during which major authors lived and wrote about significant cultural achievements.

So strong were Finley's feelings about the inadequacy of the Ancient History syllabus that he published an article in *The Times* on 22 August 1966 to share his frustrations with the public. He announced that the new JACT Ancient History A Level was imminently to be introduced: 'The traditional "outlines" of Greek and Roman history have to go ... the pace required to get through several centuries of history makes it impossible to stop and think and analyse and debate'. His old egalitarian politics shone through: a syllabus was required that was not just suitable for Classics specialists, but 'equally for the many whose one opportunity this will be to study the classical world in a systematic way'.[14]

The result was an example of outstanding collaboration between schoolteachers, academics and assessment professionals. A new JACT subcommittee, chaired until 1971 by Finley, was established, with the energetic Oxford Greek historian George Cawkwell becoming a prominent member. A meeting in 1968 acknowledged that teachers would require continuous support in delivering the radical new syllabus, which led to the publication of LACTOR (London Association of Classical Teachers – Original Records) sourcebooks (which were briefly discussed in the previous chapter) and the establishment of the Ancient History Bureau; one of its responsibilities was to respond to teachers' questions. 'Really difficult questions', it is recorded, 'would be sent to Messrs Finley, Cawkwell and Brunt ...; less difficult ones would be distributed to members of the team; easy ones would be dealt with by the Secretary [Mark Greenstock] by return of post'.[15] The Bureau also published a Broadsheet containing book reviews and short articles and ran dedicated courses for teachers in London (organised by John Sharwood Smith), Bristol and Canterbury as well as Cambridge and Oxford. The LACTORs are a series of sourcebooks published by the LACTOR committee since 1968, meaning that 'every schoolboy [or] schoolgirl could read all the inscriptions' (Oswyn Murray).[16] They are now published by Cambridge University Press.

The 19 books give translations of primary source material, accompanied by relevant annotations. They were designed so that the reader required no prior knowledge. The books cover the history of Greece between 478 and 323 BCE and the history of Rome between 113 BCE and 117 CE. The history of Roman Britain is also covered, between 113 BCE and 410 CE, as well as The Persian Empire from Cyrus II to Artaxerxes I. Former Newcastle University lecturer Maria Brosius' *The Persian Empire from Cyrus II to Artaxerxes I* (first edition 2000; revised edition 2023) exemplifies the new broadminded approach to situating the ancient Greeks and Romans in the context of their neighbours by supplying numerous Ancient Near Eastern, especially Persian and Egyptian source documents, such as the inscribed statue of Udjahorresnet; this Egyptian official records his work under Persian rule [fig. 3.2]. Despite being more than 50 years old and now in their second editions, parts of LACTORs are still used in OCR's GCE A Level Ancient History and Classical Civilisation courses (for the contents of which see Appendix III).

Specimen papers were developed to accommodate these crucial principles of accessibility to newcomers and intercultural cross-fertilisation. The revised Ancient History A Level offered by the Oxford and Cambridge Schools

3.2 Drawing by Marion Cox of the inscribed statue of Udjahorresnet in the Vatican Museum, reproduced from Maria Brosius, *The Persian Empire from Cyrus II to Artaxerxes I* (*Lactor* 16), revised edition (Brosius, 2023).

Examination Board was initially taught in twenty schools.[17] One 'period paper' was required, either:

- Greece 478–402 BCE, or
- Rome 81 BCE–14 CE

Plus one 'special subject' from:

- Herodotus and the Age of the Persian Wars
- The Culture of Athens 447–399 BCE
- The Age of Augustus
- Claudius and Nero
- Roman Britain

The first candidates sat the JACT Ancient History A Level, administered by the Oxford and Cambridge Schools Examination Board, on 26 June 1969.

The insistence on economic, social and cultural factors in driving ancient history is manifest in the formulation of the questions: for the option 'Herodotus and the Age of the Persian Wars', candidates were asked, for example, 'What inspiration and comfort will the Greeks have derived from their religious beliefs in their struggles with Persia?' In 'The Culture of Athens, 447–399 B.C.', one question was 'Discuss the view that, at the time, "the constitution of Athens was one of political equality imposed upon social inequality"'. For 'The Age of Augustus', candidates were asked 'What effect had the Augustan regime on the trade of the empire?' Candidates could no longer resort to reeling off chronologically linear narratives or lists of facts; they needed to know their sources and make convincing arguments that showed they had subjected them to rigorous critical analysis.

1969, therefore, was a watershed moment in the learning and teaching of Ancient History as a school subject. Prior to this date, syllabus content, pedagogical approaches and assessment prioritised facts, dates, military operations and political activity.[18] Thereafter *understanding*, rather than factual knowledge, was the goal. Students were required (a) to show awareness of social, economic and cultural influences and (b) to engage critically with historical sources offering personal responses. Ancient History stepped out of the shadows of History, Latin and Greek, where it was previously seen only as a supplement to these courses, and assumed a stronger identity as a standalone curriculum subject 'available to non-classicists as well as classicists'.[19] The inclusion of Roman Britain offered an archaeological dimension to the subject, as well as an obvious local interest for students surrounded by archaeological remains, which had been entirely absent from Latin qualifications. John Hart, a teacher at Malvern College, praised the success of the new A Level, thanking those involved with its creation.[20]

Oswyn Murray, Professor of Ancient History at the University of Oxford and Chairman of Examiners for OCR A Level Ancient History 1980–1984 [fig. 3.3], comments:

> Moses Finley was a pretty autocratic person. He didn't pay much attention to what other people thought but ... the people who came to the conferences were teachers who were actually engaged in designing the syllabus. They had all studied ancient history, mostly at Oxford, occasionally from Cambridge. So there was a common view of what ancient history, or indeed history, was about. It was about the methods, about understanding the past, not about facts.

Minor revisions to the syllabus were made in the late 90s after the publication in 1997 of the 'Dearing Report', the series of major reports of the National Committee of Inquiry into Higher Education in the United Kingdom. The report, commissioned by the UK government, was the most substantial review of higher education in the UK since the Robbins Committee in the early 1960s, discussed in the previous chapter. Sir Ronald Dearing, an Economics graduate and former senior civil servant, was the Chancellor of the University of Nottingham. The report made no fewer than

3.3 Oswyn Murray in 2024. Photograph by Richard Poynder, reproduced with his permission.

93 recommendations in relation to the funding and expansion of higher education and maintenance of academic standards.

One requirement was the stipulation that students of History and Ancient History should study a period lasting at least 100 years. This 'outlawed' both Ancient History period papers.[21] The necessary re-workings were undertaken by Robin Osborne and Terry Edwards, members of the JACT Ancient History Committee. The two-module course morphed into a six-module course (a structural change required for all A Levels), with the addition of a 'document study' and increased chronological coverage.[22]

The Crisis of 2007

It is difficult to overestimate the role played by Moses Finley in turning Ancient History in British schools into the intellectually stretching and fascinating subject it is. John Murrell, for many years the Secretary General of JACT, once said that Moses Finley 'revolutionised the teaching of Ancient History in schools and probably saved the subject as his successor Robin Osborne did some thirty years or more later'.[23] His reference to Osborne, Professor of Ancient History at Cambridge, related to the decision that the OCR exam board announced on 24 March 2007: they planned to discontinue A Level Ancient History as a free-standing qualification.[24] No motivating factors for this decision were made public, but the JACT Ancient History committee speculated that possible reasons included: 'the desire to save money by rationalizing the number of classical qualifications ... the prejudice of one OCR subject officer against non-linguistic subjects; and finally, a culture in OCR at the time that seemed set against listening to any but well-chosen "stakeholders"'.[25] The proposal, according to OCR, was not the abolition of Ancient History, but rather that Greek and Roman history would be included in the Classical Civilisation A Level as part of a more flexible new 'Classics suite'.[26]

The response from the Classics community was a huge advocacy campaign for Ancient History in the public, political and private spheres. Maria Miller MP tabled an Early Day Motion in Westminster on 23 April 2007:

> That this House is deeply concerned by the decision made by the OCR Examination Board to withdraw Ancient History as a standalone subject at A-level from September 2008; notes that more than 1,500 people have signed a petition on the 10 Downing Street website in protest against OCR's decision; believes that a full Ancient History

A-level can provide important insights into Western culture, values and civilisation which cannot be obtained from study of units within Classics or Classical Civilisation A-level alone; and therefore urges OCR to reconsider its decision.[27]

Michael Fallon MP, then Chair of the Classics All-Party Parliamentary Group, secured a Westminster Hall debate on 25 April 2007 to further discuss, and put on parliamentary record concerns about, the 'withdrawal of Ancient History A Level'.[28] Osborne spoke on the BBC Radio 4 *Today* programme, asking the public to help the Classics community save Ancient History. The online petition on the Downing Street website asking for government intervention had been set up by a Nottingham student. It ultimately attracted thousands of signatures.[29]

Tom Holland, award-winning novelist and broadcaster, added to the campaign with 'his socialist case for Ancient History' in the *Guardian* newspaper on 5 May 2007, entitled 'All roads lead to Rome'.[30] He cleverly linked the content of Ancient History qualifications with New Labour's policy focus on Citizenship.[31] A further press frenzy erupted when, on 14 May 2007, around 50 students from Latymer Upper Girls' School in London organised a protest in Parliament Square, outside the Palace of Westminster. They were dressed in togas, wore laurel wreaths and carried placards which read 'Caesar the day! Save Augustus!' Boris Johnson MP and Michael Fallon MP, as members of the Classics All-Party Parliamentary Group, joined the demonstration and the assembly of classicists gave interviews to newspaper and TV journalists. Lucy Westerley was one of these school student protestors. She shares her memories of the event:

> I remember my teacher Miss Gibbon coming into one of our lessons, and telling me about the Ancient History A Level being cancelled. We spent the whole lesson making a plan for the protest.
>
> The event itself was very busy. Myself and students from the AS Level class below got dressed up in chitons and made our way to Parliament Square Gardens on the tube in full costume. It felt like a great adventure! We had to push to get to the front to find Miss Gibbon. The journalists were all very loud and wanted pictures of us in our costumes. They mainly asked us why we wanted to save the A Level and I got to wax lyrical about how exciting I found the subject and how I was hopefully going to Durham to continue studying it (which I did).
>
> I made the 'Caesar the Day' sign and the scroll with Latin which were photographed next to Boris. The day before, Miss Gibbon had

asked me to make props. So I spent the night creating the scroll (which I was very proud of) and some signs (and the wreath which I don't think made it into some of the photos). Then in the morning, I remember running into the art department with a sheet, iron on interface and purple ribbon, begging them for an iron so I could attach a ribbon to Boris Johnson's toga. It was surreal to say the least!

When we got to the protest and Boris Johnson came out, I was told to wrap him in the toga and hold the wreath over his head, whilst he declaimed in Latin. He got about halfway through 'we shall fight them on the beaches' in Latin before we all got called into the parliamentary building itself.

When we got inside, we were ushered into a medium sized room and began to debate. I remember feeling very shaky when I was called to speak but I got through it ok and I even argued back to a point made by one of the proposers. I was so nervous!

I do clearly remember the feeling when the A Level was saved. Thanks to Miss Gibbon letting us all be involved to such a degree, we honestly had never felt more powerful and confident. It was such an incredible experience to be a 17-year-old girl and to be invited to speak up about your views inside the houses of parliament by the shadow minster for education, and for that to actually contribute to saving a subject you are passionate about![32]

This photo opportunity [fig. 3.4] raised the stakes for a debate in the House of Lords led by Lord Andrew Adonis, History graduate and Labour Peer of Greek Cypriot heritage, on 16 May 2007.

Adonis declared that he was 'not content to see the withdrawal of Ancient History as a free-standing A Level'. The numbers of candidates had been increasing, and this had much to do with the Cambridge School Classics Project, outstandingly successful books such as Robert Harris's *Imperium* and Tom Holland's *Rubicon*, and films such as *Gladiator*. He agreed with Baroness Walmsley that the 'study of the roots of our democracy through ancient history is crucial', but sardonically added that 'the Romans were also quite good at dictatorship and subverting established governments, so, as ever in history, you can take your pick'. He said that he was 'at one with Cicero: "To be ignorant of what occurred before you were born is to remain always a child. For what is the worth of human life, unless it is woven into the life of our ancestors by the records of history?"' He asserted that it was 'our responsibility to safeguard' minority subjects.[33] An interview on Radio 4 followed, in which he made a compelling case for the continuation of

ANCIENT HISTORY EDUCATION

Ancient History as a standalone qualification.

Two days later, on 18 May, OCR confirmed that both GCSE and A Level Ancient History would continue as qualifications in their own right, overturning the proposals to absorb their content elsewhere in the new 'Classics suite'. The JACT Ancient History committee had led a masterful public relations campaign. By leveraging existing expertise and knowledge, making new connections and developing and sharing a small number of 'key messages', they secured a successful outcome. Since 2007, relations between OCR and the Ancient History subject community have been cordial, even collaborative (see Chapter 5).

3.4 Photograph of Boris Johnson outside parliament on 14 May 2007. Photographer David Sandison.

A *Private Eye* cartoon published in the same week as the demonstration, debate and U-turn by OCR depicted two OCR staff looking out of a window at a figure lying with a dagger in his back. The caption identified the corpse as the person who had tried to abolish A Level Ancient History.[34]

Crisis of 2012–2017: Re-writing of Subject Criteria

Five years after the Classics community had rallied in support of Ancient History at parliament, in newspapers and on the airwaves, it looked likely that either Ancient History or Classical Civilisation qualifications, or both, might disappear. Michael Gove, then Secretary of State for Education, wrote on 30 March 2012 to the Chief Executive of Ofqual. He expressed concerns about the standard of A Levels and whether they properly prepared students for university study.[35] The Chief Executive responded on 3 April that Ofqual 'would develop reformed A levels, through consultation, to address these concerns'.[36] This was followed by the statement made by the then Schools Minister, David Laws, in a Westminster Hall debate on 16 April 2013 on AS Levels and A Levels: 'We want to give students a better experience of post-16 study, ensuring they are studying for rigorous qualifications that will provide them with the right skills and knowledge to allow them to progress'. Neil Carberry, the Confederation of British Industry's director of employment and skills, said, 'Businesses want more rigorous exams'.[37] Curriculum subjects were reviewed for 'rigour' in 'tranches', with Classical Civilisation and Ancient History in tranche 3, for first teaching in 2017. Caroline Bristow was one of two subject advisors at OCR (from 2015) and she explains: 'the Department (for Education) was not convinced that Ancient History and Classical Civilisation met their criteria. The greatest concern was that the two overlapped, and were not really separate, distinct subjects in their own right. If the Department could not be convinced of the legitimacy of these subjects, no GCSE or GCE in them would be offered post reform'.[38]

Steven Hunt describes how these subjects avoided 'sudden death' by a combination of judicious lobbying of the Department of Education by university academics[39] and the examination boards, whose subject officers had 'travelled all over the country to lead around 40 Teacher Advisory Groups: events usually hosted by a school and attended by teachers from all over the local area. Decisions on the specifications were influenced directly by the feedback we received'.[40] The outcome this time was positive; the subjects 'were reformed and received accreditation in 2016'.[41]

Ancient History fared rather well in this reform. To reinforce perceptions of its rigour in comparison to that of Modern History, its assessment objectives and aims were tied to those of Modern History, including the use of period and depth studies and scope for the study of any geographical location in the period 3000 BCE to 500 CE.[42] Since it had already been decided that History would be included in the English Baccalaureate (EBacc), this meant that Ancient History was automatically eligible too; a big win, in both policy and practice.[43] The EBacc encouraged students to study from a range of subjects (so-called 'facilitating' subjects, as preferred by Russell Group universities) and allowed schools to be compared locally, regionally and nationally on their students' performance at GCSE in these subject areas:

- English language/English literature
- Maths
- Sciences: Biology/Chemistry/Physics/Computer Science
- History/Ancient History or Geography
- A language [including ancient languages]

AQA had, until this point, offered a Classical Civilisation A Level which allowed teachers to combine historical and literary components. But the board decided to withdraw the qualification, leaving OCR as the only provider of A Levels in Classical Civilisation and Ancient History. Peter Wright, Teacher of Classics at Blackpool Sixth Form College, gives a personal view of how the AQA withdrawal process affected him:

> The AQA Classical Civilisation course was perfect for our students. The beauty of it was that you could blend the literature and the history together. Our students haven't had any opportunity to study Classics or Ancient History at high school so the brilliant thing about the old AQA Classical Civilisation course was that you could have a couple of history units and a couple of literature units, and there was a sprinkling of archaeology. It was perfect.
>
> It was such a brilliant gateway into the subject because it had so many different strands to it and a teacher could pick and choose the modules to suit the learners. From the AQA course you had two writers for each module then the reform came in and you look at the specification for the Ancient History and you're talking 10 to 15 writers. I thought I can't afford that or how are we going to make this accessible? I was like, where the hell do we get Macrobius from? And so I'm sitting at my kitchen table at like half 11, just typing up stuff.[44]

Oswyn Murray, who examined A Level Ancient History in the 1980s, believes that 'there must be one main source. You can only study a historical period if you have a main source. Too many bitty sources distracts students from getting to know the personality of the author, which is so important'.[45]

Peter Wright continues:

> We chose to do the OCR Ancient History because knowing what our Blackpool learners are like, if I've plonked a bit of Homer or something in front of them to start off with, they would run a mile! Whereas with the units that we're doing with the Ancient History, we start with the Politics of the Late Republic. Reading Cicero is basically a glorified soap opera. And before you know it, 6–7 weeks in and they're all making jokes about Clodius and Pompey. And then we're fine. But it is a real pity that we lost the course which was much more accessible for students and had more variety.

Regarding the appeal of Ancient History to Wright's learners, he says:

> I teach in a very white working class area. Ancient History really opens up our learners' eyes to the world around them. Blackpool can be quite an insular place, but our whistlestop tour of Egypt, Iran, Iraq and Afghanistan broadens their horizons and builds cultural capital. Ancient History has a big impact on my students' aspiration and also gives them a safe arena to discuss a whole range of different topics from slavery to homosexuality.

Grounds for Optimism: 2017–2024

From an advocacy perspective, the inclusion of Ancient History on the EBacc has been transformative. School leaders can more easily create curriculum time for a subject which has policy support and which 'counts'. Teachers of Classical Civilisation have defected to Ancient History, sometimes by choice but more often by necessity, as their school attempts to compete with others in the EBacc points league. History teachers have also found it easier to introduce Ancient History because the subject content criteria align neatly across both subjects and they have equal status in the EBacc.

The subject community has worked tirelessly to provide additional support to teachers of Ancient History, new and experienced. The Classical Association Teaching Board has created A Level sourcebooks for Greek and Roman period studies.[46] This project has been a collaboration between university academics and school/college teachers and is an excellent model for the development of future co-produced resources.

It was H.W.C. Davis, a distinguished Professor of Modern History at Oxford, who remarked that Ancient History supplies the finest discipline that can be offered to the historical beginner.[47] While there remains work to be done in terms of securing policy support for Ancient History at Key Stage 3 (KS3, the beginning years of secondary school, when learners are 11–14 years old) (there is currently none), the Classics teaching community has responded in practical ways to ensure that this policy 'gap' does not become a barrier to the subject's growth in schools. The Classical Association has been increasingly active in this area since JACT 'merged' with the CA in 2015.[48] In recent years it has professionalised as a national subject association, representing educators in schools and communities, as well as universities.

The Cambridge School Classics Project has developed a free online Ancient History resource aimed at KS3 teachers and students. The Amarantus project[49] explores life in Pompeii using chapters from a novel by Caroline Lawrence entitled *Amarantus and his Neighbourhood*,[50] and archaeological research from Pompeii. Students can explore six key aspects of Pompeian life via enquiry questions such as, 'What might meals have been like for different members of Pompeian society?' They investigate a range of sources in their historical contexts to uncover evidence to help them formulate answers. Teachers are supported with lesson plans, additional notes and pedagogical advice.

Hands Up Education, a not-for-profit organisation and international community of practice, helped shift the focus of KS3 beginners beyond Greece and Rome with the publication of their textbook *Investigating Civilisations: The Persians*.[51] Designed to engage students aged 11+, *The Persians* contains 26 topics, each double-page spread focussing on one topic, which provides material for one or two lessons. Topics include:

- Geography of Iran
- Sources of knowledge
- Cyrus' empire
- Persepolis
- The Ionian revolt
- Xerxes' invasion of Greece
- Alexander the Great
- The Parthians

Priced affordably at £6 per copy, this book acts as an ideal introduction to Ancient History. Its author expected that it would be used by non-specialist teachers so created a companion website with a *free* online guide to using *The Persians* in the classroom.[52]

The *Advocating Classics Education* project has partnered with the Classical Association and Historical Association to engage History teachers who have become fatigued by teaching the world wars and the Norman conquest, for example by providing podcasts and webinars (see Appendix I). Via Classical Association talks (Arlene Holmes-Henderson spoke at the Manchester Classical Association about 'Introducing Ancient History' in July 2020), arguments have been put that have led History teachers to turn to Ancient History in increasing numbers. Hall and Holmes-Henderson have given talks at the Schools History Project and the Historical Association annual conferences, engaging directly with hundreds of History teachers, and then following up with a package of support.

Teachers in a small number of independent schools have provided significant additional support and deserve special recognition for their contributions. James Renshaw, Teacher of Classics at Godolphin and Latymer School in London, and Examiner for OCR Ancient History, founded an informal network of Ancient History teachers across England. He created an online resource bank and set up regular digital TeachMeets to ensure that teachers new to the subject had a community of practice to provide advice and help. This developed into the Classical Association podcast Season 1,[53] which covered some of the key events, themes, sources and debates in the OCR Ancient History A Level. Featuring six episodes on Greek history, it explores the three interpretation questions on the syllabus, centred on the Persian and Peloponnesian Wars, and three key types of source that feature prominently in the course – Attic inscriptions written and preserved on stone; the comic plays of Aristophanes; and the biographies of Plutarch (who is also an important source for the Roman Republic Depth Study). Commentary is provided by leading thinkers such as Professor Paul Cartledge and Dr Rosie Wyles. Season 2, expanded to a huge 20 episodes, focussed on bitesize revision for key topics in the Greek Period Study. The podcast episodes are free to access and have been warmly appreciated by staff and students alike.

Dr Steven Kennedy, Head of Classics at Harrow School, organises and hosts an annual Ancient History Teachers' day, which is free to attend. In 2024 (30 January) it included a variety of GCSE and A Level topic seminars, general plenary lectures on the specifications and teaching resources related to Ancient History in schools, and the opportunity to discuss exam technique, teaching methods and approaches to the course. To make this event fully accessible to teachers in state-maintained schools/colleges, the Classical Association offered funding (up to £150 per teacher) for travel costs. While at Harrow, the in-person networking and the opportunity to view Harrow's collection of antiquities in the Old Speech Room Gallery[54] makes it a particularly valuable, and enjoyable, professional meeting of minds.

Looking ahead, Wright would like to see the current A Level specification made more accessible, with better support materials from the examination board. He would also like to see a return to modular examinations instead of the current linear model since they 'basically just reward those that have got good memories and can write fast'.[55]

Oswyn Murray's hope for the future of Ancient History is 'there will be as few textbooks as possible. Textbooks are there to produce facts which can then be examined and quantified, whereas what you need to do is let people loose on the original evidence and see where the hell they get'.[56]

The Impact of Advocacy for Ancient History

The number of students studying Ancient History at GCSE and A Level is at an all-time high in the 21st century. Numbers at GCSE have increased 780% since 2011[57] and at A Level the increase is 241% since 2004.

Examination Year	Number of GCSE candidates	Number of A Level candidates
2004 entry	-	416
2005 entry	-	542
2006 entry	-	530
2007 entry	-	584
2008 entry	-	682
2009 entry	-	818
2010 entry	-	608
2011 entry	200	671
2012 entry	350	754
2013 entry	1,037	700
2014 entry	1,257	717
2015 entry	1,072	659
2016 entry	1,084	755
2017 entry	919	650
2018 entry	901	584
2019 entry	904	701
2020 entry	907	676
2021 entry	1,144	660
2022 entry	1,131	699
2023 entry	1,257	837
2024 entry	1,564	1,002

Table: Number of candidates for GCSE and A Level Ancient History

In the next chapter, we explore the memories and motivations of Classical Civilisation and Ancient History students and teachers, and showcase their reflections, covering seven decades of these subjects at the secondary level in schools and Sixth Form colleges.

Notes

1. Board of Education (1937) 414, 417.
2. Board of Education (1937) 417.
3. Board of Education (1937) 408.
4. IAAMSS (1954) 118.
5. Sparrow (1965) 28–29. See e.g. the University of London papers set in the summer of 1963, published in 1965 in *Didaskalos* 1(3) 31–34, with Liddel and Harrison (2013) 20.
6. Classical Association (1962); Liddel and Harrison (2013).
7. Lister (2015) 214.
8. Thompson (2016).
9. Cartledge (1994).
10. Cartledge (1994) 4.
11. Finley (1965).
12. Sparrow (1965) 28.
13. Finley (1965) 71.
14. Thompson (2016) 142; on the letter in *The Times* see also Osborne and Claughton (2003) 117; Liddel and Harrison (2013) 20.
15. Thompson (2016) 142.
16. The comments of Oswyn Murray are transcribed from an interview with him conducted by the authors on 29 August 2024.
17. Osborne and Claughton (2003) 117.
18. Liddel and Harrison (2013).
19. Osborne and Claughton (2003) 117.
20. Hart (1969).
21. Osborne and Claughton (2003) 118.
22. Liddel and Harrison (2013) 21.
23. Thompson (2016) 143.
24. Liddel and Harrison (2013).
25. Liddel and Harrison (2013) 22.
26. The OCR Ancient History subject update text from 2007 is no longer accessible on the OCR website, but its contents are discussed in detail in Hansard, vol. 459, viewable online at https://hansard.parliament.uk/commons/2007-04-25/debates/07042552000005/AncientHistoryA-Level.
27. UK Parliament Early Day Motions, Ancient History A Level, 1333 https://edm.parliament.uk/early-day-motion/33108/ancient-history-alevel.
28. As footnote 25 above.
29. Liddel and Harrison (2013) 22.
30. Harrison (2009).
31. Harrison (2009) 177.

[32] Personal communication to the authors, March 2025.
[33] Hansard, vol. 692, viewable online at https://hansard.parliament.uk/lords/2007-05-16/debates/07051670000007/SchoolsAncientHistory.
[34] See Harrison (2009) 181.
[35] Long (2017) 14.
[36] Long (2017) 14.
[37] Transcript at https://publications.parliament.uk/pa/cm201213/cmhansrd/cm130416/halltext/130416h0001.htm#13041622000001.
[38] Bristow (2021) 60.
[39] Hunt (2018) 20.
[40] Bristow (2021) 62.
[41] Hunt (2018) 20.
[42] Bristow (2021) 61.
[43] Department for Education (2019).
[44] These and the following comments of Peter Wright are transcribed from an interview the authors conducted with him on 21 August 2024.
[45] Oswyn Murray's comment is transcribed from an interview the authors conducted with him on 29 August 2024.
[46] https://classicalassociation.org/a-level-sourcebooks/
[47] Colman (1962) 24.
[48] Lister (2015).
[49] https://cambridgeamarantus.com/
[50] Lawrence (2021).
[51] Wilson (2019).
[52] https://www.the-persians.co.uk/persiaTG/overview.htm
[53] https://classicalassociation.org/the-classics-podcast-does/
[54] https://www.harrowschool.org.uk/learning-2/arts-and-culture/old-speech-room-gallery
[55] For more information on this change to assessment, see OCR (2016).
[56] Interview with the authors, summer 2024.
[57] The qualification did not exist in its current form prior to 2011.

CHAPTER 4

Voices of Experience

Introduction

Chapters 1–3 of this book traced the institutional and curricular changes that led to the emergence of modern Classical Civilisation and Ancient History teaching in British Secondary Education. Pioneering steps towards the establishment of the subjects were taken in secondary modern schools and even a few technical schools in the 1950s. Under the leadership of John Sharwood Smith, the broad-minded and imaginative Joint Association of Classical Teachers and its journal *Didaskalos* were founded in the early 1960s and Classical Studies was first examined at CSE Level in 1965, followed by the JACT Ancient History A Level in 1969 and the first A Levels in Classical Civilisation in 1970. Some of the more modern universities, especially Kent, Liverpool and Warwick, began to offer degrees in classical subjects emphasising cultural history, material culture and comparison of source material, without disproportionately privileging the ancient languages. Admissions tutors at these HEIs welcomed applicants with Classical Civilisation A Level, not only in the case of those intending to study for degrees related to the ancient world, but in other subjects as well.

But how did it feel to be a teacher or teenager experiencing these pedagogical experiments? Anecdotes tell of such phenomenally committed teachers in the early days that their enthusiasm affected even pupils not studying classical subjects. James Brabazon, a distinguished frontline documentary film-maker who has made acclaimed programmes, especially about Africa, notably in Channel 4's *Unreported World Series*, said on the BBC World Service on 4 April 2015, 'When I was in a "sink" comprehensive school in South London, the only teacher who was nice to me was the Classical Civilisation teacher'. The teacher lent him books about myth and history, totally inspiring him, so that he ended up passionate about history and got a place (against all odds) at Cambridge. He said it was 'all down' to that particular teacher.[1] Thousands of other living individuals have engaged with classical subjects, whether as students or teachers, in the post-war period, including the inspirational and award-winning leaders of the Network for Working-Class Classicists and the community group Working Classicists.[2] But very few records remain of their subjective experiences, their memories or their views on how studying classical material affected their lives at the time or subsequently. In this chapter, we supplement the institutional, cultural and intellectual narratives of the previous chapters with the thoughts of a variety of individuals, derived from online questionnaires and interviews, on what Classical Civilisation and Ancient History has meant to them personally and professionally. The tone is more colloquial and informal than in earlier chapters, reflecting the personal nature of the material presented.

Witnesses from the Coal Face

Many of the first generations of new British classicists are sadly no longer with us now, half a century on, but we interviewed Ben Andrews, who taught Classical Civilisation in the 1970s. Ben did study Latin A Level, including some Roman history, at his school in North Essex, but his passion was for geography, and in the early 1970s he read for a degree in Geography with European Studies at the University of Sussex. After his Postgraduate Certificate in Education (i.e. teacher training), in 1977 he was employed as a Geography teacher at Peter Symonds College in Winchester, which had been a Grammar School since 1944 and had just become a state Sixth Form college in 1974. The college did not have quite enough Geography classes available and he was asked to fill his timetable up with various other things, including a class in Classical Civilisation. He says that he felt 'like a complete imposter!', especially since the other two Classics teachers were specialists – a young man and an older woman who had been Head of Classics at Winchester County Girls' High School, which was now a comprehensive.

The subject had been introduced the year before and his approximately 23 students, 'a really nice bunch', and mostly girls, were now in the seventh year of their secondary education, or the 'upper sixth'. He remembers being impressed with the syllabus because it centred on social history rather than a linear top-down historical narrative about the Roman Empire and the wars it waged. He was struck by how genuinely interested the students were in the material, rather than just focussing on getting high grades. Ben really enjoyed teaching the subject and thought it was a much better way of approaching the ancient world through the everyday life 'of ordinary Roman people' than by the traditional ancient history he had experienced himself at school, which involved somewhat uncritically reading Tacitus on emperors and their wives.

Ben left teaching altogether a few years later. After working in IT he retired, and has now volunteered as an archaeological archivist in West Berkshire Museum for a decade and a half. He is certain that his encounter with Classical Civilisation spurred him on to take such a strong interest in archaeology. And while he found it intimidating, at first, to be asked to teach classical antiquity as a non-expert, he enjoyed the background reading he needed to do. He also thinks that the plethora of easily locatable sources of information that are available today, free and online and in broadcasts, would make it much easier for a teacher of Physics or Business Studies or any other subject to turn their hand to Classical Civilisation, and would encourage them to do so.

A quite different career path lay in front of Nigel McFarlane, who studied A Level Classical Civilisation in Salford, Greater Manchester, in the mid-1980s. Afterwards, he immediately went to work in a theatre; he has been a Repertory Theatre professional, a journalist and employed in public policy and the Civil Service. He has very distinct memories of the lessons, which he puts down to the novelty of the subject for him and 'the skill and personality of the teacher', Mike Billinge, who was 'simply fantastic. His enthusiasm for the subject and encouragement of us all lit a fire in me which never went out. I still remember him quoting the opening lines of *Oedipus Rex* to us as we began to study it'. Nigel thinks that the skills imparted by the subject affected him in a 'subtle' way that has been manifested in his varied career; he wryly recalls being reminded of Cicero when navigating office politics! And he is one of many to whom we have talked who enjoyed Classical Civilisation so much that they have retained an interest in it all their lives. Nigel is, at the time of writing, completing a part-time BA in Classical Studies with the Open University.

Nigel's is one of the voices of experience to which we have been able to listen through the network of contacts built up by our initiative *Advocating Classical Education*, social media and an advertisement placed in the *New Statesman* inviting individuals who have personally taught or studied at the coal face of the new Classics qualifications to contact us. We have succeeded in painting a more grassroots picture of the stimulating atmosphere in the classrooms where these subjects have been and are being delivered. Our participants' ages range from teenage years to late 80s. They studied at all types of educational establishment: Comprehensive School, Free School,

Academy School, Convent School, Sixth Form College, State Grammar, Private Grammar and Direct Grant-funded. We designed a questionnaire asking them to share their memories; almost all agreed to be named in this book, but a few anonymous quotations are also included.

The questionnaire, included in this book as Appendix II, contained 33 questions. Besides requesting personal details and information about where and when the respondents had studied classical subjects, the questions were designed to elicit subjective answers about private experiences and views. What were the most and least enjoyable elements of the courses? Were the respondents affected personally or professionally, and if so, how and why? Would they encourage young people to choose these subjects today? An important part of the questionnaire entailed identifying the skills and competencies which the respondents believed classical subjects could bestow on those who took them. Honest responses to the current content of the syllabuses were also requested.

When we asked why they chose to enrol for a classical subject, the answers were diverse. One of the older ones had been listening to Thomas Babington Macaulay's *Lays of Ancient Rome* (1842) recited by 'an inspiring teacher', which encouraged her to seek out historical novels, especially those by Mary Renault, and fall in love with Alcibiades as portrayed in *Last of the Wine* (1956).[3] One 'entered the Classics room where students were dressed in togas and acting out an Aristophanes play – it seemed such a contrast with my experiences of education to date. The students also looked like they were having so much fun and that instantly appealed to me. Within weeks of starting the course, I had found my academic calling'.[4] Another was interested in English Literature and started delving into the various ancient texts referenced by T.S. Eliot in 'The Waste Land': 'Once I did that, I was hooked on the ancient texts, too'.[5] A participant who studied Latin and was *not* offered Classical Civilisation at school, but now teaches it, writes, 'In Year 7 we did *The Tale of Troy* in English,[6] and History started with pre-History and took us through Greeks and Romans. I loved making the links between what I knew of mythology or history and what we were learning in literature, particularly when it came to the *Aeneid*. I also enjoyed having knowledge that connected to other subjects, especially English Literature and French'.[7] Such responses reveal the importance of non-classical literature that has used classical material creatively in attracting children to the ancient world and the rich possibilities for cross-fertilisation with other academic subjects that studying the ancient Greeks and Romans offers.

A typical response from one who had embarked on Classical Civilisation at 16 years of age reads, 'I had no prior knowledge of the subject as it wasn't offered at GCSE or lower down the school. I thought I might find it interesting and it complemented my English and History'.[8] But where the subject has been well established in a school or college for some time, it can feel like a natural and far from unusual choice. Gemma Adams worked in retail for four years after her Classical Civilisation degree at Leeds, but eventually did teacher training and successfully introduced the subject to Allerton Grange School in Leeds in 2018. She is insistent that it was the respect that the subject was held in at the school she attended that enthused her and made it possible for her to become such an advocate for the subject. There were large classes and no fewer than three excellent teachers: 'When I was at school, I had no idea that Classics was not a subject that was taught everywhere – it had the same status as every other subject in the school … It is because of my experience that I am now so driven to support the fight for Classics in more schools'. Her experience shows that where classical subjects are available and seen as a normal part of the curriculum, children opt to choose them, regardless of how little exposure they might have had to them at home.

Laura Jenkinson took A Level Classical Civilisation at Cardinal Vaughan Memorial School in 2000, but she had been inspired much earlier at Drayton Manor High School by an introduction to classical mythology in Year 7; she was also motivated by Adrian Spooner's *Lingo: A Course on Words and How to Use Them* (1991), which explains, without needing to study the languages, how to improve your English by understanding the principal Greek and Latin roots of words. She chose Classical Civilisation at 16 because it was 'on offer and nothing I'd ever studied before – it seemed magical to be able to take an interest and turn it into a qualification'. She had 'heard the myths growing up but now we got to study them'. It was 'really enjoyable, and I remember thinking this was what school was actually for'. She was particularly enthused by 'the gods and the stories' and 'learning about the plays and studying art and architecture'.

Sometimes parents played an important role. Another respondent says that she just loved classical subjects. 'They were my favourite from year 8. It was my Dad who got me into the Romans, though. I've loved them for as long as I can remember, always visiting sites and reading about them'.[9] But more often it was the quality of the Classics teachers and the enticing promise of visits to Italy or Greece: one loved 'the culture that surrounded the subject, often somehow more nurturing than other subjects, with teachers who cared passionately about their subject but also about their students. There were also some great trip opportunities both in the UK and abroad!'[10] Another, now a teacher of these subjects, states, simply, 'My Classics teacher … was the most inspirational of teachers and is the reason I do what I do today'.[11] Teachers were 'really inspiring; passionate about the subject and [taught] interesting lessons'.[12]

Memories of classroom experiences once our respondents had embarked on a classical subject become quite specific and reveal the perennial magic of truly great works of literature and art if they are only made available to the young. For one, Greek comedy was thrilling: 'I will never forget reading Aristophanes' *Women at the Thesmophoria* in sixth form!' Tragedy is a perennial first choice: 'We read *Hippolytus* and I fell in love with the subject. I also loved all of the connecting myths'.[13] The ancient epics have always been firm favourites: '[I remember] reading the *Odyssey* as a class, discussing different aspects of heroism and having strong views as a class on Odysseus as a character'.[14] One participant says there are 'too many things to remember', but she 'enjoyed making films of Greek legends with Playmobil' and has particularly vivid memories of A Level Ancient History in the 1980s: 'There were a number of Goths ... I remember "Doc" (our teacher) asking one of them to fix an iron in class that she'd broken at home ... she called it "The Ionian Revolt"! We also had a Classics song that we always used to sing, with the lines,

> I've got a brand new red tractor;
> I keep it outside in my barn.
> Euphrates river in my barn.
> Alexander Helios in my barn, etc...

We made it up on a trip to York once and it is always sung when I see old friends!'[15] One teacher, a vicar's wife, is remembered as 'very keen on Plutarch'; she 'had recently come over from the Falkland Islands so at least when Argentina invaded we knew where they were. We spent a lot of time writing practice essays on Alcibiades'.[16] An examiner would have been impressed if an answer on Alcibiades drew a parallel with the motivation behind the sending of a British taskforce to the Falklands. The opportunity to draw parallels and contrasts between ancient and modern current affairs is one of Classics' chief advantages.

Alexandria Rooke studied Classical Civilisation at St Bernard's Catholic Grammar School in Slough. She was inspired by Greek theatre: her 'eccentric' teacher 'Dr Pamela Barratt used to take us to the theatre regularly, even when it wasn't part of the course, just for fun; it was on a visit to see the *Oresteia* at the National Theatre that I decided to study Drama at university with a focus on Greek Tragedy. She was deeply passionate about the subject and that rubbed off. She took us all around Greece and this experience was also incredibly formative for me'. For Francesca Grilli, a deep impression was made by 'the strong sense of community amongst A Level Classicists. I loved how multi-disciplinary it was and the often risqué nature of the content!' For her, it was material culture that first created the greatest excitement: 'Greek art was my favourite since it opened my eyes to the world around me. I suddenly noticed the classical influence on buildings I have seen hundreds of times before in my own town and I enjoyed feeling like an expert when I visited galleries and museums with friends'.

Grilli attended comprehensive school and Sixth Form college in Southport, Lancashire, taking A Level Classical Civilisation; she graduated from Nottingham (BA) and the Open University (MA) and has taught at Runshaw College for more than a decade (since 2012):

> My A Level Classics teacher is the reason I chose to study the subject at university level and also why I teach it myself today. Her passion for the subject was infectious and I loved her relaxed nature and good sense of humour. Her lessons are the only ones I remember from my time at Sixth Form. Absolutely (and this is true for most Classics teachers I have met) there is an inherent love for their subject that is unique. [They] really do live and breathe the ancient world. It's also something I'm pleased to say my own students note about me today.

Teachers' command of their subject is often praised as much as their enthusiasm: 'Both were fantastically knowledgeable'.[17]

We asked our participants about the skills, competencies and perspectives they believe that studying Classical Civilisation and Ancient History confer. We often use the image of a Swiss army knife: one multi-tool entity can equip you to perform many different kinds of intellectual action. One teacher agreed: 'I love this for explaining to students the vast array of skills they will gain from ancient subjects. I tell them that they will not only enjoy the content and have fun along the way but become well equipped for any future career path'.[18] All the respondents agreed emphatically that the following skills, which we had identified in the course of our own pedagogical experience, are nurtured by these courses:

1. Cultural literacy: understanding the significance of key figures and events in world history and literature.

2. Source evaluation: interrogating reliability and authority of evidence and propaganda.

3. Critical comparison of competing authorities in a complex society.

4. Articulating arguments: familiarity with great ancient speechmaking and persuasive communication.

5. Overview of long-term human history: the place of ancient history in human development.

6. Understanding of competing identities: national, European, cosmopolitan, ethnic, political and religious.

7. Interdisciplinary skills: thinking about a whole civilisation in the round, both society and art.

8. Political sophistication: approaching original development of ideas about democracy, republics, empire, citizenship and gender roles.

Some remarked on one or more of these individuated skills. On source evaluation, one commented that the current OCR Ancient History specifications (for the content of which see Appendix III), which they are now teaching, is 'my first ever time doing this, never touched in English A Level, or History GCSE'. Another recalled 'considering Tacitus and Suetonius in this light when using them as sources for the Julio-Claudian Emperors. Also the artwork and building programmes of Augustus. In a world of "fake news" it is becoming increasingly important to understand provenance of sources and why the author is saying what they are – the image that they are trying to project to the world'. In Classical Civilisation, respondents think that the module 'Imperial Image' is particularly stimulating because it asks students to identify and evaluate the propagandistic techniques deployed in both visual and written sources, which is a skill needed to navigate modern advertising and marketing strategies.

The Athenian Democracy option in A Level Classical Civilisation is singled out for praise in terms of delivering the ability critically to compare competing authorities in a complex society, especially 'when we study what the Athenians thought was good about their democratic system and then why it was criticised … healthy free speech! Recent years have seen the rise of the demagogue again with Trump/Boris/Farage. Wonder what Cleon would make of them?!' Several respondents mention how in class there are constant 'references to ways in which ancient history affects our current way of life', especially modern politics, and explaining 'major institutions in this country' which 'owe their very existence to a connection to the ancient world', such as the church.

On 'articulation of arguments', some provided specific memories of exciting lessons where students put their new grasp of rhetorical tools into practice: 'I remember a memorable lesson giving speeches after we'd studied both rhetorical devices AND Cicero's gestures'. 'I was a keen debater in school so was interested. I remember thinking about the speeches in comedy and the arguments about clever speaking. I also remember talking about the speeches in *Medea* in detail'. 'Getting students to make up their own speeches was an exercise that was encouraged in Ancient Roman schools! We like doing it today ... we put Dikaiopolis on trial (was he really a traitor to Athens?) and asked students to make up speeches for and against!'

Understanding competing identities struck a chord with several teachers: pupils are 'always exploring identity of different cultures and different points of view. The tragedies are particularly helpful to do this! The themes of the plays never grow old because they were written to explore political dilemmas in the first place, e.g. *Antigone* explores resistance to authority'. An example of the honing of interdisciplinary skills was 'utilising literature such as Pliny and Pseudo-Lucian for a better understanding of the reception of Greek art'. Jo Hobbs, now Chief Executive of the charity *Classics for All*, who studied Classical Civilisation at both GCSE and A Level before taking a degree in what she sees as the 'allied' field of Theology, believes that interdisciplinarity, the opportunity to study an entire culture in the round, is one of the chief merits of classical subjects: 'All of it – the multi-disciplinary approach – art and architecture, literature, drama, religion'.

Some participants would like to see the list of skills that we proposed expanded. Although there is no component of either subject exclusively dedicated to philosophy, sooner or later the birth of philosophy in classical Greece is always encountered on these courses. One teacher added 'a Philosophical viewpoint: an understanding of how Western philosophy has developed from the metaphysics, ethics and epistemology of the classical world'. Cultural intelligence was mentioned by several: 'these subjects enable students to have enquiring minds, open minds and broad minds. The world can be looked at objectively'; 'recognising what is cultural difference, even when there is a seeming (superficial) similarity, and valuing different outlooks/perspectives'. One respondent enjoyed a talk given by 'Prof Peter Stewart (Oxford) on Roman art from Gandhara and China and the influence of Greek sculptors on Buddhist art which really opened my eyes'. The sheer range of skills imbued by classical subjects is often said to have built self-belief: 'The confidence and variety of study I think have helped me as part of being an all-rounder. I am adaptable'.[19]

Several respondents commented on how much they enjoy engaging with other ancient civilisations with which the Greeks and Romans interacted: Achaemenid Persian texts in 'Invention of the Barbarian', and Egypt and Parthia in the Augustus module. 'Classics helps us to connect the modern world with the foundations that it is built on. With the decolonisation and expansion of the subject there is even more relevance to the modern world as we recognise that Classics isn't just about old white men in togas!'[20] Juvenal's *Satires* and especially Petronius' *Dinner with Trimalchio* are thought by one respondent to help understand class distinctions and the ways in which they are discussed in both ancient and modern societies.[21] One teacher particularly emphasises how useful the portrayals of gender and sexuality in ancient texts can be in the modern classroom, singling out the variety of female and gay characters in the *Aeneid*. The GCSE module 'Women in the Ancient World' is a strong favourite, as Edith Hall discovered when delivering several sessions to Hope Valley College, Derbyshire in 2019, where the students were all taking the course voluntarily as an 'extra' outside timetabled hours. Caron Downes, who has taught this module at The Mount School, York, writes: 'My dissertation was in scheming women from Greek lawcourt speeches and I still relish the opportunity to look at anything to do with Greek / Roman law and women. The new GCSE module on women is a brilliant opportunity to introduce students to so many fascinating stories'; it is 'well written and I feel the literature supports the course'.

Penny Whitworth, a teacher at Newcastle Royal Grammar School, thinks that 'close analytical reading of texts' is another core skill implanted by Classical Civilisation:

> It requires examination of plot, theme, character, use of language and you need to be able to pick apart a text and consider the author's motivations/narrative skill. For example, in a text like Euripides' *Medea*, we have to consider what we make of Medea as a character, as a woman, as an outsider, as a barbarian, as a 'witch' etc. and consider what Euripides is trying to say through her – and through the way she is whisked away at the end of the play – and how the audience might have responded with their particular worldview, and what all of it is saying about the gods.

This skill is highly transferable, she adds, not only to analysing the literary works of other and more modern cultures, 'but also in understanding the way communication happens more generally, both in the written and spoken word'.

Another thinks that emotional literacy, developed by discussing the depiction of rage, revenge and grief in, for example, the *Iliad*, is as important a life skill as all the others. Cheryl Juckes, teacher at La Sainte Union Catholic School in North London, agrees about the *Iliad*: 'I love the stories and the sense of lives of passion, humour and pain, and also the parallel world of the gods, who are far more petty and vengeful than human beings'. And Sian Squire, who teaches Classical Civilisation at Shrewsbury Sixth Form College, is fascinated by the rich and versatile skillset which the subject seems to have developed in her students: 'I am constantly in awe of the types of jobs my ex-students go into, from being the Associate Director of Tranmere Rovers football club to performing *Hamilton* on the London stage! One old student runs a well-known travel agency and has chosen as the symbol for his company an ancient Greek helmet'.

The breadth of the modules which teachers and students say have been their favourites to experience is testament to the inherently interdisciplinary nature of study of the ancient world. Nancy Moore is in no doubt that it is ancient Greek theatre: she always goes back to 'Euripides. Because he speaks truths'. One specifies examining ancient coins on the Imperial Image option and the various opportunities for studying ancient food (for example, in Greek comedy). Ancient Greek art, especially vases, and Roman architecture in 'City of Rome' are always popular ('I love its architecture and the deep richness of its history').[22] For others it is one of the great works of literature: Homer's *Iliad* and Euripides' *Medea* ('Both are such astonishingly relevant and beautiful works of literature'[23]), or the lyric poetry of Sappho or Catullus.

Ancient religion, especially in the GCSE 'Myth and Religion' and the A Level 'Greek Religion', finds many fans. Teachers and students enjoy the emphasis on specific sanctuaries such as the sanctuary of Zeus at Olympia and the Acropolis,[24] and especially Delphi: 'My absolutely favourite topic has to be the site of Delphi itself. It's such a spiritual place with so much to discuss; from Greek religious practices, to inter-city rivalries and examples of stunning Greek art and architecture'.[25] The 'Greek Theatre' option is praised by many not only for the choice of plays and artefacts, but for including secondary scholarship, 'a positive step in preparing students for university'. This option 'contains a wonderful mixture of character, plot, themes which engage the modern audience in their contemporary relevance but also necessitate learning and understanding the historical, social, performative context of – primarily – 5th-century Athens'.[26]

In Ancient History, 'Fall of the Roman Republic' and 'Alexander the Great' attract special praise: 'The narrative of a variety of huge personalities, the mixture of complex causation, political dealings. The huge wealth of information available means that you can always go into greater detail. I also love teaching this to Year 13; although challenging, it is accessible and engaging to students';[27] 'I have most enjoyed teaching ... the life and times of Cicero, Augustus, Alexander'.[28]

Would our respondents, whether teachers or students, encourage others to take these courses? Every single one replied in the affirmative, but for a variety of reasons. Frances Shaw, who took her A Levels in 1970 and taught Classical Civilisation for decades, answered this question eloquently:

> Wholeheartedly! There is such a breadth of interest in Classics; the literature contains so much profound thought about the human condition and has influenced so many artists and writers up to the present day. Studying Classics gives you a frame of reference, a lens through which to view the world: for example, I'm sure no classicist can hear about the Brexit referendum and ensuing debacle without thinking of the Mytilenean debate. I would wish the same satisfaction that I have had from Classics for everyone else. Another consideration is that in all the years I have taught and examined Classical Civilisation, I have never encountered anyone who regretted studying the subject; when I was an examiner, I found even those who were not particularly successful appeared to have enjoyed the course.

Christina Gooptu believes that the A Level is not only 'academically rigorous', but 'hugely interesting and accessible to students whatever their previous contact (if any) with the classical world'. Adam Mason stresses the training in skills in both subjects, at both GCSE and A Levels, which he says 'are incredibly valuable for sending young people out into further education and employment post 16 and 18'. Juckes focusses on 'the cultural capital they provide – without it huge swathes of literature and art are inaccessible', as does Helen Mars, who says it also enhances English vocabulary: 'It's not just for posh kids!' For Whitworth, these subjects are the ultimate Humanities: 'Students can see that very little has changed in human behaviour and I think that's important!' Downes emphasises the importance of understanding classical myths and stories because they pervade our culture and 'are around us all the time'. Matthew Gee, who took the A Level at Xaverian College, an inner-city Catholic Sixth Form college in Manchester, and now teaches it, says that he 'would argue Classical Civilisation is a very adult course, and makes you look deep inside yourself – especially Greek tragedy'.

Our respondents also wrote about how they felt studying and/or teaching Classical Civilisation and Ancient History has affected their lives and personal development. Almost all described how enthusiasm for antiquity has informed their recreational activities: 'I visit museums all over the world, especially for their Greek vase collections'.[29] 'I mostly holiday to countries with Classics sites ... I draw comics of Greek myths'.[30] Another writes, 'I love theatre and attend as much as I can, particularly Shakespeare and anything Greek – the classical passion links these two. I can answer lots of classical questions so I am invaluable at quizzes. I am doing a Latin course at University College London next week!' Whitworth reads 'fiction inspired and influenced by the ancient world, and I'm always looking out for productions of Greek tragedy'. Mars translates classical literature for pleasure and writes creatively about it.

Some of our respondents have found that their training in the classical world has helped them professionally. One respondent, who left school at 18, worked as a Teaching Assistant, but then in Verulamium Museum, with its splendid Roman mosaics and artefacts,[31] while studying for her BA and MA in Classical Civilisation at the Open University and becoming a subject lead in History at a primary school.[32] Juckes worked as a journalist, where she found 'it was extremely helpful to be able to recognise classical allusions and use them myself. I was a very useful resource to my colleagues'. Moore, who studied Classical Civilisation at King George V College in Southport and at university, found her training useful in all kinds of ways when she worked for six years for major corporations in the City, but she could not get Classics out of her system and now teaches it at St Mary's College, Crosby. But some were sufficiently inspired by studying classical subjects at secondary level that they elected to pursue a career teaching them straightaway. Grilli became determined 'to help as many other state school students study the ancient world as possible'. Mason is clear that 'without having access to this at 6th form my whole career would be noticeably different. I probably would not have taken Classical Studies at university, possibly not even chosen a career in teaching'. And Downes believes that 'Classics teachers appreciate the need to be involved in extracurricular projects so much more than other subjects', so offers masterclasses and a summer school in Classics and also teaches GCSE Latin to students from other schools for free. 'I think we all know how much needs to be done to spread the word about our brilliant subject'. Squire puts it simply: '32 years after doing my own A Level I am still teaching it!'

Case Study: Emma Bridges

Out of many inspiring personal stories, Emma's stands out, partly because she is one of the most committed patrons of our initiative; she was one of the main speakers, along with Newcastle-based working-class poet and classicist Tony Harrison, at our first Durham ACE public outreach event

4.1 Photograph of Emma Bridges by Edith Hall.

at Durham Cathedral on 4 July 2018 [fig. 4.1]. Emma's secondary education began at Willington Parkside comprehensive, where there was no Classics provision at all. She was excited by the 'enthusiasm and joy' of the 'inspiring' Classics tutor, Ken Parham, at an open day at Durham Sixth Form Centre (and attracted by the free bus pass!). Reassured that she did not need to have had any prior experience of the subject, she decided that Classical Studies (as the qualification she took was called) would complement her other A Level choices (English Literature and History), and in 1993 she opted to embark on the course. She had never even encountered the idea that one could study the ancient Greeks and Romans before, despite, as she now laughs, 'living a stone's throw from Hadrian's Wall and two miles down the road from Binchester Roman fort'.

Emma is still in touch with friends who took the same A Level at the same time; all say that they were infected by the teacher's 'enthusiasm and how much he loved it [i.e. classical antiquity], and what a massive advocate he was for the subject'. As for Emma, by the end of the first term, having previously assumed she would probably study English at university, 'I knew I had found my thing and that I wanted to do more of it. I loved it'. She realised that she could continue to study literature and history, but also learn about architecture and art – and she had an 'arty' side after taking Art GCSE. In Classical Civilisation, she says, all these things are 'tied together'.

It was from Mr Parham, who had studied Classics at Bristol University, that Emma first began to understand that she could take up the languages at degree level. 'None of us would have ever had a clue about that before hearing him talk about it'. Then Emma faced her first obstacle. Parham suggested she should think about applying to Oxbridge. Oxford had just introduced a new pathway through the degree in Classics, called Course II, which enabled students without an A Level in either ancient language to be admitted, except that they still needed a GCSE in one of them. Having not had an opportunity to study the languages formally even to GCSE level, Emma had also missed the Oxbridge Open Days because her college was not 'plugged into' the necessary network of contacts. She wrote to some of the admissions offices at several Oxford colleges, and most said that the GCSE was a requirement, full stop. Others said that they were not even considering applicants for Course II, but that they would still only take students with at least one ancient language A Level. But at Brasenose College, the Ancient History tutor, Dr (now Professor) Greg Woolf (who is one of ACE's patrons, as we will see in the following chapter), as well as the people Emma wrote to at a couple of other colleges, said that if she attended a summer school in one of the ancient languages, they would take it as evidence that she was interested in it and capable of studying it.

So at 17 years old Emma enrolled for the inaugural Durham summer school in ancient Greek, and it was a life-altering experience. She met people from schools 'the like of which I had never encountered before' – private schools; these teenagers were 'doing the summer school basically as a bonus for their UCAS [Universities and Colleges Admissions Service] applications'. But Emma did Beginner's Greek with a few others, and the part she remembers loving was that I 'felt like I was discovering a bit of me ... a thing that I could explore that was new to me'.

Emma went to Oxford, consolidated her Greek, began to study Latin and took First Class Honours in 1999 – the first student ever to get a First on Course II. This was a remarkable achievement, but Emma says that she was *not* a natural language learner and found it difficult: 'For me, language learning was a means to an end. I was expected to do it as part of my degree and personally have always been very glad I did as it gave me some important tools for thinking about the texts I'm interested in. This meant that I was well equipped to research the things I've tended to focus on since then. But I do feel strongly that there are lots of different ways to be a classicist, all of which are valid and important – and not all of them involve having to read Homer or Virgil fluently in the original'.

She followed her undergraduate degree with an Oxford MSt in Classical Languages and Literature in 2000 (she is keen to stress that her generation still did not need to fund tuition fees in Higher Education). She then won a scholarship to read for a PhD at Durham University on the figure of Xerxes the Persian king in ancient and more recent cultural history. She was supervised by Professors Peter Rhodes and Edith Hall and in due course the thesis resulted in a monograph published by Bloomsbury in 2015.[33]

Emma is now a Senior Lecturer and Staff Tutor in Classical Studies at the Open University. She regards the OU as her 'spiritual home', because she is now teaching people who might not have had access to the classical world by traditional means – a world that she has found 'so fulfilling and enriching'. This 'aligns so well with everything that I've experienced myself in the past'. She says, 'I never had an *intention* of being an academic ... I thought I was going to work in publishing, journalism, something like that'. But gradually she realised that she loved studying Classics 'and I just didn't want to stop'; 'I never quite felt that I'd got enough of it'. In her spare time she loves reading fiction set in the ancient world and she has a keen interest in the ways in which creative practitioners work with classical themes; alongside her Classical Studies PhD students, she also currently supervises a Creative Writing PhD student whose work centres on Cassandra.

Although Emma herself stresses that she (and the other people with whom she is in touch who studied Classical Civilisation A Level alongside her) did not choose it because she was thinking in terms of transferable skills, she agrees with those identified earlier in this chapter. What she would personally add to that list is something to do with emotions: 'I don't know whether I'd call it emotional literacy, but certainly an emotional intelligence. Empathy'. She does not think that this is unique to Classics and believes that it applies broadly to some other Humanities subjects. Yet she does think that the ancient world, taught well, can nurture sympathy for how 'people from different societies and cultures think and feel and express themselves, as well as understanding your own society or your own emotions'.

Emma's second monograph, *Warriors' Wives: Ancient Greek Myth and Modern Experience* (2023), exemplifies this conviction. Emma's husband was an RAF pilot who saw active service; her personal experience and emotions, as well as those of other military spouses, are interwoven with the ancient epic and dramatic presentations of the anxiety and ordeals undergone by wives during the Trojan War, above all Penelope in the Homeric *Odyssey*. Little surprise, then, to discover that her favourite author is Homer. His poems, for Emma, are 'about the entirety of life, about everything that makes us human. They encompass the full spectrum of human emotions. They're about grief and love and fear and anger and joy and loss and familial relationships and so many different aspects of life ... how we organise our societies, how we treat one another as humans ... and how we think about morality. There's always something else to discover in Homer'.

Case Study: Peter Wright

Blackpool-born Peter Wright, like Emma, has devoted his life to improving the accessibility of the ancient world to people who might never have been able to enjoy it otherwise. He went to a state primary school and remembers being inspired by Homer when he was only in Year 3: 'I still remember my teacher wheeling out this big TV and there was some chap and he was reading sections from the *Odyssey* with pictures in the background. And I was like, "Oh my gosh, this, this!"' After Catholic High School, he attended Blackpool Sixth Form College, where he took A Levels in English Language and Sociology as well as Ancient History. He chose Ancient History because he had been intrigued by the local Roman archaeological sites to which his father had taken him as a child, and because the Ancient History teacher, Derek Slater, was 'a wonderful chap': Peter remembers being in a group of just six and taught in a room so small he compares it to 'a broom cupboard'!

But he was bowled over by what he calls the 'romantic' element of studying antiquity. He recalls his excitement when, having been aware of the importance of Julius Caesar to the history of his own region, he first read a text written by the great Roman himself. For him, it was the titanic figures, 'the big hitters', as he calls them, of Roman History – Cicero, Pompey – that proved to be his 'gateway' into a passion for antiquity, and a fascination with the 'literature and society of this massively colourful world'.

Peter progressed to Lancaster University, where he had initially enrolled to study English, but within days had changed to History, partly because the curriculum included units in Ancient History (as it still does). Inspired by the internationalism of the university, and hearing so many languages spoken, he eagerly embraced the chance to learn Latin as well. Straight after graduating he studied for the PGCE in History because he wanted job security. He knew that he wanted to stay in the North-West and got married at only 22. He feels he was lucky because there was an opening for a History teacher at the end of the teacher training course at the Sixth Form college which he had attended, and the Head Teacher asked him at interview whether he would teach the Ancient History A Level, which was attracting far too few students and was in danger of being cut. Peter was given a year to turn it round. And turn it round he did! The following year no fewer than 50 signed up. He remembers being called into the Head Teacher's office in the summer of 2007 to be told this news, and the enormity of his excitement and relief.

How did he achieve this? He is very modest about it, saying he simply implemented his 'learning and teaching skills' and acted on his commitment to 'making the vocabulary accessible'. 'The beautiful thing about teaching this stuff is that as a teacher you don't have to work very hard at making it awesome and interesting: the material itself is ... One of the best things as a teacher is when you're walking around the room and you can hear students making little 'in' jokes about the texts that they've been reading or the people that they've studied'. He acted on his instinct to put the students into direct contact with the ancient sources that had so excited him as a teenager, like Herodotus, because it is the authentic voices of ancient individuals that make the subject so vivid. He asked the college to buy him 20 copies of Cicero's letters, which provide a uniquely thrilling portrait of life in the last years of the doomed Roman Republic: 'It all stems from actually finding out who these people are and engaging with them'.

4.2 Photograph of Peter Wright in York beside the Statue of Constantine in 2023. Reproduced with his permission.

After 17 years of delivering the ancient Greeks and Romans to several thousand Blackpool teenagers, in different periods via both the Classical Civilisation and the Ancient History A Levels, he currently (2024) has 120 students studying Ancient History A Level. The number involved means that he has had to train up other teachers at the school to meet demand. He stresses the importance of building up relationships with local 'feeder' schools, both primary and secondary; he has developed appealing 'taster' sessions, often focussing on the Battle of Actium in 31 BCE, when Augustus' fleet defeated the combined forces of Antony and Cleopatra. This can be angled to appeal to either a history class or literature students, since so much Roman poetry, especially Vergil's *Aeneid*, responds to the battle and its personalities. Word of mouth and sibling relationships have helped build up recruitment, too: many students say they were encouraged to try a subject they knew little about by an older friend or brother or sister. Peter finds that students say that someone has told them about the exciting field trips they can go on if they do Ancient History – not just the trips abroad, but the museums and sites and classicising architecture on their doorsteps in Preston, Chester and Ribchester, to which 'the vast majority of students, even though it's a 25-minute drive away, have never been' [fig. 4.2].

Peter's remarkable achievements in promoting education in classical subjects in a socio-economically deprived area have won him recognition. In 2008, Blackpool Sixth Form College was named in the *Good Schools Guide* as achieving the highest results by male students in Ancient History. Two years later, Peter was named Outstanding Teacher of the Year at the college. He hit national headlines in 2015 when he was not only shortlisted for the *Times Educational Supplement* award for making an Outstanding Contribution to his subject, but was named *TES* Teacher of the Year; the trophy was bestowed on him at the awards ceremony by the comedian, presenter, screenwriter and author David Baddiel.[34] And in 2023, Peter was delighted to be named Community Classicist of the Year by the Working Classicists initiative.[35]

An Interview with Shirley Barlow

One significant figure in the emergence of Classical Studies at university level, a development which had a knock-on effect in terms of bringing the subject to the attention of secondary education professionals, was Dr Shirley Barlow, and she agreed to be interviewed by us [fig. 4.3]. She was appointed Lecturer in Classics at Kent at the time the university was founded in 1965, which coincided with the inaugural school CSE examinations in Classical

4.3 Photograph of Shirley Barlow with Edith Hall in 2020, taken by Sarah Poynder and reproduced with her permission.

Studies in the UK. The Kent department set the tone from its inception by labelling itself the Department of Classical Studies.

Barlow, who was born in Surrey, had received a conventional education at Sutton High School, a girls' selective Grammar School which was then a state Grammar School in which some pupils, like Barlow, were receiving a free education funded by Direct Grant from the government. She took degrees in Classics first from UCL, where she remembers feeling somewhat restricted by the narrow, philological focus of the curriculum taught at that time, and subsequently from Cambridge. She then studied and taught at the University of Ann Arbor, Michigan for four years. Despite loving the USA and being promoted to an Assistant Professorship, she was yearning to implement a change in the way the subject was taught, and when she heard about the plan to open a university in Canterbury, she says, 'I was drawn to the idea of a new initiative and couldn't resist applying'.

She found it exciting to design a brand new curriculum alongside her original colleagues. At that time the university ran a compulsory course for all Humanities students entitled 'Britain in the Modern World', which she remembers broadening her students' horizons immensely. Interdisciplinary courses were also encouraged, so she introduced pioneering modules that were clearly important forerunners of the emergence of Classical Reception Studies in other institutions, especially her 'Ancient Greece in the Modern World', which traced the reception of classical culture from the 18th to the 20th centuries, and on which she collaborated with colleagues in the departments of English and Modern Languages. Since many students were applying by the early 1970s with qualifications in Classical Civilisation or Ancient History, the department never offered courses requiring specialist knowledge of ancient Greek or Latin, such as textual criticism, prose composition or palaeography, although the ancient languages were available to learn if students so wished at both beginner level and more advanced levels. Mark Drakeford, Former First Minister of Wales (2018 to 2024), studied Latin alongside other classical courses there.

While colleagues taught historical modules such as ancient slavery and philosophy (all available to be taken in translation), Barlow pioneered courses on classical literature and myth in translation. Her own research specialism was Greek tragedy, and besides her evergreen *The Imagery of Euripides* (1971), she made a point of publishing editions of two important plays in the 'Aris and Phillips' series, which has a unique format that makes the plays as useful to readers without ancient Greek as to those studying it in the original. This format consists of a long, accessible introduction, with facing translation in contemporary English and – crucially – a commentary keyed to the translation rather than the Greek text. Her *Euripides' Trojan Women* (1986) was followed a decade later by *Euripides' Heracles* (1996). The *Trojan Women* edition was instrumental in that play frequently being adopted on A Level courses in Drama and its regular productions by theatre companies. Unsurprisingly, her Kent modules on ancient drama were extremely popular, prompting many applicants to choose that university and students from other departments to participate.

One of them was Alan Davies, a comedian, writer and TV presenter best known for acting the lead in the BBC mystery drama series *Jonathan Creek* (1997–2016) and as a permanent presence on the panel show *QI*. He studied Drama & Theatre Studies at Kent in the mid-1980s, and remembers Barlow with gratitude: she was the best teacher he had at university, since she was 'engaging and knowledgeable and [someone who] inspired commitment to her subject, classical drama'.[36] Barlow herself is clear about the merits of studying classical literature in translation: 'I think that all the arguments that apply to studying [texts in the original] languages apply to Classical

Civilisation in the sense that the literature is so good that if it is well translated you can still get a massive amount out of it'.

An Interview with Penny Murray

While Shirley was pioneering new degree courses at Kent, Penny Murray [fig. 4.4] was involved in similar initiatives at the University of Warwick, which had also been founded in 1965 in response to the Robbins Report. Penny had the opportunity to learn Latin at a very early age at a Froebel primary school, where the teaching followed the enlightened principles formulated by the 19th-century Friedrich Froebel, who invented the term 'Kindergarten'. As a result, she knew she loved languages and in due course took the traditional Classics triad of A Levels in Latin, Greek and Ancient History at a private school before studying Classics at Newnham College, Cambridge.

Her tutor there was Pat Easterling (later Regius Professor of Greek at Cambridge), who, as was noted in Chapter 2, was an energetic supporter of Classical Civilisation qualifications in schools. Although Penny loved language work, she says that she began to realise that many of the academic classicists, with honourable exceptions,[37] while brilliant at editing texts, had 'very little interesting to say about the content of it'. She related to the feelings W.B. Yeats expressed in his poem 'The Scholars':

4.4 Photograph of Penny Murray in 2024 by Richard Poynder, reproduced with his permission.

> Bald heads forgetful of their sins,
> Old, learned, respectable bald heads
> Edit and annotate the lines
> That young men, tossing on their beds,
> Rhymed out in love's despair
> To flatter beauty's ignorant ear.
>
> They'll cough in the ink to the world's end;
> Wear out the carpet with their shoes
> Earning respect; have no strange friend;
> If they have sinned nobody knows.
> Lord, what would they say
> Should their Catullus walk that way?[38]

Penny reminds us that this was the late 1960s, when there was 'the beginnings of a realisation' that there was more to 'reading really exciting texts like Euripides' *Bacchae*', because they were 'about real, living human beings. They are about humanity'.

Having decided that she did not want to spend her life focussed on editing texts (although her edition of Plato's reflections on literature in the *Republic* and *Ion* is indispensable to scholars),[39] for her Cambridge PhD she chose concepts of inspiration, such as the Muses, which she traced well beyond antiquity under the supervision of a classicist who has been key to studying Greek and Roman literature from a Comparative Literature standpoint, Michael Silk. That research in due course resulted in volumes on both the Muses and the idea of Genius.[40] She feels that 'the ancients thought so much about what it is to be human – more so than, say, many medieval authors', and she is 'not terribly interested in God!' The ancient Greek gods, however, she thinks are perennially fascinating, because they behave like outsize humans, with the crucial difference that they do not age or die. What is it, then, to be human?

Penny is worried that some modern approaches to ancient literature overlook their aesthetic aspects, their sheer beauty, and wanted to teach it in ways that make these qualities accessible to a wider range of students. So after a Junior Fellowship at Oxford, she applied with alacrity for a newly created post at the recently founded University of Warwick. There was no department of Classics, but an inspirational Professor of English, George Hunter, one of the 'pioneering academics who, in the wake of the 1963 Robbins Report, were tasked with tackling elitism, gender discrimination, and class-and-culture prejudice in higher education by widening participation', and asked 'to imagine a new Humanities ethos for a changing world'.[41] Hunter left Warwick for Yale in 1976, but not without leaving his mark on future developments.

Thanks to his vision of English literature as part of a cultural continuum which could only be properly understood in a European context, there was already a strong classical component in the syllabus: for example, a core course for all students was the European epic tradition, from Gilgamesh, Homer and Vergil to Dante and Milton. In this enlightened atmosphere, the development of Classics was strongly supported not only by Humanities teachers, notably Tom Winnifrith and Ken Gransden in English, and Andrew Barker, an ancient music expert employed in the Philosophy Department, but also by scientists and mathematicians. So in 1976, the Joint School of Classics was set up with two young lecturers at the centre, supported by colleagues with a classical background in other departments. Penny was appointed as the literature specialist, together with another new lecturer who specialised in Ancient History, Sam Lieu, who brought a fascinating comparative perspective resulting from his Hong Kong Chinese heritage.

Penny found the position of Classics not consisting of a separate department, but being deployed as a foundational subject across the Humanities, most congenial. She also enjoyed the diversity of the students she was teaching. Still in her mid-20s, in her very first year, she taught three highly appreciative old age pensioners.

The first degree courses were introduced that year, one in English and Latin, the other in Classical Civilisation. At the outset, there was a requirement that applicants for Classical Civilisation had O Level Latin, but this was rapidly abandoned, 'partly for practical reasons (not enough candidates around) but also because it would put off precisely the people we wanted to attract, i.e. those who hadn't had the opportunity to do anything classical at school'. By abandoning the requirement and welcoming students with qualifications in any subjects whatsoever, the application numbers increased, so that while the initial intake in 1976 was ten, applications had risen to 72 by 1981. It was a very popular degree course, even though, as Penny recalls with a smile, 'word went round Oxford that in Warwick University library, St Augustine's *City of God* was catalogued under "Town Planning" – quite a good joke, but indicative of a certain attitude'. She also remembers one student transferring into it from after a year of reading Classics at Cambridge and finding Warwick much more inspiring.

The introduction of a degree in Classical Civilisation necessitated the speedy development of a new syllabus and modules 'on the societies of Greece and Rome as unified cultural wholes, not merely as unrelated fragments of "literature", "history", "philosophy" and so forth'.[42] She became certain that seeing civilisations in the round rather than narrow linguistic training was what was required by the majority of graduates: 'What about the people who will go out into the world and become civil servants, politicians, captains of industry, management consultants, experts in human resources, publishers, media tycoons, TV producers, script writers etc.? Better that the future bank manager should read the *Iliad* or the *Aeneid* in translation than not read it at all'.[43] Penny did discuss the exciting developments at Warwick with Shirley Barlow and share ideas when they were teaching together on summer courses; she also visited Cardiff University in order to discover what similar courses taught by teachers including Nick Fisher looked like there. There had been a Cardiff tradition going back decades earlier to a lecturer named Kathleen Freeman,[44] who taught there between 1919 and 1946, and also lectured to miners' groups locally. The new Warwick syllabus was originally based on Greek and Roman literature in translation, but soon metamorphosed, with modules on culture and society.

Penny remembers some interesting characters among the Warwick students. One, Robert Thirtle, went off to be a puppeteer and theatre professional. Stephanie Norgate is a poet and author of plays broadcast on radio and was for many years Reader in Creative Writing at the University of Chichester. Tim Loughton, who gained a first-class degree in Classical Civilisation in 1983, was a Tory MP and Parliamentary Under-Secretary of State for Children and Families from 2010 to 2012. Neil Masuda worked as a journalist for *The Sun* newspaper after studying for an MA with a thesis on the poet Ovid, later moving to the *Mirror*. Penny feels that studying Classical Civilisation opened up her students' eyes 'to a whole new world, which was actually a world that was the foundation of the world that they lived in. It was both like it, but different'. They might be 'bowled over' by Homer or tragedy, but also learned a great deal from 'understanding it on a human level'. 'It just speaks to them', partly because the centrality of family relationships to ancient Greek literature is fundamental to its perennial appeal. When it comes to issues around difficult topics such as sexuality, she believes that 'it's much safer to discuss them in relation to the ancient world than to discuss them as things are now because of everybody being so polarised'. On the other hand, if the discussion of sexuality occurs in the context of another time and place, 'you can really talk about the issues'.

Conclusion

People who have studied Classical Civilisation or Ancient History at school, Sixth Form college or university, have become teachers and academics, but they have also become journalists, politicians, IT specialists, archaeologists, theatre professionals, poets, business people, sports stars, musicians, civil servants, advertising executives, hospital administrators, travel company owners, lawyers and broadcasters. The personal themes that recurred in their almost exclusively positive views of classical subjects are the self-confidence and cultural literacy that these subjects bestow, the enhancement of understanding of other academic subjects, as well as the utter delight in the sheer beauty and brilliance of the works of art and literature to which they offer access. But many have commented on how well engagement with the ancient Greeks and Romans has equipped them for critical analysis of current affairs and politics; classical material offers a safe arena for talking about 'difficult' and divisive social issues – gender, race, sexuality – and encourages a broadminded, relativist attitude to cultural difference. But we had not expected quite such an insistence from our respondents and interviewees on the human values, moral sensibility and emotional literacy that they associated with the classical courses in which they had participated. The ancient world can help make us wiser and better people and the modern world perhaps a slightly more tolerant and hopeful place to be.

Notes

[1] BBC World Service 'Weekend' programme, 28 minutes 23 seconds in at http://www.bbc.co.uk/programmes/p02ngjt1.
[2] https://www.workingclassclassics.uk/#:~:text=An%20intersectional%20lens%20that%20acknowledges,Network%20for%20Working%2DClass%20Classicists. https://www.workingclassicists.com/
[3] Frances Shaw.
[4] Francesca Grilli.
[5] Sian Squire.
[6] Green (1958).
[7] Cheryl Juckes.
[8] Adam Mason.
[9] Becky Milne.
[10] Penny Whitworth.
[11] Catharine Jessop.
[12] Becky Milne.
[13] Nancy Moore.
[14] Adam Mason.
[15] Sian Squire.

[16] Cheryl Juckes.
[17] Adam Mason.
[18] Francesca Grilli.
[19] Jo Hobbs.
[20] Jo Hobbs.
[21] Clare Jevon.
[22] Anna Karsten.
[23] Christina Goopta.
[24] Becky Milne.
[25] Francesca Grilli.
[26] Penny Whitworth.
[27] Adam Mason.
[28] Catharine Jessop.
[29] Frances Shaw.
[30] Laura Jenkinson.
[31] https://www.enjoystalbans.com/listing/verulamium-museum/
[32] Clare Jevon.
[33] Bridges (2015).
[34] https://www.tes.com/magazine/archive/tes-fe-teacher-year-i-was-hugely-honoured-and-thrilled-win-award
[35] https://www.workingclassicists.com/post/working-classicists-awards-2023-the-results-are-in
[36] Davies (2009) '1986'.
[37] She mentioned E.R. Dodds, whose *The Greeks and the Irrational* (1951) had argued that Greek reason and logic had been over-emphasised, to the detriment of understanding the mystical, spiritual and transcendent elements of the ancient Greek experience, such as maenadism.
[38] This is the revised version of the poem which Yeats published in the second edition of *The Wild Swans at Coole* (Yeats (1919) 25).
[39] Murray (1996).
[40] Murray and Wilson (2004); Murray (1989).
[41] Rutter and Howard (2008).
[42] Penelope Murray in Murray and Murray (2001).
[43] Penelope Murray in Murray and Murray (2001).
[44] See Irwin (2016).

CHAPTER 5

Advocacy for State School Classics Education

In the previous chapters we have presented the results of our research into the history and development of secondary qualifications in Classical Civilisation and Ancient History in the United Kingdom, and have attempted to describe how they have been experienced by teachers and students over the decades. This book is the result of an Arts and Humanities Research Council (AHRC) Leadership grant, which commenced in 2017, entitled *Studying Classical Civilisation in Britain: Recording the Past and Fostering the Future*. But the campaigning component of our project, *Advocating Classics Education*,[1] entailed setting up partnerships with 15 institutions across the UK's four nations, where colleagues would engage with schools in their region to draw attention to the advantages of Classical Civilisation and Ancient History and support their introduction across a growing network of diverse educational settings.

Disappointed by the dearth of detailed accounts and photographs of the seminal meetings and events that took place in the 1960s and 1970s at the dawn of the democratisation of Classics education that we describe in Chapters 2 and 3, we here provide a record of some of the exciting initiatives that took place 'on the ground' all over the four nations during the first years of ACE's activities as it built up a network of grassroots partnerships. The tone is informal, reflecting the atmosphere of the events as they took place. We offer this account in case it is of interest to those who are motivated to help grow such educational opportunities in the future.[2] The chapter then traces developments subsequent to the project's initial funding, as ACE expanded its activities to include outreach in collaboration with museums, its move to the North East of England and new horizons including the teaching of classical subjects in prisons.

Phase One

Pilot events and sessions with school students were run throughout 2016, including a gathering that featured activities and discussions with London Sixth Formers on 17 June 2016 [fig. 5.1].

5.1 Caroline Bristow, Arlene Holmes-Henderson, Edith Hall and Mai Musié at an outreach event at KCL on 17 June 2016. Photograph by Steven Hunt.

The project was officially launched at a major event at KCL on 1 July 2017, where speakers included Dr Maria Haley and Professor Emma Stafford (Leeds). A panel of schoolteachers (Steve Mastin, Paul Found, Stephen Dobson, Ken Pickering, Simon Beasley, Ed Bragg and Jo Lashly) explained to university partner representatives what was currently missing in terms of support and advocacy, to inform future directions of the project at local, regional and national levels [fig. 5.2].

5.2 The Teachers' Panel at the official launch of ACE, KCL 1 July 2017. Photograph by Edith Hall.

ACE Partners

University partners included Queen's University Belfast, University of Bristol, Durham University, University of Exeter, University of Glasgow, University of Kent, University of Leeds, King's College London, University of Nottingham, Open University, University of Reading, University of Roehampton, University of St Andrews and University of Swansea.

ACE Researchers

Edith led the project from its inception in 2015. Arlene began as AHRC Research Fellow in Classics Education at KCL from 2017 and continued as Senior Research Fellow until 2022. She worked part-time on this project throughout (averaging 2.5 days a week). Thereafter she became co-director of the ACE project at Durham University and Professor of Classics Education and Public Policy there.

The project has benefitted from the input of postgraduate and postdoctoral research fellows, with Dr Rory McInnes-Gibbons the latest addition. Dr Peter Swallow was webmaster for the *Advocating Classics Education* project as a PhD student working on the reception of Aristophanes,[3] and a member of the team since 2017. He is currently MP for Bracknell [fig. 5.3] and Chair of the All-Party Parliamentary Group for Classics at Westminster. But Peter was previously a Research Fellow at Durham University working on the popular reception of Aristotle's natural science on the Leverhulme-funded *Aristotle beyond the Academy* research project.[4] Before that, he held a postdoctoral position at the Centre for Hellenic Studies, King's College London (KCL), and taught at both KCL and Goldsmiths. He has also taught at Notting Hill and Ealing High School.

5.3 Peter Swallow MP. Photograph reproduced with his permission.

Marcus Bell was a Public Impact Researcher for the ACE project. They completed their BA and MA at King's College London, focussing on 20th-century receptions of ancient dance, and a DPhil at Oxford on Euripides' *Bacchae*. Marcus teaches in the Department of Theatre and Performance at Goldsmiths University of London and remains dedicated to outreach and activism inside and out of the classroom. Their current research examines chorality at the turn of the 21st century by considering the work of dance practitioners, performance artists and activists. With ACE, they travelled across the country attending events with each partner university [see below fig. 5.16] and collated and analysed the feedback from those events to inform a larger understanding of the impact this project has created.

Samuel Agbamu was an ACE Public Engagement Assistant while completing his PhD at King's College London. He travelled with the team to events hosted by our partner universities, where he represented the project admirably to educational audiences and members of the public [fig. 5.4]. Sam is now Lecturer in Classics at the University of Reading and is writing a book on Italy's ideological use of the Roman Empire during its colonial endeavours in Africa in the 19th and 20th centuries.

5.4 Samuel Agbamu at Leeds University event. Photograph by Edith Hall.

Bella Watts completed her undergraduate studies at Barnard College in New York, majoring in Ancient Studies. Her focus was gender and sexuality in the ancient world, having previously studied Latin and Greek at school. She supported ACE's mission to make the study of classical subjects more accessible and inclusive [fig. 5.5]. Bella collaborated with Arlene on an article

5.5 Bella Watts. Photograph reproduced with her permission.

surveying the UCAS entry tariffs for classical courses at British universities[5] and now works in the banking sector.

Nimisha Patel completed her PhD exploring the presence of Classics material in Post-Independence Indian school textbooks [fig. 5.6]. 'Nimi', dedicated to changing education to accommodate a wider demographic of students who feel marginalised in mainstream education, volunteered with ACE as she believes that Classics offers students the opportunity to develop skills in synthesising large quantities of multi-disciplinary data. This is a skill which she thinks is beneficial and unfortunately slowly fading in an education system focussed on creating 'worker bees'. She now works for a charity supporting expansion in affordable housing.

5.6 Nimisha Patel. Photograph reproduced with her permission.

Kitty Cooke was an Ancient World student at UCL. She attended the state-sector Parrs Wood High School in Manchester, where she was inspired to study Ancient History by her teacher David Midgley, and is passionate about expanding the teaching of Classics to all [fig. 5.7]. She lectured on ancient coins at an ACE event held at the British Museum, having previously volunteered at the British Museum in the Department of Coins and Medals. Kitty is now Development Manager at the Museum of the Home in London.

5.7 Kitty Cooke. Photograph reproduced with her permission.

Our researchers included Caroline Latham, who studied English at Queen Mary University of London, taught drama in London state schools for decades, took Classical Civilisation A Level, learned Greek, enrolled at the Open University and was awarded her PhD at King's College London for an excellent thesis on translations of Greek drama for the professional stage. Caroline conducted archival research for the project, delving into old textbooks and exam papers for all exam boards since Classical Civilisation and Ancient History qualifications were first introduced [fig. 5.8]!

5.8 Caroline Latham. Photograph reproduced with her permission.

5.9 Sarah Poynder. Photograph reproduced with her permission.

Sarah Poynder [fig. 5.9], now a civil servant, was a History undergraduate at UCL and conducted research on the backgrounds of people with experience of Classical Civilisation and/or Ancient History secondary qualifications, collecting, analysing and interpreting data and compiling statistics supplied by our survey and questionnaire.

ACE Patrons

The ACE project has six official patrons who support our work and offer invaluable advice. Professor Paul Cartledge was the inaugural A.G. Leventis Professor of Greek Culture in the Faculty of Classics at the University of Cambridge and a Fellow of Clare College [fig. 5.10]. He has also been the Hellenic Parliament Global Distinguished Professor in the History and

5.10 Paul Cartledge. Photograph: public domain.

Theory of Democracy at New York University. He has written and edited over 20 books, many of which have been translated into foreign languages. He is an honorary citizen of modern Sparta and holds the Gold Cross of the Order of Honour awarded by the President of Greece.

Natalie Haynes is a writer and broadcaster and – according to the Washington Post – a rock star mythologist. Her first novel, *The Amber Fury*, was published to great acclaim on both sides of the Atlantic, as was *The Ancient Guide to Modern Life*, her previous book. Her second novel, *The Children of Jocasta*, was published in 2017. Her retelling of the Trojan War, *A Thousand Ships*, was published in 2019. It was shortlisted for the Women's Prize for Fiction in 2020. It has been translated into multiple languages. Her non-fiction books, *Pandora's Jar: Women in the Greek Myth* (2020) and *Divine Might: Goddesses in Greek Myth* (2024) enjoyed great success in the New York Times Bestseller list. Her novel about Medusa, *Stone Blind*, was published in 2022 and Margaret Atwood liked it. So did Neil Gaiman.

Natalie has spoken on the modern relevance of the classical world on three continents, from Cambridge to Chicago to Auckland, and tirelessly advocates for us at state-sector schools and colleges [fig. 5.11]. She writes for the *Guardian*. To date, 11 series of her show, *Natalie Haynes Stands Up for the Classics*, have been broadcast on Radio 4.

5.11 Natalie Haynes speaks at Redborne Upper School in Bedfordshire. Photograph by Edith Hall.

Our philosopher is Malcolm Schofield, Professor Emeritus of Ancient Philosophy at the University of Cambridge. He is the author of a number of definitive texts in his areas of expertise: *Saving the City: Philosopher-Kings and Other Classical Paradigms*, which provides a detailed analysis of the attempts of ancient writers and thinkers, from Homer to Cicero, to construct and recommend political ideals of statesmanship and ruling; and *The Stoic Idea of the City*, which offers the first systematic analysis of the Stoic School.

Dr Emma Bridges (whom we met in Chapter 4) completed her PhD in Classics at the University of Durham (2000–2003), with a thesis on the ancient reception of the Persian king Xerxes. Prior to that she studied Classics, first for a BA (1995–1999) and then for an MSt (1999–2000), at Brasenose College, Oxford. She spent three years at the Institute of Classical Studies (School of Advanced Study, University of London) as Public Engagement Fellow in Classics, but has been at the Open University since 2021 as Staff Tutor and Senior Lecturer in Classical Studies. As well as focussing on research and teaching in Classical Studies, she is committed to making Arts and Humanities research accessible to audiences beyond academia, and to fostering collaboration and conversation between academics and wider communities. She gave the keynote at ACE's event in Durham in 2018 (see above, fig. 4.1).

Charlotte Higgins is the chief culture writer of the *Guardian* newspaper. She is the author of six works of non-fiction, five of them about the classical world. *Under Another Sky: Journeys in Roman Britain* (Jonathan Cape), was shortlisted for the 2013 Samuel Johnson Prize, among other awards, and in 2010 she won the Classical Association Prize. She believes everyone, whatever their background or income, should have the chance to learn about (and through) the classical world [fig. 5.12].

5.12 Charlotte Higgins at the Exeter University Event. Photograph by Arlene Holmes-Henderson.

Charlotte was born in the Potteries, studied Classics at Oxford, and was awarded an honorary doctorate from Staffordshire University. She lives in London.

Professor Greg Woolf is now Leon Levy Director of the Institute for the Study of the Ancient World at NYU [fig. 5.13]. As a cultural historian of the Roman Empire, he has a longstanding interest in the culture of empire in the ancient world. Much of his work considers the Roman world in a global perspective. He has written on literacy, knowledge cultures and libraries, ethnography, the Roman economy, gendered Roman history and the emergence of religions. Currently he is working on a book on migration and mobility, and also on urban resilience as one aspect of the environmental history of antiquity. Greg writes:

> It is a privilege as well as a pleasure to be associated with *Advocating Classics Education* which will fight to give as many as possible the opportunities I first enjoyed in the 1970s. I learned Latin and Greek at Bexhill Sixth Form College, and then at Christ Church, Oxford. I learned to dig on the Sussex Downs as a schoolboy, and later wrote a doctorate in Cambridge. Classics is the most naturally interdisciplinary subject it is possible to study or teach. I still enjoy going back and forth between history, archaeology and classical literature in my writing which has touched on literacy, economics, imperialism, libraries, pottery and hillforts. My work takes me around the world, because academic Classics is a truly international community.

5.13 Professor Greg Woolf, Leon Levy Director of the Institute for the Study of the Ancient World at NYU. Photograph by Genevieve Shiffrar.

ACE Events

Soap Operas and Goddesses in Kent

On Saturday 30 September 2017, we held our first ACE event at Kent University's lovely campus in Canterbury. Hosted by Dr Rosie Wyles, it was attended by teachers and secondary-level students from all over the county, notably the legendary Paul Found, who single-handedly built up classical subjects from scratch to huge numbers of students at Norton Knatchbull School in Ashford [fig. 5.14]. The entertainments included our Natalie Haynes, who delivered a hilarious talk on what Aristotle's analysis of Sophocles' *Oedipus Tyrannus* (a set text for the A Level Classical Civilisation option on Greek theatre) could tell us about how soap operas are written. First rule: Aristotle's *'Unity of Place'* explains why most of them are named after the locations in which they are set, for example, the East End of London, Coronation Street in working-class Manchester and Emmerdale in the Yorkshire Dales.

5.14 Paul Found in action. Photograph by Edith Hall.

One of the most famous ancient objects in the local Roman museum is a figurine of the Dea Nutrix, or Nursing Goddess, who holds twin babies. Rosie asked everyone to suggest a caption for a photo of the deity. First prize went to Vicky Stone from Simon Langton Girls' Grammar School for the witty one-liner, 'The third triplet's under my chair'. The fun continued with a film recorded by Paul Found's students. They had made an episode of the *Jeremy Kyle Show* (a British tabloid talk show) in which Orestes had an altercation with the Furies over whether he had been entitled to kill his mum Clytemnestra. It made the scene of Orestes' trial in Aeschylus' *Eumenides* look like a vicarage tea party.

The hilarity was balanced by two moving talks. Kent University lecturer Dr Christopher Burden-Strevens recounted how it was only the study of Classical Civilisation which had rescued him during a tough adolescence. He went on to learn ancient languages at university and now is flourishing in his permanent academic post. And Caroline Ball's discovery of the Greeks and Romans through Classical Civilisation at her comprehensive school led to her winning a place to study at Oxford. Comic and serious by turns, the day covered archaeology, philosophy, literature, history and languages; it was enhanced by the warm hospitality we all enjoyed from our hosts at Kent University.

Coins and Captions in Leeds

Our partners in Leeds provided a range of engaging Classics activities for teachers and students on a wet Wednesday in darkest December 2017. Participants had travelled from schools across Yorkshire, Derbyshire, Humberside and Lancashire. Then postgraduate student (now school teacher) Maria Haley described how she had been educated at a state-maintained school in Sheffield. Gemma Williams (whom we met in Chapter 4, now Gemma Adams), a History teacher from Allerton Grange School, summarised her motivations to introduce Classics to the curriculum and provided tips including how to optimise communication with senior leaders, promote the subject to students and source funding to set up a new subject. Lucy from Dixons Trinity Academy explained the role of Classical Civilisation and Ancient History in broadening the cultural horizons of students in Bradford. Participants then transferred to the Brotherton Gallery, where they enjoyed two handling sessions of ancient artefacts led by postgraduate student Elinor Cosgrave and Professor Emma Stafford. This opportunity to connect with the material past in a tangible way ensured smiles all round.

Hilary Hodgson from the charity Classics for All (CfA) led a session with teachers to establish what help they may need to introduce Classical Civilisation / Ancient History. The University of Leeds and the Yorkshire Classics Network agreed to support these teachers. Charlotte Higgins closed the afternoon event with a talk entitled 'Four things I learned from Classics and it's not what you think!' Her illustrated talk covered art, history, literature and politics. She then chose the winner of the Roman mosaic caption competition. One of the most famous artworks in Leeds City Museum is a Roman mosaic of a female wolf, discovered in the 1840s near the town of Aldborough, North Yorkshire. Participants were asked to provide a caption: what was the she-wolf saying?[6] Signed books were given as prizes and participants left feeling inspired and entertained.

Walking in the Footsteps of the Romans in Bath

On Monday 29 January 2018, our Bristol University partners hosted their ACE event in the Roman Baths at Bath. They invited a number of decision-makers in education to attend, including chief executives of multi-academy trusts in the South West, Head Teachers, teachers and policymakers. The evening started with an overview of the project by Hannah Walsh, then coordinator of the Bristol and SW Classics hub.[7] Teachers of Classical Civilisation from local state schools gave presentations on Classics in their curricular structures. Rob Flitton from Orchard School in Bristol explained

5.15 Attendees at Bristol University ACE event at Roman Baths. Photograph by Arlene Holmes-Henderson.

that all students study Latin and Classics at KS3. Funding from Classics for All had made possible the introduction of Classics as an extra-curricular club and follow-up funding had allowed it to be included in the mainstream curriculum.

Jo Carrington explained how classical literature is read in translation as part of the English curriculum at Clevedon School, North Somerset. She and her pupils wrote a play based on the life of Socrates and performed it in Greece. The teachers' enthusiasm for Classics was infectious.

The evening finished with a torchlit, after hours, behind-the-scenes private tour of the Roman Baths [fig. 5.15]. This was a spectacular experience. Our tour guide, Lindsey Braidley, the education manager at the Baths, picked out highlights from the museum collection for the ACE group, describing ways in which the Baths could enrich the study of Classics in local schools. Participants left with goodie bags including stickers, pens, pencils and information on upcoming events at the hub.

Battle Strategy and the Great Roman Bake-Off in Exeter

On Saturday 3 February 2018, our partners at the University of Exeter hosted a whole day of classical activities. Because this event was held at the weekend, students did not come in school/college groups but rather arrived as individuals (they left as friends). Some participants had travelled 80 miles, taking two buses and a train. The day started with an introduction from Professor Sharon Marshall, a member of the Classics Department. The first interactive workshop was led by Laura Jenkinson from GreekMythComix.[8] She explained that designing comics can aid engagement with the key characters and plot developments of any story. She challenged participants to create their own, with prompts from Greek art.

Attendees enjoyed three further interactive workshops. The first was focussed on ancient architecture. Dr Chris Siwicki explained the contribution of Vitruvius to architectural theory and practice. His drawings (not so scientific) of the Vitruvian man and of column capitals prompted laughter, including his own! He vowed to stick to writing about architecture in future, rather than attempting to draw too many images freehand. The second workshop was led by another Exeter Classicist, Dr Nicolò D'Alconzo. He sought volunteers to perform a scene from Euripides' *Helen* after discussing characterisation, both ancient and modern. The acting talents of Professor Marshall and Dr Siwicki rendered the performance hilarious.

5.16 Marcus Bell leads the hoplite phalanx at Exeter. Photograph by Arlene Holmes-Henderson.

The final interactive workshop, on the Battle of Thermopylae, was run by A Level Classical Civilisation students from Exeter College. They recreated the Spartan fighting formation (the phalanx), complete with replica armour and weapons [fig. 5.16].

Exeter students had been encouraged to enter the Great Roman Bake-Off competition which was judged by Charlotte Higgins and Arlene. Entries included Odyssean cupcakes (coconut and lime curd), Seaton hoard coin cupcakes (chocolate and orange), iced Roman shortbread biscuits (butter lemon) and a spectacular model Pantheon (vanilla and lemon). The judges gave first place to undergraduates Matt Noble and Nicole Browes for their cake depicting the Pantheon building in Rome. This cake was a deserving winner both for aesthetics and taste. The day finished with Charlotte Higgins explaining how she had benefited from studying Classics. She demonstrated, with examples, how the skills she learned have been valuable throughout her journalistic career.

Celebrating Classics in Belfast

On Friday 9 February 2018, Legion XX pitched camp at the Ulster Museum in Belfast for a whole day of activities for young people aged 6–18. The day started early (8am) when BBC Radio Ulster Breakfast did a live broadcast from the museum. Dr John Curran and Helen McVeigh, our ACE partners at Queen's University Belfast (QUB), arranged a morning for primary school children of handling sessions, classical drama in translation and mask-making, helped by volunteer student teachers from Stranmillis University College [fig. 5.17].

5.17 Students in the masks they had created in Belfast. Photograph by Arlene Holmes-Henderson.

The afternoon session was aimed at secondary-school pupils and included a performance of classical drama from QUB English and Drama undergraduate students, a talk on the *Aeneid* by Dr John Curran and a hilarious comparison of ancient and modern life by Natalie Haynes. Buses brought students and teachers to the event from all over Ireland, demonstrating the demand for Classics education.

This event was a spectacular example of partnership working. The Ulster Museum provided exceptional facilities, QUB staff organised the event, colleagues at Stranmillis University College contributed teaching expertise and resources, the Classical Association of Northern Ireland (CANI) led handling sessions (including artefacts borrowed from Trinity College Dublin) and Legion XX travelled for more than seven hours each way to bring the classical world to life [fig. 5.18]. They transported 20 large crates of armour, weapons, equipment and replica items. With more than 250 attendees (including both primary and post-primary learners and their teachers), this was one of the largest and most successful ACE events.

5.18 Legio XX in Belfast. Photograph by Arlene Holmes-Henderson.

ACE Goes to Parliament

On Monday 19 February 2018, Edith and Arlene spoke at a meeting of the Conservative Education Committee in the House of Lords, at the invitation of Ancient History teacher and consultant Steve Mastin. This was an excellent opportunity to discuss the project's aims and objectives with Peers interested in both Education and History [fig. 5.19]. We discussed the opportunities and challenges we had encountered, and were given substantial encouragement by the meeting's attendees to keep going!

5.19 ACE at a Parliamentary Education Committee meeting. Photograph by Sarah Poynder.

Glasgow ACE Event: Rome's Final Frontier

The University of Glasgow hosted its ACE event in the spectacular Hunterian Museum on Thursday 22 March 2018. Attendees included teachers, local authority representatives, Head Teachers and policymakers from across Scotland. Professor Matthew Fox, our host, had devised a fun quiz for attendees to complete while they explored the Hunterian's Roman exhibition, 'Rome's Final Frontier', showcasing archaeological finds from the Antonine Wall.

Arlene surveyed the role of Classics in Scotland's *Curriculum for Excellence* – her specialist subject![9] Gillian Campbell-Thow from Glasgow City Council summarised the introduction of Latin as L3 (the third language learned by pupils after English/Gaelic [L1] and a modern language [L2]) in selected Glasgow City Council primary schools, as well as plans to introduce Classical Studies as part of Broad General Education in selected secondary schools. These projects had been made possible by a grant from Classics for All.

Professor Do Coyle from Moray House School of Education, Edinburgh University, shared news of a new teacher training route for teachers of Latin and Classical Studies in Scotland. The University of Edinburgh planned to offer a Masters in Transformative Learning and Teaching and would allocate a few places to Latin with Classics. Creating a home-grown supply route for Classics teachers in Scotland would be vital to the continuation of the subject in Scottish schools in the decade ahead (unfortunately, this promise was not fulfilled, as we explain in Chapter 7).

Andy McKellar, from the Scottish Qualifications Authority, summarised the syllabus content for Classical Studies in Scotland. The topics available for study in Scotland are interesting and varied (see Appendix IV).

Ann Cunningham, a teacher of Classical Studies at Calderside Academy in Blantyre, South Lanarkshire, explained the value of Classical Studies for pupils in local authority schools. She brought four pupils to tell their own compelling stories: they each described eloquently how studying Classics made them more informed citizens and better communicators. Alex Imrie from the Classical Association of Scotland described the financial help available from Classics for All to schools and/or local authorities keen to introduce Classical Studies.

Natalie Haynes did a super job of summarising the value of studying Classics in the 21st century and reduced the audience to fits of laughter describing her experiences of studying and teaching Classics. Her segment on Aristophanes' sexy comedy *Lysistrata* particularly lightened the mood!

Professor Fox closed the event with a rallying call to turn the evening's enthusiasm into action. The policy support exists in Scotland: Classical Studies qualifications are available at all levels. We just need to secure curriculum time and more teachers!

Campaigning for People's Classics in Swansea

Our partners at Swansea University funded buses to bring in dozens of teenagers from all over Wales to think about ancient Greece and Rome on Friday 11 May 2018. This made the event accessible for students in rural and coastal areas, and became an exemplar for future ACE events. We explored big questions via poetry, music and art workshops. Did women in Greek myth get out of the kitchen/boudoir into heroic action? Which city had the coolest foundation tradition – Athens or Rome?

5.20 Chris Pelling and Edith Hall at Swansea. Photograph by Maria Oikonomou.

The highlight was the keynote speech by Christopher Pelling, Emeritus Regius Professor of Greek at Oxford, who honoured us by returning to what he always calls 'God's Own Country' of Wales [fig. 5.20]. He recalled growing up in Cardiff and eventually deciding to be a scholar/teacher rather than a lawyer. Fascinated by modern as well as ancient history, he gradually became aware that the ancient world could be used for good causes, like fighting tyranny (as in many productions of *Antigone*) or very bad ones, like fomenting hatred (Enoch Powell quoting the *Aeneid* in 1968).[10] Celebrating the success of Swansea's ACE event, and the national campaign, the university's social media team quoted Freddie Mercury in Welsh, *Peidiwch â fy stopio i nawr!* DON'T STOP ME NOW! [fig. 5.21].

5.21 Some of the Swansea attendees. Photograph by Edith Hall.

ACE Classics Festival at the University of Reading

On Thursday 17 May 2018, 60 students and six teachers from schools in Oxfordshire, Surrey and Berkshire attended a day of Classics-themed activities hosted by the University of Reading. Participating schools were the Oxford Spires Academy, Trinity School, Newbury and the Winston Churchill School, Woking. The Department of Classics at the University of Reading worked together with the university outreach team to provide sessions including artefact handling from the Ure Museum, an introduction to Spartan military tactics, Greek drama, epic poetry and interactive activities, including designing a Greek shield and decorating a theatre mask. The Virtual Rome project was showcased on iPads and students were able to embark on personal tours of the ancient city using new technologies. Edith provided the closing keynote on 'Reactionary and Progressive uses of Classics in Berkshire', in which she highlighted the strong history of people's Classics in the Reading area.

Edith and Arlene judged the artwork competition, awarding the prizes to Ella Wood and Ben Bower from Winston Churchill School for their excellent Medusa-inspired shield designs. Feedback from both students and teachers was universally positive: many students commented that they were now much more likely to consider applying to university and many teachers

5.22 Reading planning meeting. Photograph by Amy Smith.

said that they were interested in introducing Classical Civilisation or Ancient History qualifications in their schools. Many thanks to our partners in Reading: Professors Peter Kruschwitz and Barbara Goff, Jackie Baines and Tom Gidlow [fig. 5.22].

Pompeii, Herculaneum and Classics after the Classroom at Roehampton

The University of Roehampton Department of Humanities held their ACE event at Grove House on Thursday 21 June 2018 in the Adam Room, a location decorated with classical motifs and relief panels. The event attracted practising teachers from Surrey, Sussex, West London and Kent, as well as undergraduates, graduate students and trainee teachers. The programme included panel presentations by experienced teachers on setting up Classical Civilisation and Ancient History courses. Edith and Arlene gave a lecture on Classics and 21st-century skills. An update on the Roehampton-based 'Classics after the Classroom'[11] project was provided, which gave an insight into the careers chosen by classicists after university. Compelling testimonies were shared from a prison chaplain, an asset manager and an educational leader. The climax was a fascinating, illustrated talk from Professor Andrew Wallace-Hadrill (Cambridge) on Herculaneum and Pompeii [fig. 5.23]. A drinks reception followed, with Roman-style nibbles, provided by the University of Roehampton students' Classics Society.

5.23 Tony Keen, Kathryn Tempest, Arlene Holmes-Henderson, Edith Hall and Andrew Wallace-Hadrill at Roehampton. Photograph by Susan Deacy.

Emperors, Coins, Frogs and Oracles: ACE at Warwick

On Monday 2 July 2018, our partners at the University of Warwick hosted their ACE event, in conjunction with the Warwick Classics Network and Classics for All. The event attracted 200 students aged 14–18 and around 40 teachers from schools all over England, including Berkshire, the East Midlands, Essex, London, the West Midlands, Wiltshire and Yorkshire. The day was opened by the then Provost of Warwick University, Professor Christine Ennew.

Students enjoyed interactive sessions including:

- *'From Emperors to Slaves: Inscriptions in the Roman World'* (Professor Alison Cooley)
- *'Coins and the Ancient World'* (including a handling session, with Dr Clare Rowan)
- *'Aristophanes' Frogs'* (Dr Emmanuela Bakola)

While students were enjoying these sessions, the teachers got together to plan strategies to grow the study of Classical Civilisation and Ancient History at GCSE and A Level [fig. 5.24]. This opportunity for knowledge exchange and professional learning was valuable for teachers, many of whom are the sole Classics teacher in their school.

5.24 Teachers' workshop at Warwick. Photograph by Arlene Holmes-Henderson.

A highlight was the opportunity to use Oculus Go Virtual Reality (VR) headsets to explore ancient Athens in VR. Teachers and students marvelled at the wonders of this innovative technology and enjoyed experiencing ancient sites in a new way. Dr Robert O'Toole, Warwick's academic technologist, explained how the University of Warwick planned to make this technology available to schools through the Warwick Classics Network. The plenary lecture *Delphi: Centre of the Ancient World*, given by Professor Michael Scott, transported us to ancient Delphi, home of the famous oracle and the religious centre of the Greek world [fig. 5.25].

5.25 Michael Scott, Arlene Holmes-Henderson and Paul Grigsby at Warwick. Photograph by Robert O'Toole.

Opening up Classical Studies at the Open University

Our Open University partners hosted their ACE event on Monday 1 April 2019, in conjunction with the Student Hub Live team in the university's studio in Milton Keynes. The event attracted a live audience from Redborne Upper School and hundreds of participants in the livestream from UK schools and worldwide. The event included these sessions:

- The World of Greek drama (Dr Christine Plastow and Dr Jan Haywood)
- Exploring the Classical World (with Edith and Dr Henry Stead)
- The Votives Project (Dr Emma-Jayne Graham and Dr Jessica Hughes) [fig. 5.26]

5.26 Emma-Jayne Graham and Jess Hughes describing the Votives Project at the Open University. Photograph by Arlene Holmes-Henderson.

There was a panel session for teachers new to Classics teaching with Classics for All (Charlie Andrew), Redborne Upper School (Stephen Dobson) and ACE (Arlene).

An exciting highlight was the opportunity for remote participants to ask questions via the livestream 'hotdesk'. The technology also facilitated quizzes, votes and 'shout-outs' to school Classics departments who were watching. [fig. 5.27].

5.27 Henry Stead organises filming of Emma Bridges at the Open University. Photograph by Arlene Holmes-Henderson.

St Andrews: Introducing Classics into Scottish State Schools

ACE, in conjunction with the Classical Association of Scotland and Classics for All, ran an event at the University of St Andrews on Wednesday 11 March 2020. This date was the 'day which changed everything'[12] when the World Health Organisation declared Covid-19 a global pandemic, but not until after we had concluded the business of the day. This was actually our second attempt, after a day-long event for teachers and pupils in 2018 was postponed by bad weather.

Edith introduced ACE, acknowledging structural differences between the Scottish and English curricula, while also highlighting the rich bank of resources that were easily translatable across the curricular divide. Seb Sewell (Royal High School, Edinburgh) explained how he had embedded

Classical Studies at RHS, emphasising the need to secure support from school senior leadership. He embraced a whole-school initiative to digitise resources, developing materials that his pupils can access online. This demonstrated how Classics can be aligned with school-wide priorities, like any other subject.

Next was Jennifer Shearer (Kirkcaldy High School), whose success in making Classics accessible to pupils in Fife is well-known across Scotland. Outside the population centres of Glasgow, Edinburgh, Dundee and Aberdeen, Kirkcaldy High School represents a beacon of excellence in making classical subjects accessible to young people in a non-selective local authority school. She offered an insight into a typical day's activities for her Latin learners, showing how classical subjects are useful even beyond the subject-specific benefits they bring, addressing neatly the wider objectives of Scotland's *Curriculum for Excellence.* Lucy Angel (Mackie Academy, Stonehaven) shared her experience of getting Classics into a school from scratch, assisted by the Classical Association of Scotland (CAS) and ACE, developing an S2-elective option (for students aged 13–14) into a fully fledged set of senior classes, boasting over 30 pupils across National 5 to Advanced Higher. Lucy's case is noteworthy: she did not possess the credits to be recognised by the General Teaching Council of Scotland (GTCS) as a Classical Studies teacher. Taking advantage of financial assistance from CfA, however, she undertook a Masters degree which was accredited by the GTCS. Lynne Pratt and Mike Lynch (Moray House School of Education, University of Edinburgh) explained the pathways that teacher training candidates in Latin and Classical Studies could follow (although no such pathway has yet been opened).

Alex Imrie explained that the Classical Association of Scotland has an ever-expanding network of Classics teachers, working with schools, universities and the Scottish Qualifications Authority (SQA) to develop materials combining the latest research with robust classroom pedagogy. CAS has projects at all levels; thanks to CfA, it can offer funding to help new centres open. The day celebrated collaboration across the sector, identifying new directions for Classical Studies in Scottish schools.

Phase Two

The project's tendrils (appropriate to our vine leaf logo) extended to the national conferences of allied organisations. Edith, Arlene and project postgraduate assistants took every opportunity to engage new audiences with our aims to widen access to Classical Civilisation and Ancient History in schools. This phase was generously funded by an anonymous donor, King's College London's Department of Classics and the Classical Association.

Outreach as Activism: ACE at the Women's Classical Committee (WCC)

On 18 April 2018, ACE was invited to contribute to the Women's Classical Committee's (WCC) Annual General Meeting. ACE's Public Impact Researcher, Marcus Bell, represented the project on a panel on Outreach as Activism [fig. 5.28]. The day offered an excellent opportunity to reflect on how Classics can productively make a difference within society, but also how we can improve Classics itself by critically examining our own positionality within the discipline. The day entailed important conversations about race, through a critical whiteness workshop, and was bookended by two keynote speeches. Professor Nancy Rabinowitz discussed her work within American prisons and the benefits of using Greek tragedy for outreach and activism. Donna Zuckerberg, Editor in Chief of the online journal *Eidolon*, encouraged everyone to analyse the way they interact on social media.

The panel on outreach as activism facilitated a discussion about the practicalities of engaging in a mode of outreach that makes a tangible impact. Attendees discussed how we can 'burst out of our bubbles' – a phrase deftly coined by Paulette Williams – to make positive changes in the wider community, whether an individual school or a marginalised social group. The WCC AGM allowed the ACE project to collaborate with academics, teachers and other activists who work in the UK and the USA.

Showcasing Ancient History in Stratford-upon-Avon

Edith and Arlene attended the annual conference of the Historical Association (HA) in Stratford-upon-Avon (18–19 May 2018). ACE had been collaborating with the HA over many months and embraced the opportunity to showcase Ancient History at the event attended by 250+ History teachers and enthusiasts. Arlene led a workshop on numismatics, 'Exploring historical significance through coinage', helping teachers grapple with the notoriously challenging concept of historical significance and showing how coins could enrich students' understanding of historical periods. Edith delivered the keynote address, *Classical Education in the Wooden O: Shakespeare's Groundlings go to Rome*, to promote the study of Ancient History in schools.

She showed how Shakespeare was influenced by his study of ancient Rome and how both *Cymbeline* and *Coriolanus* highlight his framing of contemporary events in historic settings, for example, the food riots across Warwickshire, Northamptonshire and Leicestershire after the enclosure of common land in 1607.[13] Her keynote included the acting out of Act 3 Scene 1 of *Cymbeline* to bring the Roman context to life. Ably assisted by teachers Steve Mastin (Cymbeline) and Richard Kerridge (Cloten), Edith (Caius Lucius) and Arlene (Queen) made their Stratford stage debut. ACE's collaboration with the HA has continued, including journal and magazine articles, webinars and podcasts, all designed to support History teachers' professional learning.

ACE Visits Oxford, Cambridge and RSA (OCR)

On 11 June 2019, Arlene and Edith visited Alex Orgee, Subject Manager for Classics at exam board OCR in their headquarters in Cambridge [fig. 5.28]. OCR are now the sole provider of qualifications in Classical Civilisation and Ancient History (for the contents of their syllabuses see Appendix III). Arlene and Alex had interacted several times previously via the OCR Classics Consultative Forum and the Classical Association's Teaching Board, but this was Edith and Alex's first meeting and was dedicated to discussing Classical Civilisation and Ancient History at GCSE and A Level. OCR was also keen to increase uptake of these subjects. As readers will discover, some of the ambitions discussed in this initial meeting came to fruition in Phase Three of the ACE project.

5.28 Edith Hall, Alex Orgee and Arlene Holmes-Henderson at OCR, Cambridge.

ACE at King's College London Teachers' Day

King's College London hosted a subject enrichment day for teachers of Classics on 19 June 2018, superbly organised by Dr Emily Pillinger. The theme was the learning and teaching of Classics using archaeological sites and material culture. The morning included a visit to London's Mithraeum and the afternoon showcased a series of linked lectures by King's Classics academics (Professor Hugh Bowden and Dr John Pearce) and a roundtable discussion with Arlene (representing the ACE project) and Dr Aisha Khan-Evans (KCL Latin with Classics PGCE subject director). More than 70 teachers and trainee teachers attended from the London area and beyond. A number of ACE partners had held handling sessions, so Arlene was able to reflect on the pedagogical value of teaching through objects. Visits to archaeological sites were much discussed, from Caerleon to Vindolanda to Lullingstone and the Roman Baths in Bath, a spectacular site with a thriving educational programme for schools.

Cultivating Classical Connections with #TeamEnglish

Arlene spoke at the Team English National Conference held in Peterborough at Jack Hunt School on Saturday 13 July 2019. The conference attracted 450 English teachers from around the UK keen to learn about innovative approaches in the English classroom [fig. 5.29]. Arlene's session was 'Connecting Classics: Enriching English teaching with help from the Greeks and Romans'. She showcased Classics activities at Key Stage 3 (KS3, learners aged 11–14), Key Stage 4 (KS4, learners aged 14–16) and Key Stage 5 (KS5, learners aged 16–18) and outlined avenues to funding for teachers in non-fee-paying schools. At KS3, she suggested storytelling with Homer's *Iliad* and *Odyssey*. At KS4, she made links between Ovid and Shakespeare. At KS5, she traced the birth of classical rhetoric and stressed its importance for cultivating critically literate citizens. This single event led to 15 schools introducing Classics to their English curriculum and kept Arlene busy with school visits for months afterwards.

Further engagements with the English teaching community took place when Arlene delivered a keynote at TeachMeet English Icons in Sheffield (March 2020) and at the Litdrive national conference in July 2023 at Aston University. She collaborated with the English and Media Centre to produce teaching and learning resources for use in the English and Drama classroom. 'The Facility' is a collection of new writing, inspired by Sophocles' *Antigone*,

5.29 Attendees at Team English National Conference. Photograph by Arlene Holmes-Henderson.

partly funded by the Classical Association. It is available as a digital download or printed book and has been used extensively in schools, including for theatrical productions. With funding from AHRC, the English and Media Centre (EMC) produced and hosted a free digital resource 'Approaches to Rhetoric for 11–14-year olds' in collaboration with Arlene. Lucy Webster (EMC) and Arlene co-presented this publication and modelled some of its many interactive activities at the Voice 21 Speaking Summit in London in March 2024.

Aware that Classical Civilisation and Ancient History can be taught by teachers with a range of disciplinary expertise, Arlene gave presentations at national events which attracted teachers of varied specialisms. In 2023, she gave presentations at two ResearchEd conferences (in Leicester and Birmingham) as well as Teaching and Learning Leeds and WECollaborate (Rickmansworth). The combined audience for these 2023 conferences was over 5,000.

ACE Panel at Classical Association/FIEC [International Federation of Associations of Classical Studies] Conference

On Sunday 7 July 2019, delegates of the FIEC/CA conference attended a panel in the Logan Hall at the Institute of Education in London on the work of ACE [fig. 5.30]. Edith spoke about establishing ACE and treated the audience to the premiere of the ACE film. The events featured in this film were the subject of our second talk by Arlene, 'The Achievements of the ACE project to date' (policy, pedagogy and press coverage). Dr Paul Grigsby of the University of Warwick spoke on 'Getting Classics into schools: experiences

5.30 Gemma Williams, Paul Grigsby, Edith Hall and Arlene Holmes-Henderson.

from the first year of the Warwick Classics Network', created by Professor Michael Scott in April 2018 following discussions with ACE.

Finally, in an inspirational closing contribution, Gemma Williams of Allerton Grange School (whom we met in Chapter 4) spoke on 'Classics in the comprehensive classroom: getting Classics started from scratch'. Gemma described introducing Classics in a city where only three of 41 non-fee-paying schools currently offer the subject. From her initial approach to her Senior Leadership Team (SLT) through to selling Classics to her GCSE and A Level students, Gemma's enthusiasm lit up the hall and reminded everyone of the key role played by dedicated teachers.

British Museum: ACE 'World of the Hero' Event

On Monday 13 January 2020, Edith and Arlene collaborated with the Schools and Young Audiences Team at the British Museum to provide a lecture for teachers of Classics, Ancient History, Drama and English, and accompanied them on a free visit to the Troy exhibition. Teachers, researchers and home educators travelled from Birmingham, Leicester, London, Manchester, Norfolk, Reading, Southampton and Southport to attend the event. Arlene facilitated a pre-lecture discussion about the A Level Classical Civilisation course and pathways to its introduction. Edith selected pivotal lines of Vergil's *Aeneid* Book 3 which link the *Aeneid*, *Odyssey* and *Iliad* through Helenus the seer's speech. Feedback from the event was universally positive:

> 'Best afternoon of free CPD ever. More like this please.'

> 'Edith Hall is a wonderful speaker. So enthusiastic and inspiring. Thank you for organising this, and for all you're doing to change the landscape for Classics in state schools. As a pair you are seemingly tireless. Involving the British Museum is SO GOOD.'

> 'Great lecture. First class academics who are approachable and don't make school teachers feel silly for asking basic questions. If only I could attend more afternoon events like this!'

> 'Well organised. Easy to book and interesting. Ideal for me as a home educator.'

> 'Loved the Troy exhibition. Can't wait to bring my students to the next

ACE event at the museum on 24th February and visit the exhibition with them. Geek fest.'

British Museum: ACE's 'OCR Classics in 20 Objects' Event

Described by some as 'Glastonbury for Teachers', we collaborated with the British Museum to run an event for students and teachers on 24 February 2020, focussing on prescribed objects for Classical Civilisation GCSE and A Level held in the BM collection [fig. 5.31].

Lidia Kuhivchak, Classics Hub Ambassador at Lionheart Trust Schools (in 2020) summarised the day:

> As an Academy Trust that has recently introduced Classics, it is particularly helpful for our students to have access to Classics events which do not focus on Latin and Greek language …
>
> We started with the GCSE Classical Civilisation session, where Edith Hall took our students through the Parthenon Friezes and was very emphatic that these would have been originally brightly coloured – a fact often neglected in GCSE study and in reproductions of the images. Second was the Theseus Kylix, looking in detail at the labyrinthine imagery and the deeper symbolism of civilisation versus barbarism. Our students particularly enjoyed the emphasis on barbaric or animalistic characters as furry and hairy, which could be seen on the high quality images (much better than looking at a tiny image in a textbook!)
>
> It is clear that students will benefit in their Classics exams, both at A Level and GCSE, from exposure to sources beyond the syllabus, and Edith took us through some useful comparative objects. My favourite was the little Italian oinochoe with a Xanthias figure, which implied Greek drama was possibly performed in Oscan. It was a pleasure to see my students taking notes without prompting from us; even more

5.31 Pupils from Beauchamp Academy in Leicester visit the British Museum. Photograph by Lidia Kuvichak.

happily, our GCSE students said that this taste of the A Level syllabus made them keen to take the option in Year 12 – something every Classics teacher hopes to hear!

Many of our students would never have the chance to go to the British Museum unless we took them and it's this opportunity to develop their cultural capital that makes trips like this more than worthwhile; they are essential for our students to develop into keen and knowledgeable classicists who can rival their privately schooled counterparts.

Classical Associations of Scotland and Northern Ireland

Partners in Scotland and Northern Ireland have been central to the vision and aims of ACE since its inception. In April 2021, Arlene spoke to CAS about the opportunities to integrate Classical Studies in Scotland's *Curriculum for Excellence* (especially the Broad General Education phase). In March 2023, she spoke to a highly engaged online audience of CANI members about the progress made by ACE and its collaborators. This was an opportunity to celebrate the progress made in primary classrooms in Northern Ireland, and conjecture how this momentum could be transferred to post-primary settings.[14]

Classical Collections Network

On 7 October 2022, the Classical Collections Network (CCN) hosted an online conference 'Opening up the conversation: diversity and classical collections'. The CCN aims to advance education for the public benefit in archaeology and the study of the languages, literatures, material culture and history of the ancient world by supporting the study and use of classical collections in UK museums. Arlene gave a keynote under the 'widening participation' strand which focussed on helping museum professionals explore ways they could collaborate with the ACE project. The AHRC follow-on project *Improving Access to Classical Studies in Museums and Schools* formed a case study, with contributions from curators Dr Susanne Turner (Museum of Classical Archaeology, Cambridge) and Dr Chrissy Partheni (Liverpool World Museum).

ACE Classical Civilisation Teachers' Summer School

This exciting course (fully funded thanks to the Classical Association, the Society for the Promotion of Hellenic Studies and KCL's Widening Participation Fund) provided a comprehensive introduction to topics studied during GCSE and A Level Classical Civilisation. The summer school was open to all teachers in secondary schools and Sixth Form colleges and ran from 22 to 26 July 2018 at KCL. Topics covered were:

- Myth and Religion
- Women in the Ancient World
- Roman City Life
- War and Warfare
- The World of the Hero: Homer's *Iliad*
- The World of the Hero: *Odyssey*
- The World of the Hero: *Aeneid*
- The World of the Hero: material contexts
- Greek Theatre
- Imperial Image
- Invention of the Barbarian
- Greek Art
- Greek Religion
- Love and Relationships
- Politics of the Late Republic
- Democracy and the Athenians

In the River Room at KCL, with its spectacular views, a heroic band of teachers [fig. 5.32] met KCL academics in scorching heat to think about how teenagers would respond to texts from Homer to Horace and images from Mycenae to Hadrian's Wall. Participating teachers ranged from someone still training, to non-classicist educators hoping to introduce Classical Civilisation, to people already experienced in it.

Our exemplary KCL colleagues had read the OCR teaching materials carefully and delivered bespoke sessions. Dr Ellen Adams showed for

5.32 Teacher Training Summer Course at KCL. Photograph by Mike Taylor.

'Homeric World' the importance of thinking about the size and setting of early Greek towns; Dr Nicola Devlin packed the entire history of Greek vase-painting into 90 lucid minutes for Greek Art; Dr Emily Pillinger enthralled on Sappho and Catullus for 'Women in the Ancient World' and made the *Aeneid*'s message on migrants compelling for 'World of the Hero' [fig. 5.33]; Dr John Pearce showed how the Colosseum revealed almost everything we need to know about 'Roman City Life'; Dr Lindsay Allen had everybody thinking like an Achaemenid Persian in 'Invention of the Barbarian'; for 'Imperial Image', Professor Dominic Rathbone made Edith

5.33 Emily Pillinger on Sappho and Vergil. Photograph by Michael Taylor.

dislike Roman emperors even more than before; Dr Pavlos Avlamis won the prize for Most Popular Activity when he got everyone to draw Achilles' shield from *Iliad* XVIII for 'World of the Hero'; Professor Mike Trapp made Plato comprehensible for 'Love and Relationships'; Professor Hugh Bowden sorted out myth and religion for both GCSE and A Level; Arlene had everyone turning into classically trained orators for 'Politics of the Late Republic' and conducted overviews of curricula and resources; Edith held forth on 'War and Warfare' (with outstanding prior assistance from Dr James Corke-Webster), 'Greek Theatre' and the *Odyssey*. Legacy assets in the form of films of the presentations were created by BigFaceArt and posted online afterwards on the ACE website.

But the real efforts were made by the extraordinarily committed teachers who attended the whole course or parts of it: Charlotte Cannon, Will Dearnaley, Edda-Jane Doherty, Jenny Draper, Laurence Goodwin, Chandler Hamer, Rob Hancock-Jones, Pantelis Iakovou, Susan Jenkins, Jo Johnson, Lidia Kuhivchak, Jo Lashly, Lottie Mortimer, Judith Parker, Alex Rooke, Saara Salem and Helen Turner.

Several of the participants have since progressed significantly in their careers and we celebrate their successes; Lottie Mortimer leads the PGCE Latin with Classics course at the University of Sussex, Jo Lashly is Chief Examiner for Eduqas Latin (and Roman Culture/Civilisation) and, with Rob Hancock-Jones, is a member of the Classical Association's Subject Advisory Teams. Pantelis Iakovou won a Classical Association Teaching Award in 2024 for 'Outstanding State Sector Initiative' for his tireless efforts to expand access to Classics across the Harris Foundation Multi-Academy Trust. Reflecting on these successes, we believe that ACE has played an important role in nurturing professional development across the sector and creating communities of practice. It was a privilege to spend the week with such inspiring educators and we look forward to seeing how their careers continue to progress.

ACE The Film

In collaboration with BigFaceArt and Henry Stead, we produced a film which highlights our campaign to expand access to the study of the ancient world, spotlighting young people on their experiences of studying Classics. It features Edith and Arlene, the poet Tony Harrison, Natalie Haynes and Olympic-medallist-turned-Classics-teacher Jack Oliver talking about their love for Classics. They are joined by students from Redborne Upper School

(Milton Keynes), Norton Knatchbull School (Ashford), Nower Hill High School (Harrow), Christ the King Sixth Form College (Lewisham) and former pupils from Calderside Academy (Glasgow). These students speak passionately about how the study of the ancient world has enriched their educational experience and given them transferable skills. The film received its premiere screening at the 2021 Classical Association Annual Conference and was highly praised. We are thrilled that it has also been nominated for film festivals, including the AHRC Research in Film Awards, the Lift Off Spring Showcase, the London International Web and Short Film Festival and the Screen Power Film Festival, where it won second prize. Following these successes, the film has even earned its own official IMDb page.[15] 'I'm really pleased and proud to have made this documentary about the importance of Classics in the curriculum', said Michael Taylor, the film's director.

Phase Three

In 2020 Arlene secured approximately £100,000 AHRC Follow-on Funding for Phase Three of the project. She led a team of academics, museum curators, outreach coordinators and assessment professionals on the project 'Improving Access to Classical Studies in Museums and Schools'. Our new partners included OCR exam board, the Liverpool World Museum and the Cambridge Museum of Classical Archaeology. We developed:

1. New teaching and learning resources for the A Level Classical Civilisation Greek theatre component
2. A museum education project which uses classical bodies to explore body positivity with teenage audiences
3. Digital sourcebooks to enhance the learning and teaching of GCSE and A Level Classical Civilisation
4. Classics advocacy in connection with the 'Return of the Gods' exhibition of classical antiquities at the Liverpool World Museum

OCR Translations

Teachers had often expressed frustration that the prescribed translations for the Greek Drama module in A Level Classical Civilisation were of poor quality. Budgetary limitations had restricted OCR subject managers to copyright-free translations. In practice, this meant online versions which were, in many ways, unsuitable. With AHRC funding, Edith produced new, copyright-free translations and accompanying notes for all three plays: *Oedipus Rex*, *Bacchae* and *Frogs*. These are now being used successfully by the exam board, teachers and students across the country.

Everybody is a Classical Body? Outreach Via a Cambridge Museum

Since March 2020, 'Everybody is a Classical Body?' has been an outreach project at the Museum of Classical Archaeology (MoCA) at the University of Cambridge [fig. 5.34]. The idea for the project was born from a conversation between the museum curator Dr Susanne Turner and Arlene. The museum holds a collection of over 500 plaster casts, most of which represent bodies in various degrees of nakedness. Clearly, the collection is a fertile resource for talking about bodies, body image, body aesthetics and wider topics such as gender, objectification and gaze.

The project used classical casts to create spaces to explore a range of body-relevant themes for teenage audiences. We wanted to create workshops and resources to engage young audiences through an issue important to them. A broader goal was to increase young people's engagement with the classical world.

The first stage was the most challenging. We needed to identify ideas and concepts specific enough to create concise sessions. This could not be an eight-week-long university course, but a two-hour introduction, accessible to all young people, while making an impact. We needed an expert. The museum's Education and Outreach Coordinator Justyna Ladosz worked closely with a Relationships and Sex Education expert throughout the scoping phase.

We settled on creating two sessions. One on the theme of 'Posing Power' about body shapes and sizes, focussing on five statues from the collection. This session also explores how we, as an audience, instinctively 'read' and make assumptions from the way the statues pose. The second theme, 'Body Parts',

5.34 Poster advertising workshop for teachers.

focusses on specific parts of the body, such as abdominal muscles. These themes work together but can also be delivered separately.

Secondary schools could book these as in-person or online workshops. Alongside these, we created resources for teachers who preferred to deliver the session in their own classrooms – old-fashioned paper worksheets, high-resolution images, videos and fact files. Mentimeter, an online presentation-making tool with built-in functions for quizzes, questions etc., made online sessions fun and interactive. We delivered trial sessions for teenagers and teachers online. We collected feedback using Mentimeter which allowed us to evaluate the efficacy of the sessions, influencing future directions of the project.

The first trial workshop with teachers helped us define the sessions more clearly. Overall, audiences were receptive to the idea of using statues to talk about bodies. Here are some of the teachers' responses: 'It was a great way to be educated about today's (and past) society and how we view others'; 'A superb and innovative way to engage young people in conversations about bodies and body image'; 'Seeing how people have always strived for a perfect body helps to show that even sculptures portray an unrealistic and unattainable beauty standard'.

Filming at the Liverpool World Museum: Co-producing Digital Sourcebooks

With the Liverpool World Museum, we produced digital sourcebooks based on their world-class collection of ancient artefacts. These sourcebooks gave teachers and students access to relevant material beyond the prescribed sources, an essential requirement of the Classical Civilisation syllabuses. In June 2021, we filmed the first tranche of educational videos about Greek pottery techniques and Roman funerary practices, which are included in the digital sourcebooks for A Level 'Greek Art' and GCSE 'Myth and Religion'. We also produced short films on polychromy in Greek art and depictions of gender and sexuality in Roman statues (for A Level 'Love and Relationships'). The opportunity to get so close to such incredible artefacts was electrifying and underlined the unique power that museums have to make the ancient world tangible.

Dr Chrissy Partheni [fig. 5.35], the museum's Curator of Classical Antiquities, guided us through the museum's collection. Highlights included a black-figure amphora depicting Ajax and Achilles playing dice and a Roman ash chest dedicated by one C. Minicius Gelasinus to himself! Filming

5.35 Filming with Dr Chrissy Partheni at the Liverpool World Museum. Photograph by Peter Swallow.

was expertly handled by local film company Half Cut. With movement restrictions caused by the coronavirus pandemic, it was especially hard for young people to access museums. These digital sourcebooks brought the classical antiquities in the Liverpool World Museum to young people wherever they were.

These open-access interactive sourcebooks, which can be used freely worldwide,[16] include learning activities, videos, simulations, 3D scans and close-ups of objects. They can be used flexibly as revision material, for teaching beyond the curriculum, or to complement the sources prescribed by OCR. They were produced by Peter Swallow (ACE) and Chrissy, with

5.36 Front page of an ACE digital sourcebook featuring the Ince Athena designed by Hardeep Dhindsa. Reproduced by kind permission of Becky McLoughlin, graphic artist at Iconicus Design.

contributions from Arlene, Hardeep Dhindsa (KCL) [fig. 5.36] and Dr Gina Muskett (University of Liverpool). We hope that students who use them will be inspired to visit the Liverpool classical collections.

Preparing for Your First Classical Association Conference as a Teacher

On Monday 14 June 2021, the Classical Association (CA) hosted a virtual event for schoolteachers designed to provide information and dispel myths about presenting at a CA conference as a teacher. Hosted by Arlene, a former schoolteacher herself, the event exemplified knowledge exchange across educational phases.

The organisers of the Swansea CA conference in 2022, Ian Goh and Maria Oikonomou, gave a short presentation explaining the difference between a paper and a panel, outlining what makes a successful abstract and charting the process from abstract submission to conference presentation. Three teachers then provided personal testimonies of their CA conference experiences: Peter Wright (Blackpool Sixth Form College), Gemma Williams (Allerton Grange School, Leeds) and Andrew Christie (formerly of Streatham and Clapham High School). They shared their top three tips for aspiring teacher presenters. Because this event was the first of its kind, the organisers were keen to gather feedback from participants. When asked what they found most surprising, comments included: 'how many people attend the CA conference' and 'that academics are keen for school teachers like us to get involved and have our say'. Since this myth-busting session was recorded and the video made available online (via the Classical Association website), the number of teachers attending and presenting at CA conferences has risen sharply.

Phase Four

ACE Moves to Durham University

In September 2022, ACE moved its host institution to Durham University and launched Phase Four of the project, focussing especially on the North East of England. Arlene and Steven Hunt have identified how 'Classics poverty' (the uneven distribution of access to classical subjects) has affected the North East in particular.[17] The move to Durham provides ACE with an exciting opportunity to address this severe lack of provision.

Edith, Arlene and Peter Swallow became members of the Durham University Department of Classics and Ancient History in 2021–2023 and immediately started work to form new collaborations with the many brilliant organisations working to promote Classics in the North East. These included Classics for All North, Durham's Public Policy Hub, English Heritage, the Great North Museum, the National Trust, Schools North East, the Historical Association and Association for Language Learning North-East branches and of course the recently launched Hadrian's Wall branch of the Classical Association. Durham introduced a new Postgraduate Certificate of Education (PGCE) course in Latin with Classics in 2022 and ACE team members worked with colleagues in Durham's School of Education as well as mentors in schools to support and enrich the year-long teacher training experience. Durham threw a mini-bash, organised by Dr Rory McInnes-Gibbons, to celebrate ACE's new institutional home, alongside other exciting initiatives, complete with a cake baked by Edith [fig. 5.37]!

On 19 October 2023, Arlene spoke to 600 Head Teachers from across the North East of England at the Schools North East Summit, held at St James' Park in Newcastle. She enthused Head Teachers (of both primary and secondary schools) about the rich landscape of classical presences in the region, then outlined ways in which the ACE project and the Durham Classics for All hub would support them (and their teaching staff) to integrate these into their curriculum. Arlene provided reassurance that Classics is valued by policy officials and that parents/young people are generally supportive too (based on case studies from previous schools). Dr Laura Hope,

5.37 Celebrating ACE's move to Durham.

the Durham CfA hub coordinator spoke to more than 30 enthusiastic school leaders on the day and followed up with school visits.

In April 2023, ACE and Durham Classics hosted a two-day event for local Sixth Form students in collaboration with CfA and English Heritage at the university's Oriental Museum (OM), welcoming 23 students from the Durham Sixth Form Centre, Durham Johnston comprehensive school and St Anthony's Girls' Catholic Academy in Sunderland. Day one was museum-based and day two was a trip to Housesteads and Chesters Roman Fort. On the first morning we met at the Oriental Museum, where co-organisers Laura Hope and Ross Wilkinson greeted the group. Rory McInnes-Gibbons outlined the history of Hadrian's Wall and its popular reception in the 20th century. This introduction included strands of research conducted during Edith's project *Classics and Class in the North East*, such as the Historical Pageant of Newcastle and the North, staged at Leazes Park in 1931, which gave 6,000 local people the chance to bring history to life. This demonstrated to students how Hadrian, and the Wall, have exerted influence over the region's identity.[18]

The group then split into two for the workshops hosted at the Archaeology Department and at the Oriental Museum. Karl Racine (Archaeology) led an object handling session with a collection of Roman artefacts from Pompeii to the Severn Valley, which saw students select an object and explain what they thought it was, before Karl explained their original function in antiquity. Meanwhile, Ross Wilkinson's session at the Oriental Museum saw students darting across the collections in pursuit of Cleopatra. Her portrait was located by one keen-eyed student on a contemporary coin next to a denarius showing her notorious lover, the Roman general and triumvir Mark Antony. Students and teachers also looked at x-rays and discussed the practices (good and bad) of previous curators and professors who mistreated these 'mummified' human remains. This was a good moment to showcase how the study of Classical Civilisation provides opportunities to expand discussion to wider issues such as, in this example, the ethics of curatorial practices.

Day two started early for an hour's bus ride to Housesteads Fort where we met Helen Klemm, Education Officer for English Heritage. The group examined artefacts including a miniature spoon for earwax removal which left most dumbfounded. Exploring the ruins [fig. 5.38] was followed by the pursuit of murder mystery clues (trialling one of English Heritage's experiences for school groups) after two 'bodies' had been discovered in a house to the south of the fort.

Durham University, Classics for All and the Classical Association supported the event to ensure that it was free to schools. Student feedback

5.38 Teachers and students on ACE study visit to Hadrian's Wall. Photograph by Frances McIntosh.

was 100% positive and teachers requested further opportunities to join educational visits. By bringing together stakeholders across the Classics community in the North East, the ACE project continues to advocate locally and regionally for wider access to the study of Classical Civilisation and Ancient History.

Classics in the North East Film

This film is based on research from the book *A People's History of Classics* (2020), written by Edith and Henry Stead and augmented by further engaged research by Arlene and Rory [fig. 5.39]. It explores North East England's unique links to classical art, literature and architecture, and its influence on the contemporary arts scene. Designed to share research findings with members of the public, Edith outlines how Athenian democracy inspired the Penshaw Monument in Sunderland and how the region's coal miners discovered Roman artefacts, some of which are now displayed in museums across the region. The poetry of Tony Harrison, the literature of award-winning author David Almond OBE, the collections of the Great North Museum in Newcastle and the testimony of Cathy Bothwell, a teacher in a local state-maintained school, weave together to showcase the depth and variety of classical presences. As Edith comments in the film: 'Temples and fish markets, poetry and paintings, theatres, museums and schools: the North East is the country's leading regional centre for Classics'. The team wanted

5.39 Rory McInnes-Gibbons, Edith Hall and Arlene Holmes-Henderson filming at the Penshaw Monument. Photograph by Alan Fentiman.

the film to be useful to a wide range of stakeholders as an introduction to the rich history and contemporary vibrancy of Classics in the North East of England. Since it was made publicly accessible, it has been used by teachers, local history groups, playwrights, actors, museum and heritage professionals, policy officials, artists, authors, researchers and even the Visit North East England tourism authority.

Impact

The AHRC selected our project as an example of successful engaged research with significant societal impact.[19] The Museums Association commissioned us to write an article about our innovative model of working collaboratively with museum curators and museum education specialists. 'The benefits of improving children's access to the classics' was published in the Museums Journal;[20] more detailed insights into our project collaborations with museums have been published as book chapters.[21] Greatest attention has, rightly, been paid to the impact of our advocacy and training on the uptake of Classical Civilisation and Ancient History in secondary schools and colleges. The results are spectacular.

The graphs below show the trends in GCSE and A Level uptake of Classical Civilisation and Ancient History over the last 20 years. In this chapter we described in detail the programme of advocacy which we embarked upon in 2017. With a 2–3 year lag between schools introducing these subjects and students sitting the exams, the steepest GCSE increase starts from 2022. This filters through to an increase in A Level numbers from two years later.

While we are absolutely delighted with the measurable outcomes of our advocacy campaign, we acknowledge with gratitude the roles played by all patrons, supporters, collaborators and funders. These results are testament to what is possible when academics, charities, museums, assessment professionals and subject associations collaborate and share information in a structured way.

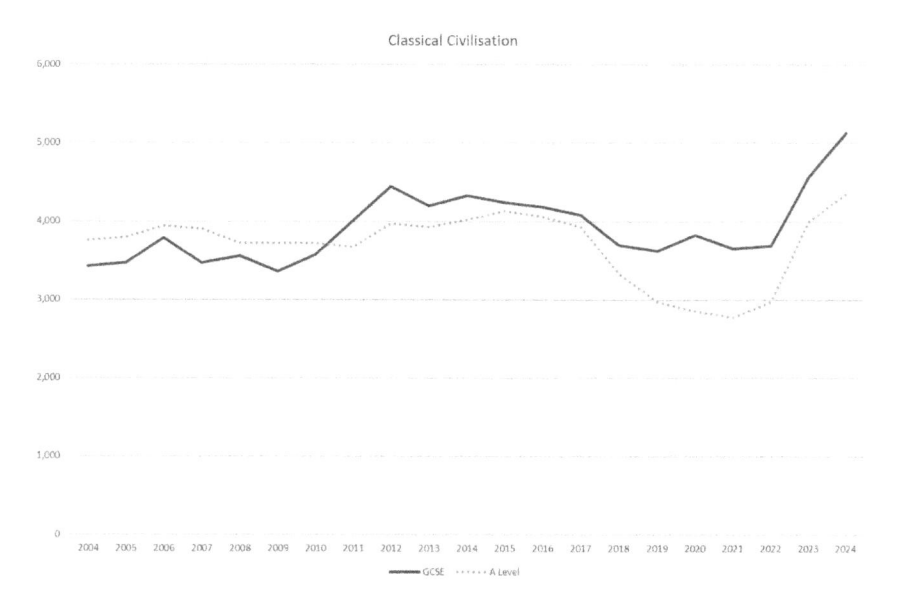

5.40 Graph showing trends in GCSE and A Level Classical Civilisation uptake (2004–2024).

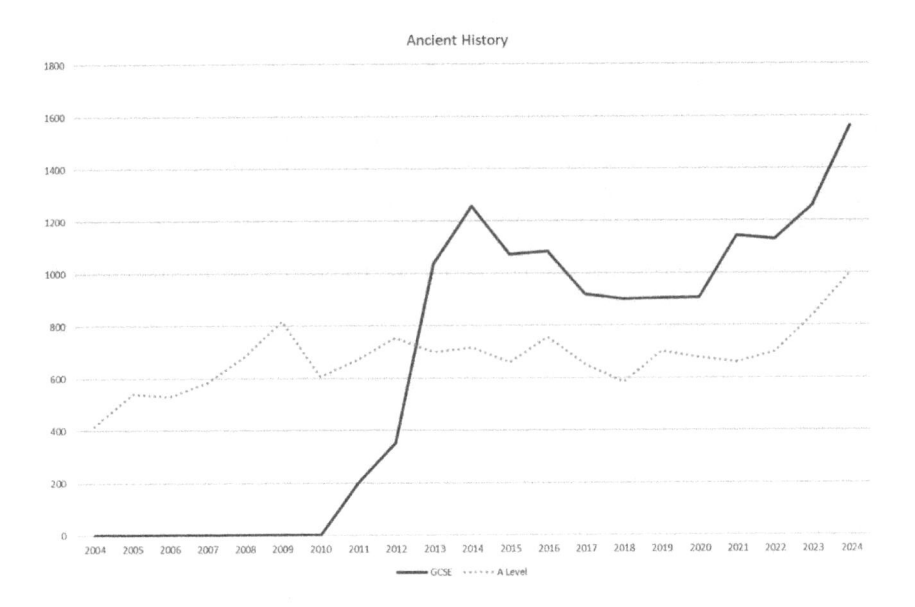

Ancient History

5.41 Graph showing trends in GCSE and A Level Ancient History uptake (2004–2024).

In 2023, Arlene was awarded an MBE for Services to Education. A recipient of one of King Charles' Birthday Honours, Arlene attended an investiture at Buckingham Palace with her family. In a Durham University press release about her royal honour, Arlene commented, 'I enjoy using my experience, knowledge and skills to make a positive difference. I collaborate with inspiring colleagues in academia, schools, charities and museums. This award is a reflection of our collective achievements'.

In the same year, Edith won the Classical Association Prize. Awarded annually to the person who has done the most to raise the profile of Classics in the public domain, Edith's leadership of the ACE project was particularly praised by the judges: 'all her outreach and public engagement work is firmly rooted in her belief that Classics should not be the preserve of the elite'.[22]

Phase Five

ACE in Prisons

Advocating Classics Education has, since 2015, been designed to widen access to the study of Classical Civilisation and Ancient History. Having achieved significant success in our initial phases focussed on teenagers in schools and colleges, we then turned to the most marginalised members of society.

With funding from Durham University, the ACE project took Classical Civilisation and Ancient History into prisons in September 2024. Working initially with learners in an all-male prison in the North East of England (which houses young offenders as well as older prisoners), Edith, Arlene, PhD students and postdocs delivered a four-month programme which covered an introduction to the ancient world, rhetoric and communication, art and architecture, ethics, drama and podcasting the past.

Teaming up with the prisons education organisation NOVUS, our series of lessons focussed on essential life skills such as oracy and emotional intelligence, as well as virtue ethics to explore what it means to be happy. By working with NOVUS, we supported their mission to help their learners develop skills and confidence that improve employability post-release from prison and to reduce re-offending. Feedback from the learners at the end of the course was universally positive, with 100% of the cohort recommending it to learners in other prison contexts.[23] Three benefits were identified in particular:

i) social cohesion: the course enhanced communication skills (especially listening) and diffused conflict leading to better relationships between prisoners (and staff)

ii) intellectual stimulation: learning about philosophy was a highlight and was identified as a 'treat' compared to the existing educational programmes (including tiling, decorating and construction). Access to Classics ignited a love for learning which had never existed for many members of the group

iii) mental health and wellbeing: learners reflected that the drama performance component (Sophocles' *Philoctetes* – play in a day) helped them consider their actions, and sentences, in new ways. This project is an excellent case study of how HEIs can form partnerships to deliver benefits for the good of the people who need it most, deepen their civic impact and amplify their contributions for the local community. In April 2025, the *Guardian* newspaper published a story about the work of the ACE project team in prisons. Written by the education correspondent Sally Weale, it quoted Sarah Hartley from NOVUS: 'The prisoners involved in this project have found it engaging, and through Classics have reflected on how to improve their decision-making, persuasion and active listening'.[24]

All-Party Parliamentary Group for Classics

In October 2024, Arlene[25] supported Peter Swallow MP to re-establish the All-Party Parliamentary Group for Classics at Westminster.[26] With more than 20 members of Parliament (representing all parties, in both the Commons and Lords) committed to the group, there now exists a national strategic forum to discuss issues facing Classics in schools, colleges, universities, museums and communities. In its first year, the Classics APPG held a policy roundtable to influence and inform how Classics fares in the Curriculum and Assessment Review process. It also convened key stakeholders to discuss Greek culture and language education in schools and communities. The list of future discussion topics is long.

Notes

1. https://aceclassics.org.uk/
2. Many photographs were taken on these occasions of students engaged in the activities, but, unfortunately, many cannot be reproduced because the subjects, most of whom cannot now be consulted, did not at the time grant written permission.
3. This resulted in two books: Swallow and Hall (2020) and Swallow (2023).
4. https://aristotlebeyond.co.uk/
5. Holmes-Henderson and Watts (2021).
6. The wolf is viewable online at https://news.leeds.gov.uk/news/setting-the-record-straight-on-legend-of-the-citys-wonky-wolf.
7. https://classicsforall.org.uk/what-we-do/our-networks/bristol-and-south-west
8. Laura Jenkinson-Brown has taught Classical Civilisation and Introductory Latin for the past decade and a half, focussing on KS3–4 Classics and A Level Literature. She has created a website full of resources to support the teaching of Classical Civilisation and Ancient History (for teachers, learners and home-schoolers). More information can be found at https://greekmythcomix.com/.
9. Holmes-Henderson (2013).
10. See further https://edithorial.blogspot.com/2013/04/how-enoch-powell-got-vergil-wrong.html.
11. For the project report, see Christoforou and Tempest (2018).
12. Cucinotta and Vanelli (2020).

[13] Published as Hall (forthcoming b).
[14] For more information, see Chapter 7 and Taylor et al. (2022).
[15] https://www.imdb.com/title/tt14258132/. Watch here: https://vimeo.com/540080441.
[16] All ACE digital sourcebooks can be accessed at https://www.aceclassics.org.uk/resources-financial-support/digital-sourcebooks.html. They function optimally on a desktop computer rather than a mobile device.
[17] Hunt and Holmes-Henderson (2021).
[18] To be published by Routledge Taylor Francis as a volume entitled *Classical Encounters in England's North East*.
[19] Holmes-Henderson (2023b).
[20] Holmes-Henderson (2023c).
[21] For more information about the ACE partnership activities with the Museum of Classical Archaeology in Cambridge, see Turner (2023). To learn more about the ACE collaboration with the Liverpool World Museum, see Holmes-Henderson, Partheni and Swallow (forthcoming).
[22] https://www.durham.ac.uk/news-events/latest-news/2023/05/professor-edith-hall-wins-the-classical-association-prize/#:~:text=We%20are%20delighted%20that%20Professor,of%20Classics%20in%20the%20UK
[23] For some reactions to the course as articulated by the students, listen to this episode of the *Against the Lore* podcast: https://open.spotify.com/episode/6OSGyxVVITxs5PyBVbpsZR?si=NNCUPy-nTlOTy6vApyWkNg.
[24] Weale (2025).
[25] Professor Tim Whitmarsh (Regius Professor of Greek at the University of Cambridge) and the British Academy Policy Team provided significant assistance, as did the Classical Association which acts as secretariat to the group.
[26] For more information, see https://publications.parliament.uk/pa/cm/cmallparty/241120/classics.htm.

CHAPTER 6

Getting Started

Previous chapters have recounted the history of qualifications in Classical Civilisation and Ancient History and the pioneering personalities who secured the preservation of these subjects in British classrooms through resource creation, project management, knowledge exchange, assessment expertise, policy engagement and advocacy. The authors built on these activities via the *Advocating Classics Education* project and have supported hundreds of schools to introduce and/or extend the teaching of Classical Civilisation and Ancient History.

6.1 ACE Impact Map (dropped pins represent the locations of schools/colleges, stars represent partner institutions and squares in circles represent summer school participants' institutions).

In this chapter, we provide advice to school leaders, teachers, parents and students on how to boost provision and widen access to the study of classical subjects. This advice is based on our experience of working with schools intensively over the last decade and is designed to be easily implementable.

School Leaders

As decision-makers on what is taught, to whom, by whom, when, where and for how long, school leaders are vital stakeholders in the ongoing efforts to widen access to Classical Civilisation and Ancient History. School leaders, in our experience, are generally receptive to the idea of introducing Classics as part of a broad and balanced curriculum. They are always keen to know, though, how classical subjects 'fit' into the curriculum and they usually ask about the teaching model adopted by other schools. They appreciate the flexibility on offer: of course Classical Civilisation and Ancient History can be allocated discrete curriculum time from Year 7 to Year 13, but it's also possible to teach these subjects as 'electives' for a half term (or more). For example, Anna McOmish describes how Ancient History is taught in Years 8 and 9 as part of History at Aldridge School in Walsall.[1] The positive outcomes for students are manifold. Bloor, McCabe and Holmes-Henderson explain how Classical Civilisation can be used as a literacy intervention for newcomer students with English as an Additional Language, requiring no additional curricular time commitment.[2] The Classical Association's 'Introducing Classics by Stealth' video (2022) showcases a range of ways in which Classics in translation can be taught via other curriculum subjects at KS3, before occupying allocated timetable space at KS4 for GCSE. Off-timetable teaching is also an option: some schools offer a Classical Civilisation breakfast club or an Ancient History after-school club. It is often via these extra-curricular sessions that students work towards GCSE and A Level qualifications.

We have witnessed school leaders making space for Classical Civilisation as an extra-curricular club as a 'trial'. If the club proves popular, and there is a viable cohort for GCSE/A Level, the subject can be 'promoted' onto the timetable. ACE partner school Cambourne Village College followed this route to introducing Ancient History and Allerton Grange School in Leeds established Classical Civilisation by gauging demand via an initial extra-curricular activity. School leaders see the value of creating opportunities which excite and motivate both staff and students, helped no doubt by Ofsted's requirement for 'a broad and balanced curriculum'.[3]

Funding is, naturally, a major concern. New curriculum subjects need to be resourced with books/posters/online materials and teacher training. This is where Classical Civilisation and Ancient History are in a stronger position than many others. There exist a number of funding sources which cover all these costs and even extend to travel costs to local sites/museums for educational enrichment. For further details on organisations across the UK, funding bodies and resources, see Appendix I.

With policy support (Ancient History 'counts' on the EBacc, as was discussed in Chapter 3) and funding, school leaders need to be sure that they identify staff members who will take ownership of this project. To ensure sustainability and resilience (staff members move schools, take career breaks etc.), it is best to involve a number of teaching colleagues from the outset (at least three per school):

1. Identify expertise in classical subjects across school community

2. Decide which classical subject you would like to introduce

3. Explore timetabling options: on timetable, extra-curricular or both, e.g. lunchtime club at KS3, on-timetable at KS4 GCSE

4. Identify teaching staff who are willing and able to 'upskill' in Classical Civilisation/Ancient History and to begin teaching it

5. Contact Classics charities to determine what financial assistance is available and how teacher training can be accessed

6. Visit a local school to discuss their previous introduction of classical subjects with school leaders, teachers and students. Ask lots of questions!

7. Start promoting Classics to students and parents

Teachers

As was explained in detail in Chapter 4, it is usually classroom teachers who drive the introduction and growth of Classical Civilisation and Ancient History in secondary schools and Sixth Form colleges. In some cases, these teachers may themselves have studied a classical subject at GCSE/A Level (and very occasionally at university), but went on to teach another subject, e.g. English, History, Philosophy, Art, Music, Physics etc. In other cases, they have no prior qualification in a classical subject but have become interested in the ancient world via television documentaries, holidays to Rome/Pompeii/Athens, books about Greek mythology and/or plays and films about the ancient world.

In England, a teacher does not require a university degree in the subject which they are teaching. It is up to academy leaders to decide whether teaching staff have sufficient expertise to lead students through the course. The ACE project has supported enthusiastic 'non-specialist' teachers via a fully funded week-long GCSE/A Level Classical Civilisation summer school in London, subject knowledge enhancement videos for each component and school talks (online and in-person).

For teachers who would like to 'upskill' on Classical Civilisation and Ancient History subject knowledge content, several colleagues have written articles and book chapters giving advice on how to introduce Classics in a state-maintained school, which offer a first-hand account of the trials and triumphs.[4] Published in 2024, *Classics in Action* showcases ideas from Jessica Dixon and Arlene Holmes-Henderson's teaching experience, plus innovative examples from a range of schools, to provide strategies for teaching Classical Civilisation and Ancient History (as well as Latin and Greek). Inspiring and practical in equal measure, it is designed to enrich, enliven and extend the teaching practice of all teachers who are currently teaching, training to teach or interested in teaching classical subjects and related disciplines, in primary or secondary schools. This fills the gap which previously existed for teachers of ancient languages, interested in introducing Classical Civilisation and/or Ancient History but lacking practitioner-focussed material.

A number of free or subsidised professional development courses also exist:

The Open University offers a free course via its OpenLearn suite of resources, 'Introducing the Classical World'.[5] This online resource offers a free statement of participation on completion of the four modules (estimated 20 hours of study) and covers topics such as 'Archaeological Evidence, the Visual Arts, Literature, Historiography and Philosophy'. This is an excellent starting point for teachers who want to become familiar with the chronology and geography of the ancient world.

The British School at Athens offers online and in-person courses for teachers (both British and Greek).[6] The four-day in-person intensive course for school teachers explores Ancient Greek history and archaeology through site tours and lectures. The course includes tours of key sites, classes on interpreting and teaching material culture, group sessions on sharing and creating teaching resources and workshops for writing lesson plans which link directly to key topics in the GCSE and A Level in Ancient History and Classical Civilisation specifications. Bursaries are available for teachers in the state-maintained sector and the course is scheduled outside term-time to minimise disruption to participants' schools. Online workshops are focussed on topics which permeate several qualification components. For example, the theme 'Democracy and Athens' shares with teachers a range of methods for approaching and studying primary sources. Participants follow a series of online presentations, introducing the main components of the module and providing new case studies beyond the school syllabus. These online courses are free.

Members of the Historical Association and Classical Association have access to webinars which provide subject knowledge enhancement on specific GCSE and A Level modules. These are led by practising teachers and leading academics and are an excellent resource for new and experienced teachers alike. Both associations offer professional development workshops and annual conferences. Teacher members usually qualify for a discounted rate. Connecting with subject communities is vital. Teachers need to make decisions about which optional modules to teach, how the content of the syllabus should be prioritised for teaching, how to assess and how frequently etc. Answers to these questions can be found via discussion with fellow professionals. Classics for All organises online TeachMeets which allow teachers to share elements of their professional practice and discuss issues of concern. Both the Classical Association and OCR exam board run continuing professional development courses which bring hundreds of teachers together and give them the chance to network with each other, building mutually supportive relationships. Finally, the Classics Library (see Appendix I) is an online platform which allows teachers of classical subjects to discuss topics and share resources online. There is always someone available to help a teacher new to Classical Civilisation and/or Ancient History who has a query.

Credit-bearing Courses

For teachers who wish to complete A Level Classical Civilisation as a student before teaching it themselves, the National Extension College (NEC) offers an online, self-paced course which confers the A Level qualification.[7] The Classical Association offers four full bursaries per year to teachers in state-maintained schools who wish to embark on this course prior to, or alongside, introducing Classical Civilisation to their classrooms. Learners enrolled on the A Level Classical Civilisation with the NEC study the literature and culture of the ancient world, from epic poetry and ancient comedy, to cults, rituals and religion. Along the way, they make fascinating connections between the culture, politics and society of ancient Greece and Rome as Homer's *Odyssey*, Vergil's *Aeneid* and the works of Euripides, Sophocles and

Aristophanes transport them to the ancient world. Via this course, learners critically analyse the issues and values that shaped classical civilisation and its influence on today's world. They develop skills in presenting coherent, well-evidenced arguments and sharpen their critical-thinking skills.

The University of Cambridge offers an undergraduate certificate in Classical Studies via its Institute of Continuing Education. This one-year part-time course gives students of any age a foundation in a broad range of analytical methods and helps them to develop knowledge of Greek literature, Latin literature and Athenian democracy in the age of empire, all studied in English. Five full bursaries are available for teachers in state-maintained schools from Classics for All. Bursaries are particularly intended for applicants working in deprived/disadvantaged settings and those who would otherwise face financial barriers that would prevent them from engaging with the course.

The Open University offers a Masters degree in Classical Studies. Thanks to funding from the A.G. Leventis Foundation, three practising teachers per year (from state-maintained schools) can embark on this part-time, online, distance-learning degree. The scholarships consist of a grant to cover the full cost of the tuition fees. They are awarded to teachers who intend to introduce or develop the provision of Classical Civilisation (or Latin) into the curriculum of the non-fee-paying school or college where they work. They are open to teachers of any discipline and at any level, including primary, secondary and tertiary, looking to develop their knowledge of the ancient worlds of Greece and Rome with this aim in mind.

Top tips

1. Identify strengths and areas for development among interested staff
2. Decide on Classical Civilisation or Ancient History
3. Explore funding options for training/resources and discuss with school senior leaders
4. Connect with local/regional/national subject teaching community to get advice re: pedagogical approaches, teaching and learning materials and promoting the subject to students/parents
5. Contact Classics charities to discuss the help available
6. Join the Classics Library to discover free resources
7. Observe good practice in a nearby school
8. Find a mentor who will offer support
9. Start teaching Classical Civilisation and/or Ancient History!

Parents

The parents of many contemporary teenagers did not themselves have access to Classics at school. As a result, some question the relevance of Classical Civilisation and Ancient History in their children's school curriculum. Our project has encountered very few such parents. More often, parents are delighted if their children are being afforded the opportunity to study something they did not. Indeed, parents also contact us to ask for advice on how to persuade their child's school leaders to introduce Classics. Many parents reflect positively on the growing public perception of Classics, thanks, in no small part, to novels re-telling Greek mythology from female perspectives by classicists such as Pat Barker, Costanza Casati, Elodie Harper, Emily Hauser, Natalie Haynes, Madeline Miller and Jennifer Saint. These books have been read widely outside educational contexts after being recommended by book clubs and have been featured in *Good Housekeeping* magazine.[8]

Parents who listen to podcasts and radio shows have contacted us to say that they have been inspired to learn about the ancient world as a direct result of listening to episodes of Radio 4's 'Natalie Haynes Stands Up for the Classics', 'In Our Time' or Greg Jenner's 'You're Dead to Me'. For individual adult learners, membership of the Classical Association offers multiple benefits. The national branch structure means that in almost all UK cities/regions, community members of all ages are welcomed to regular talks, events and visits with like-minded individuals. The cost is low and the return is great.

City Lit, based in London, offers online courses in ancient literature, history and culture as well as an annual Classics Day hosted at the British Museum. Costs are kept low to encourage participation from all those who are keen to be involved. With over 5,000 courses on offer, City Lit is one of London's largest providers of courses. Classes take place during the day, in the evenings and at weekends, to make sure there's a time which works for everyone. Since the Covid-19 pandemic, courses have taken place both in-person and online, so people living outside of London can also access all that City Lit has to offer.

Local museums also provide ways to engage with Classics. For example, Corinium Museum in Cirencester hosts Roman re-enactment days for adults and children, as well as walking tours of local Roman sites. The Cambridge Museum of Classical Archaeology (MoCA) hosts an art class 'Drink and Draw' on Friday evenings, with tuition (and wine/soft drinks), to allow members of the public to study in detail the plaster casts of Greek and Roman sculpture.⁹ During school holidays, MoCA offers family-inclusive events such as 'Urban Sprawl: Building an Ancient City' in 2024, which invites members of the local community and visitors to make their mark by creating their own building for the growing ancient city. Visitors are asked *How will you contribute to our growing city? Will you add a theatre? A temple? A sewer system? Or something else entirely? And what do your citizens need in order to thrive in your city? Ponder all that and more as you craft our cityscape. No construction experience necessary.* This activity is open to visitors of all ages and is a 'gateway' activity to further engagement with the museum, its collections and programmes in future.

Creativity and Classics is the focus of the Manchester Classical Association's public engagement programme, *Athena's Owls*. These free craft and literacy activity workshops provide a fun environment for children where they can learn a little about life in the ancient world by creating something they can take home with them at the end of the session. The 'Owls' (and their grown-ups) who come along to the workshop might have heard of some of the myths, like Hercules' terrifying encounter with the Hydra, or Perseus' defeat of the Gorgon Medusa, or they might even have covered some nuggets of ancient Rome or Egypt in school – sometimes they haven't heard of any of it. It's a family affair, with parents, grandparents and carers all warmly welcome to participate.

6.2 Logo for Athena's Owls project.

Students

Where to Access Information

For students who are interested in Classical Civilisation and Ancient History and who would like to see one/both introduced to their school, there are many possible courses of action.

The first is to make contact with the Classical Association, the national subject association for Classics. There is a network of Classical Association branches across the country (and allied associations in Scotland and Northern Ireland) which offer a varied programme of events for school students and lifelong learners. Local CA branches can make connections to Classics for All regional hubs, university Classics departments and experienced staff in local schools who can provide advice. Membership of the Classical Association is available at a discounted rate to young people.

The Classical Association also maintains up-to-date information regarding Classics-themed podcasts, summer schools and competitions. School/college students can engage with these as individuals or can suggest to their teachers that whole classes/clubs get involved. For advice on setting up a Classics club at your school, see the Classics for All website.[10]

Competitions

Many Classics charities run annual competitions, offering prizes ranging from book vouchers to trophies to publication in books. Below is a sample of those available in the year prior to publication.

Classical Association Poetry Competition

This competition invites aspiring poets either to write an original poem in English that draws inspiration from the ancient world or to translate a poem from an ancient language into English. There are three age categories: junior (aged 11 and under), senior (aged 12–18) and open (aged 19 and above). The first- and second-place winners in each category share a prize fund of £1,500 and the poems written by the overall winners of the original and translation categories are narrated by the judges on the CA's Classics podcast.[11]

Classical Association Young Speaker Competition

This competition is aimed at students aged 18–24 and invites them to prepare a presentation in any style (for example, a mini lecture, spoken-word piece, edited short film) on a topic related to the ancient world. The winner delivers their presentation at the Classical Association conference.[12]

Gladstone Memorial Essay Prize

This essay competition is also open to students under 19 and still in full-time education who have not yet completed A Levels, IB or equivalent qualifications. They are asked to write an essay not exceeding 2,000 words and can choose from a range of suggested essay titles. Previous titles have included:

- Were the ancient Olympic Games more significant to the ancient Greek world than the modern Olympic Games are to our world today?
- Why does the Trojan War provide such fertile ground for modern retellings? You may discuss more than one modern retelling of a Trojan War story.
- How shocking do you think the poems of either Catullus or Ovid would have been to their ancient audiences?
- Which one piece of artwork (ancient or modern art or sculpture) do you think best captures the telling of a classical myth which you have read? Justify your answer with reference to at least two other pieces of artwork depicting the same myth.

The first prize stands at £200, the second at £100.[13]

Lytham St Annes Classical Association Branch Ancient Worlds Competition

This competition is run by the Lytham St Annes branch of the Classical Association and is open to students aged 11–18. They are invited to pitch a documentary on any aspect of the ancient world in 15 minutes or less. The winners share a prize pot of £650.[14]

Ovid Competition

This competition is run by the Cambridge School Classics Project and is open to UK students in Year 7 or equivalent (ages 11–14). Free Classics Tales resources are provided for classwork on Ovid's *Metamorphoses* and then students produce their own creative response to the myths in one of four categories:[15]

1. Performance
2. Artefact
3. Creative Writing
4. Animation

Entries are welcome from individual students and groups of up to four. Each school can submit one entry per category.[16]

Extra-curricular Learning Opportunities

For students who wish to further their knowledge of the ancient world but whose schools do not currently, and do not plan in future, to offer classical subjects, there are in-person and online extra-curricular study options available.

In-person

The JACT Classics and Ancient History Summer School has been welcoming students aged 16–19 since 2000, whether they study Classics already or not. It is 'an inclusive and fun camp experience, with courses that cater to those interested in myth, literature, philosophy, history and ancient languages'.[17] In recent years it has been hosted at St Mary's School in Sheffield.

Online

Helen McVeigh's online Classics Academy offers a range of Classics courses such as 'Ancient Greece in modern novels' and 'Pompeii: myth or reality' at affordable prices. Live lessons are scheduled in evenings and at weekends over 4–8 weeks.

As mentioned above for teachers, the National Extension College offers an online A Level in Classical Civilisation. This is a paid option, with no bursaries currently available for teenage students. The self-paced nature of the course does, though, allow for part-time flexible study alongside school-based curriculum options.

Wolsey Hall, a former correspondence college now Cambridge International online 'homeschooling college' based in Oxford offers an online AS/A Level in Classical Studies (syllabus of Cambridge Assessment International Education, see Appendix II). Again, this course incurs costs for the student but offers similar flexibility to the NEC distance-learning option. Students targeting higher education outside the UK may prefer to undertake the international A Level in Classical Studies since this syllabus is likely to be recognised more easily by non-UK universities.

Notes

1. McOmish (2023).
2. Bloor, McCabe and Holmes-Henderson (2023).
3. Amanda Spielman (2023), Chief Inspector of Schools, *House of Lords Education for 11–16 Year Olds Committee*, Thursday 22 June 2023. Viewable online at https://committees.parliament.uk/oralevidence/13464/html/.
4. See Sanchez and Felton (2018) and Reynard (2020).
5. https://www.open.edu/openlearn/history-the-arts/classical-studies/introducing-the-classical-world/
6. For full details, see https://www.bsa.ac.uk/courses/school-teachers-course/.
7. https://www.nec.ac.uk/courses/classical-civilisation-a-level/
8. Finney (2023).
9. Turner (2023).
10. https://classicsforall.org.uk/
11. For more information, see https://classicalassociation.org/competition/2024-competition/.
12. For more information, see https://classicalassociation.org/competition/young-speaker-competition/.
13. For more information, see https://classicalassociation.org/events/2024-gladstone-memorial-essay-prizes/.
14. For more information, see https://lsaclassics.com/classics-competition/competition-2024/.
15. https://classictales.co.uk/
16. For more information, see https://classictales.co.uk/ovid-competition.
17. For more information about the JACT Classics Summer School, see https://www.classcivsummerschool.com/.

CHAPTER 7

Next Steps for Classics Education in Policy and Practice

This book has recorded the historical origin and development of Classical Civilisation and Ancient History qualifications in secondary education. We have identified heroic individuals, pivotal moments and effective interventions.

In this final chapter, we present ten recommendations. These reflect outcomes of the desk-based archival research we have completed, as well as the engaged research conducted in schools with educational professionals. Since the beginning of the ACE project, our patrons, supporters and collaborators have helped us consider how we can create conditions which allow Classical Civilisation and Ancient History to thrive in schools and colleges. Our recommendations are addressed to teachers, school leaders, policy officials, funders, assessment organisations, academics and young people themselves.

1. Conduct more research into Classics Education

Key stakeholders: Durham Centre for Classics Education Research and EngagementS (CERES) [fig. 7.1], funders, Classics and Education academics

7.1 Logo of Durham Centre for Classics Education Research and EngagementS (CERES).

Launched in 2024, Durham University's Centre for Classics Education Research and EngagementS (CERES) acts as a hub for projects relating to Classics in the curriculum, community and policymaking. With plans to offer Masters and PhD studentships, as well as postdoctoral projects, Durham is pioneering cross-sector collaboration with diverse stakeholders. Conducting and disseminating high-quality Classics Education research, the team produces findings which inform 21st-century thinking and practice.

CERES has been founded against the backdrop of Classics Education lagging behind other sub-fields of classical research in both productivity and visibility.[1] Underfunded because it exists on the periphery of both Classics and Education, large-scale research trials of 'what works' simply do not exist in classical subjects while they abound in other areas of educational research, e.g. Maths education, History education, financial literacy training etc.

Policymakers require a robust evidence base to make significant investments. Head Teachers ask for data to support the inclusion of a new curriculum subject. Teachers request information on how to optimise their pedagogies to improve student attainment.

This research can and should be done in Classics, pioneered by academics who recognise Classics Education as a valuable and rigorous area of academic research. Engaged research has been a feature of Classical Reception Studies for decades. It is hoped by the authors of this book that Classics Education is recognised as an emerging and vital area of scholarly inquiry, done by the brightest and best in our field. There is some hope that the Research Excellence Framework's emphasis on impact and engagement might improve the perception of participatory research in Classics and lead to a greater number of studies.[2] Changes will be required in the funding landscape (Classics Education is not currently a discipline in AHRC's list of subject classifications, for example), including the expansion of Classics charity grant-making criteria to include research activity and, perhaps most important of all, acceptance by the Classics community that PhD students and postdocs working on Classics Education topics are contributing just as much to the field as those working on, e.g., Pindar.

2. Give Classical Civilisation parity of esteem with Ancient History in the English Baccalaureate (and any future policy initiatives)

Key stakeholder: Department for Education

Classical Civilisation is unfairly excluded from the EBacc performance measure. School leaders sometimes interpret its absence from the EBacc as an indication that it is less academically rigorous or 'worthwhile' than Ancient History. Future curriculum policy decisions should afford them equal status.

3. Reposition Classical Civilisation and/or Ancient History as subjects open to all

Key stakeholder: School leaders and teachers

Restricting access to the study of classical subjects to 'gifted and talented', 'more able' or 'top set' pupils at any school stage (i.e. from KS3 to KS5) perpetuates their elitist image and creates further division between the 'haves' and the 'have nots'. The Voices of Experience (in Chapter 5) from Sixth Form colleges (e.g. Francesca Grilli and Peter Wright) provide compelling evidence for why this inclusive approach should be the norm.

4. Champion all classical subjects

Key stakeholders: Classicists (broadly defined, but particularly academics)

As a subject community, it is essential that the public 'shaming' of Classical Civilisation stops. Jibes like it being 'intellectual baby food' and 'Classics lite'[3] are damaging to the future of the whole subject community (including languages), particularly if they are made by classicists themselves. Policymakers will not make a major investment if classicists as a disciplinary group disagree about the value and importance of Classical Civilisation and Ancient History. We hope that this book has provided ample evidence for their value and status.

5. Ensure that GCSE and A Level (and equivalent) qualifications are attractive, but also aligned with Higher Education requirements

Key stakeholders: Teachers, academics, subject associations and examination professionals

The content of examination specifications changes in every subject. Teachers know this when they start teaching. It often requires the purchase of materials by schools and additional training and/or subject knowledge enhancement by teachers. Our research has shown that it is essential that teachers are involved in the process of syllabus revision and that their concerns and feedback are acted upon. Equally, academics in Higher Education have important contributions to make to these discussions about

HE readiness (which will affect many school students regardless of their choice of degree subject). There is scope to consider how the guidelines produced by regulatory bodies for secondary and higher education (e.g. the Department for Education's subject content criteria[4], Ofqual's subject level guidance[5] and the Quality Assurance Agency's [QAA] Subject Benchmark Statement for Classics and Ancient History)[6] align (or not). Progress is already being made; the Classical Association has convened subject advisory teams comprised of practising teachers and academics. Members of these subject advisory teams are leading sector-wide conversations about qualification reform, providing effective two-way channels of communication for knowledge exchange between schools/colleges and universities. OCR also has a Classics consultative forum with teacher and academic representatives, so it is hoped that we will, in future, avoid a crisis like the one experienced during the re-writing of subject criteria in 2012–2017.[7]

6. Collaborate with non-academic actors to improve the public perception of classical subjects

Key stakeholders: authors, employers, podcasters, broadcasters, journalists, subject associations, creative industries professionals, policy colleagues

These are many non-academic champions for Classics who can optimise the reach of our activities. The ACE project has been fortunate to benefit from the patronage of several high-profile ambassadors (see Chapter 5). In future, we should work collaboratively and cooperatively with colleagues who work beyond schools, colleges and universities to access new, broader platforms to change the narrative about what Classical Civilisation and Ancient History are and to whom they are available.

7. Normalise teacher training in Classical Civilisation and Ancient History (without Greek and/or Latin)

Key stakeholders: Providers of Initial Teacher Training and the Department for Education

Educators in English schools do not require a formal teaching qualification. Nevertheless, many teachers choose to complete a PGCE (or an equivalent degree such as a Diploma in Education and Training, PGDE or Bachelor of Education) to equip them with the skills, knowledge and expertise to teach confidently and effectively in the classroom. Most providers of Classics PGCE courses insist that applicants have Latin qualifications (at least to GCSE or equivalent) because otherwise students cannot access the tax-free training bursary offered by the DfE.[8] Trainees in 'Languages' (including Latin and Greek) qualify for tax-free government financial incentives whereas prospective teachers in Humanities (including Classical Civilisation and Ancient History) do not.[9]

This can discourage graduates of Classical Civilisation and/or Ancient World Studies courses from moving into teaching. Models do exist where Classical Civilisation and Ancient History can be combined with History or English to create a PGCE pathway (such as at the University of Leicester)[10], but this does not attract the tax-free training scholarship offered to those doing the Latin with Classics course. The data speak for themselves here: Ancient History and Classical Civilisation are increasing in popularity at GCSE and A Level whereas Latin and Greek are in decline.

Providers of Initial Teacher Education (ITE) and the DfE should rethink the allocation of financial support to reflect the areas of demand within the Classics subject portfolio.

8. Reinstate Classics teacher training courses in Scotland

Key stakeholders: General Teaching Council of Scotland (GTCS), Classical Association of Scotland, ITT providers, Independent Schools and local authorities

There have been no routes for Classics students to enter secondary teacher training in Scotland for over a decade. When schools want to teach Classical Studies (the equivalent of Classical Civilisation/Ancient History in Scotland), they need to recruit a teacher with a teaching qualification from outside Scotland or support a teacher trained in another subject to acquire sufficient GTCS credits to apply for registration in an additional subject.[11] This is a lengthy, difficult and expensive process.

A more direct solution to the expansion of Classical Studies in Scotland is the reinstatement of a teacher training degree (PGDE) in Classics at a Scottish university. Some progress has recently been made by the Classical Association of Scotland (CAS), with an Ancient History degree now 'counting' towards the credits required to teach History in Scottish schools, but even this concession remains sub-optimal. Such a move will require careful collaboration between GTCS, CAS, a willing provider and one or more local authorities which offer placements to trainees and probationers (all newly qualified teachers in Scotland are guaranteed a one-year job in a local authority school after they qualify). Independent Schools could also offer placements and their experienced teaching staff will be important mentors for new Classics teachers trained in Scotland.

9. Include the Greeks and Romans in the Northern Ireland Curriculum (NIC)

Key stakeholders: Council for the Curriculum, Examinations and Assessment, Northern Ireland Department for Education, Classical Association of Northern Ireland

The study of the Greeks and Romans does not currently appear anywhere in the NIC. Taylor et al. (2022) showed that it is possible to teach the Romans as part of the NIC's 'World Around Us' unit in primary schools, but the opportunity for progression of learning disappears in the post-primary phase. It is vital that students in Northern Ireland are given equal opportunity to study Classical Civilisation and/or Ancient History as their peers in England, Wales and Scotland.

10. Involve young people in making decisions about the future of Classical Civilisation and Ancient History in schools and colleges

Key stakeholders: students aged 14–18 across the United Kingdom

When asked, young people give excellent advice about subject content, marketing, and strategies for widening access to Classics. Adult members of the Classics community should create more opportunities for them to contribute. Classics for All's Chorus (a network for young classicists) is a positive step in this regard, as is the Lytham St Annes Classical Association branch's Classics Ambassadors Scheme.

In looking to the future, fewer decisions should be made by professional educators, academics and assessment colleagues in boardrooms and offices. Instead, we should work with the young people studying Classical Civilisation and Ancient History, many of whom have lent their voices to our campaign.

Notes

[1] Small-scale research has been conducted by practitioners in Classics classrooms for decades, with short reflective articles and case studies published in *Didaskalos* and the *Journal of Classics Teaching*, as well as *Teaching Classical Languages* in the USA. The research landscape and evidence base in Classics, however, bears no resemblance to the scale of publications and/or funded projects focussed on the learning and teaching of other curriculum subjects.
[2] Searle et al. (2018).
[3] Mount (2020).

[4] Viewable online at https://www.gov.uk/government/collections/gcse-subject-content.
[5] Taking GCSE Ancient History as an example, see https://www.gov.uk/government/publications/gcse-subject-level-conditions-for-2022/gcse-subject-level-conditions-and-requirements-for-ancient-history-2022.
[6] Viewable online at https://www.qaa.ac.uk/the-quality-code/subject-benchmark-statements/classics-and-ancient-history-(including-byzantine-studies-and-modern-greek).
[7] This crisis was discussed in Chapter 3. For more information on the short time-scales and lack of coherent communication pathways between key stakeholders, see Hunt (2018a).
[8] Hunt et al. (2024).
[9] For more information on teacher training bursaries in Classics and policy recommendations, see Holmes-Henderson et al. (2024).
[10] See https://le.ac.uk/education/study/pgce/courses/history-classics.
[11] All secondary school teachers in Scotland must hold a degree validated by a Higher Education Institution (HEI) in the United Kingdom or a degree of an equivalent standard from a HEI outside the United Kingdom. This qualification must include degree-level study relevant to their subject, up to a minimum of 80 Scottish Credit and Qualifications Framework (SCQF) credit points (including 40 at SCQF Level 7 and 40 at SCQF Level 8 or above). For further details, see https://www.gtcs.org.uk/join-the-register/secondary-teaching.

Glossary

AH. Ancient History.

AHRC. The Arts and Humanities Research Council. This organisation (part of UKRI) funds outstanding original research across the whole range of the Arts and Humanities.

A Level. The Advanced Level is a subject-based qualification conferred as part of the General Certificate of Education at a higher level than the GCSE and the O Level. It is an examination taken by students aged 17 to 18 in secondary education in England, Wales and Northern Ireland. A Levels are usually treated as a measure of attainment suitable for university entry.

APPG. All-Party Parliamentary Group. A cross-party group of parliamentarians (from the House of Commons and the House of Lords) who commit to discuss issues pertaining to a topic/country at Westminster.

AQA. The Assessment and Qualifications Alliance examinations board.

AS Level. The AS Level is a subject-based qualification taken at the midpoint of the two-year course of study which the A Level comprises. Students may complete their studies at the end of the AS Level (age 17) or use it to complete their qualification at the higher A Level standard.

BM. The British Museum.

CA. Founded in 1903, the Classical Association is the national subject association for Classics in England and Wales.

CANI. The Classical Association of Northern Ireland was relaunched in 2014 to promote Ancient History and Classical Studies in education throughout Northern Ireland.

CAS. Founded in 1902, the Classical Association of Scotland is the national subject association for Classics and Ancient History in Scotland.

CC. Classical Civilisation.

CCN. The Classical Collections Network is a charitable incorporated organisation to advance education for the public benefit in archaeology and the study of the languages, literatures, material culture and history of the societies of the ancient world by supporting the study and use of classical collections in UK museums.

CfA. Classics for All, a British charity which seeks to support the expansion of classical subjects in non-fee-paying schools.

CLC. Cambridge Latin Course.

CPD. Continuing Professional Development.

CSCP. Cambridge School Classics Project.

CSE. The Certificate of Secondary Education was a qualification offered in England, Wales and Northern Ireland from 1965 to 1987. It was a formal exam that provided a leaving certificate for students who did not achieve GCSE O Levels. The CSE was available in both academic and vocational subjects.

CUCD. Council of University Classical Departments.

DES. The Department of Education and Science (the name of the current Department for Education between 1964 and 1992).

DfE. (2010–present) The Department for Education is a department of the UK government responsible for issues affecting people in England up to the age of 19, including child protection and education. It has previously been known as the Department of Education and Science (1964–1992), the Department for Education (1992–1995), the Department for Education and Employment (1995–2001), the Department for Education and Skills (2001–2007) and the Department for Children, Schools and Families (2007–2010).

EAL. English as an Additional Language.

EBacc. The English Baccalaureate (EBacc) is a school performance indicator linked to the General Certificate of Secondary Education (GCSE). It measures the percentage of students in a school who achieve five or more A*–C grades in traditionally academic GCSE subjects.

Eduqas. An examination board that is part of WJEC. It operates under this name in England, Northern Ireland, the Isle of Man and the Channel Islands.

EMC. The English and Media Centre is a charity (based in England) with a national and international reputation for supporting teachers of English and Media through publications, training and consultancy.

FIEC. The International Federation of Associations of Classical Studies (FIEC) is an umbrella organisation encompassing the majority of classical studies associations worldwide. Its central aim entails fostering cooperation among Classics scholars by disseminating information among affiliated associations, enabling direct contact between association delegates and informing and advising governmental authorities on the importance of classical studies. The organisation hosts a tri-annual *International Congress* attracting classicists from around the world.

GCE. The General Certificate of Education is a subject-specific family of academic qualifications used in England comprised of the O Level, AS Level and A Level.

GCSE. The General Certificate of Secondary Education is an academic qualification awarded in a specified subject to students aged 14 to 16 in secondary education in England, Wales and Northern Ireland.

GTCS. General Teaching Council for Scotland.

HA. The Historical Association is the national subject association for History in the United Kingdom. It brings together people who share an interest in, and love for, the past and to further the study, teaching and enjoyment of History in all guises and forms: professional, public and popular.

HE. Higher Education.

HEI. Higher Education Institutions are universities, colleges and other institutions offering and delivering higher education.

IAAMSS. Incorporated Association of Assistant Masters in Secondary Schools.

ITE. Initial Teacher Education.

ITT. Initial Teaching Training.

JACT. Joint Association of Classical Teachers.

JCPA. Junio Cycle Profile of Achievement (Ireland).

KCL. King's College London.

Key Stages. Key Stages are the legal terms for the periods of schooling in maintained schools in England and Wales. Key Stage 2 refers to the period of four years comprising Years 3–6, when students are aged 7 to 11; Key Stage 3 refers to the period of three years comprising Years 7–9, when students are aged 11 to 14; Key Stage 4 refers to the period of two years comprising Years 10–11, when students are aged 15 to 16. Key Stage 5, referring to the period of two years comprising Years 12–13, is colloquially referred to as the *Sixth Form* when students are 17–18 years old.

LACT. London Association of Classical Teachers.

LEA. Local Education Authority. Under the Education Act 1902, education powers were transferred from school boards to local councils.

MAT. Multi-Academy Trust.

MFL. Modern Foreign Language.

MoCA. Museum of Classical Archaeology at the University of Cambridge.
NC. National Curriculum. This refers to the statutory curriculum to be studied by young people in state-maintained schools and colleges. It is devised and overseen by devolved governments in the UK.
NEC. National Extension College.
NIC. Northern Ireland Curriculum.
NWCC. Network for Working-Class Classicists.
NYU. New York University.
OCR. The Oxford and Cambridge and RSA examinations board.
Ofsted. The Office for Standards in Education, Children's Services and Skills is a non-ministerial department of the UK government. The services Ofsted inspects or regulates include nurseries, state schools, non-association independent schools, learning and skills providers (including in prisons) and teacher training organisations in England.
O Level. The O Level was a subject-based qualification taken by UK school students at the age of 16. It was superseded by the GCSE.
OM. Oriental Museum at Durham University.
PGCE. The Postgraduate Certificate in Education is a one-year higher education course in England, Wales and Northern Ireland, which provides training in order to allow graduates to become teachers.
PGDE. The Postgraduate Diploma in Education is a one-year higher education course in Scotland which leads to provisional registration with the GTCS.
POW. Prisoner of War.
QAA. The Quality Assurance Agency for Higher Education is an independent charity which ensures that students and learners experience the highest possible quality of education by setting benchmarks in each subject area.
QUB. Queen's University Belfast.
RHS. Royal High School (Edinburgh).
SCITT. School-Centred Initial Teacher Training.
SCQF. Scottish Credit and Qualifications Framework.
SD. School Direct.
SDUK. Society for the Diffusion of Useful Knowledge.
SEND. Special Educational Needs and Disabilities.
SLT. Senior Leadership Team within a school, college or MAT. Usually comprising Head Teacher/Principal and their deputies in charge of curriculum, student welfare and professional development.
UCAS. The Universities and Colleges Admissions Service is an independent charity and the UK's shared admissions service for higher education.

GLOSSARY

UCL. University College London.

UKRI. UK Research and Innovation is a non-departmental public body sponsored by the Department for Science, Innovation and Technology (DSIT). It is comprised of nine funding councils (of which AHRC is one). It funds research and engagement activities across all disciplines.

VR. Virtual Reality.

WC. Working Classicists, a hub of information, support, resources and articles designed to support working class people in Classics.

WCC. Women's Classical Committee was founded in 2015 in the United Kingdom to support those who identify as women, non-binary people and people of other marginalised genders in Classics.

WJEC. The Welsh Joint Education Committee examinations board.

APPENDIX I

Guide to Resources

This appendix provides an overview of the resources available which support the introduction and/or enrichment of Classical Civilisation and Ancient History in the secondary school and college curriculum. As with any list of digitally hosted assets, they are correct at the time of going to press but their longevity cannot be guaranteed.

We hope that this list will expand exponentially in the years post-publication.

ACE website www.aceclassics.org.uk

The ACE website is full of resources which have been designed to support the introduction and/or teaching of Classical Civilisation and Ancient History in secondary schools and colleges. These include:

- The ACE film
- Videos to support the teaching and learning of GCSE and A Level components
- Videos featuring students, teachers, patrons and collaborators advocating for Classics
- A step-by-step guide to introducing Classical Civilisation and/or Ancient History
- Advice on funding
- Shared teaching resources
- Syllabus overviews and links to OCR exam specifications
- Promotional leaflets for Classical Civilisation and Ancient History, outlining subject content and skills conferred

- Digital sourcebooks
- Relevant project publications
- Blog

OCR Classics https://www.ocr.org.uk/subjects/classics/

The OCR Classics website is the home page for all GCSE and A Level qualifications in classical subjects. Updates to the qualifications, news and opportunities for professional development are also posted here. See Appendix III for an overview of current qualification content.

Bloomsbury Textbooks https://www.bloomsbury.com/uk/discover/ superpages/academic/ocr-endorsed-resources-for-classics/

Bloomsbury publishing has a range of Classical Civilisation and Ancient History textbooks (endorsed by OCR) linked to the GCSE and A Level content.

Classical Association https://classicalassociation.org/

The Classical Association is the national subject association for Classics at all levels from primary school to lifelong learning. It maintains a list of resources for teachers and home-schoolers and publishes a range of academic journals including the *Journal of Classics Teaching* and *Omnibus* magazine, which is aimed at teachers and Sixth Form students. The Classical Association hosts annual CPD days for Classical Civilisation and Ancient History and a major annual conference (in a different UK city each year) for which teachers qualify for a reduced registration fee.

Its website contains:

- Becoming a member
- Teaching and learning materials (all quality checked by the Education Coordinator)
- Advice on funding
- Competitions
- Summer schools (including those run by the JACT Summer School Trust) (and bursary information)

APPENDIX I

- Podcasts
- Local/regional branches and their activities
- Professional development opportunities for teachers
- Teaching awards
- Conferences

Classical Association of Northern Ireland (CANI)
https://classicalassociationni.wordpress.com/

CANI provides a one-stop-shop for details of Classics-related events and opportunities across Northern Ireland. On the website you'll find:

- Membership
- CANI4Schools teaching and learning resources
- Events
- Blog
- Newsletter
- Belfast Classics summer school

Classical Association of Scotland (CAS)
https://cas.wp.st-andrews.ac.uk/

The oldest Classical Association in the UK, founded in 1902, is still going strong. On the CAS website, you'll find details of:

- Membership
- News (e.g. opportunities to advocate for Classics teacher training in Scottish education)
- Events
- Local branches
- Ancient Voices online summer school

Classics for All (CfA) https://classicsforall.org.uk/

One of the leading national charities supporting Classics in schools, Classics for All offers teachers flexible support to introduce or develop a classical subject sustainably on the curriculum. On its website you'll find:

- Advice on getting started
- Applying for financial support
- Events
- Book reviews
- Newsletters
- The Chorus – a growing network of young Classicists across the UK from Sixth Form to university graduates
- Case studies of schools which have successfully introduced classical subjects
- Regional networks with local coordinator contacts
- Welsh Classics Hwb
- Resources (a log-in is required)

The Classics Library www.theclassicslibrary.com/

This is a resource-sharing website for Classics teachers, run by former Classics teacher Stephen Jenkin. Teachers and trainee teachers can register for access via the log-in page and are then free to explore the resources that have been uploaded by practising teachers in each of the subject areas. This is an excellent time-saver for teachers new to Classical Civilisation and Ancient History. There are also discussion fora where teachers can ask questions/provide advice.

Warwick Classics Network https://warwick.ac.uk/fac/arts/classics/warwickclassicsnetwork/

The Warwick Classics Network, based at the Department of Classics and Ancient History at the University of Warwick (an ACE partner), is a network of teachers and academics dedicated to the promotion and support of Classics and Classics teaching in Coventry, Warwickshire and beyond. Launched in

2018, the network has collated a wide range of resources for teaching Classical Civilisation and Ancient History at all levels on their website.

Radio and Podcasts

Radio programmes and podcasts offer an excellent way for Classics enthusiasts of all ages to engage with ideas about the ancient world. The ACE project has worked closely with:

Our patron, Natalie Haynes, who makes the radio show Natalie Haynes Stands Up for the Classics: https://www.bbc.co.uk/programmes/b077x8pc

Against the Lore: https://podcasters.spotify.com/pod/show/againstthelore

Stupid ancient history: https://www.youtube.com/channel/UCamPyE75uCUj3BX-N6Iqf7Q/videos

Organisations

The Cambridge School Classics Project (CSCP)
https://www.cambridgescp.com/

CSCP hosts the 'Amarantus and his neighbourhood' project, a KS3 Ancient History resource, and provides links to the 'Romans in Focus' videos and 'Classic Tales' materials which can be used flexibly at KS2–KS3. These are all free of charge. The Cambridge Latin Course, although primarily a language-focussed series of textbooks, includes a range of Classical Civilisation materials both in print and online. The CSCP online annual conference also includes a number of presentations by teachers for teachers, demonstrating how these resources can be used effectively in the classroom.

Hands Up Education https://hands-upeducation.org/

Hands Up Education publishes the *Investigating Civilisations: The Persians* book and hosts an annual conference for teachers at the Museum of London.

The Open University www.open.edu/openlearn/history-thearts/headstart-classical-studies

As was mentioned in Chapter 6, The Open University provides free courses on the classical world as part of its HeadStart Classical Studies page. For teachers new to Classical Civilisation and Ancient History, these provide a pathway towards greater confidence with subject content. The Masters degree in Classics, fully funded by the A.G. Leventis Foundation for up to three teachers per year, is available for those who want to deepen their learning.

British School at Athens (BSA) https://www.bsa.ac.uk/

The British School at Athens collated 'image banks' to aid the study of GCSE Classical Civilisation topics (The Homeric World, War and Warfare, Women in the Ancient World and Myth and Religion).

The banks include images from the BSA archives. Teachers can pull these images easily into teaching materials such as Powerpoint presentations and pupil booklets. Each image bank is in the Teaching Resources area of the Classics Library (see above) under the appropriate heading.

Association for the Reform of Latin Teaching (ARLT)

The Association for Latin Teaching exists to support the teaching and learning of Latin, Classical Greek, Classical Civilisation and Ancient History in schools. The organisation is run by practising teachers for teachers, and for anyone else with an interest in Classics.

ARLT runs an annual Refresher Day which offers opportunities to share good practice in Classics Education and to stay in touch with the latest research.

It also offers a Summer School for Classics teachers which is a residential CPD course and networking event that brings together teachers at all stages of their careers. Every year practising teachers, PGCE students and prospective teachers, as well as experienced retired teachers, meet to celebrate their love for Latin, Greek and all things Classics.

From option groups to lectures, trips and even a Latin speaking table at lunch, every teacher has an opportunity to learn and share their knowledge in a friendly and welcoming environment.

APPENDIX I

Additional Classical Subject Associations

The Society for the Promotion of Roman Studies www.romansociety.org/

The 'Roman Society' offers:

- Membership
- Events
- Funding for state-maintained schools to buy books (grants range from £50–£600)
- Prize for best Classics PGCE essay
- Publications

The Society for the Promotion of Hellenic Studies www.hellenicsociety.org.uk/

The 'Hellenic Society' offers:

- Membership
- Events
- Funding for state-maintained schools to buy books and other teaching materials, host Classics days or produce Greek plays (grants up to £500)
- Hardship and access grants (up to £100)
- Publications including the excellent magazine 'Argo'
- Undergraduate essay competition

One key advantage of the above-mentioned two learned societies is membership of the Hellenic and Roman Library at Senate House in London. This library holds a stunning collection of texts and offers a scanning service and postal loans for members outside London.

Gilbert Murray Trust https://gilbertmurraytrust.org.uk/ancient-greece/

Gilbert Murray was mentioned in Chapter 2 of this book. Each year the Trust set up in his memory distributes £750 of Classical Civilisation Textbook grants in allocations of at least £100 each. These grants are to assist with the purchase of textbooks for the teaching of Classical Civilisation at GCSE, A Level and equivalents, in non-fee-paying schools in England, Scotland, Wales and Northern Ireland.

Allied organisations include:

Asterion: Celebrating Neurodiversity in Classics https://asterion.uk/
British Museum https://www.britishmuseum.org/learn/schools
The Historical Association www.history.org.uk/
The Schools History Project www.schoolshistoryproject.co.uk/

Social Media

One of the best ways to keep up to date on good practice in Classics education is to maintain an active digital profile on X/Bluesky/Meta/Instagram/TikTok. This will allow you to make connections with teachers and academics in Classics and to 'observe' classroom practice elsewhere. It is also an excellent way to build a network of colleagues for resource co-creation and sharing.

Higher Education

For a list of UK universities offering classical courses, see:

Council of University Classical Departments:
https://cucd.blogs.sas.ac.uk/

For a comparison of the entry requirements and courses available, see Holmes-Henderson and Watts (2021).

APPENDIX II

Teaching Classical Civilisation and Ancient History in Britain

Questionnaire

Thank you so much for taking the time to answer these questions. All the questions are voluntary, and you can answer or not answer as many as you feel comfortable with, with as much or little detail as you would like to give.

1. Name

2. Age

3. Part or parts of the country where you received secondary education (O Level, AS/A Level, GCSE, Highers etc.), as well as the name of the school(s) if possible

4. What type of school (private or state-sector, Secondary Modern, Technical, Comprehensive, Grammar, Direct-Grant, Academy, Night-School, Sixth Form college etc.)?

5. Was it selective?

6. What qualification – e.g. GCE, GCSE, O Level, Certificate of Education, AS or A Level, Higher – and in what subject – Classical Civilisation (or Classical Studies) or Ancient History?

7. Can you remember which examination board(s)?

8. What dates did you do these qualifications?

9. What other subjects did you do at each level?

10. Did you go on to tertiary education? If not, what did you go on to do?

11. If you did go on to tertiary education – where, what, which degrees? Bachelor's, Master's, Doctorate, Diploma, Certificate of Education?

APPENDIX II

12. What job experience have you had/professions have you gone into?

13. If you are a teacher, have you taught Classical Civilisation or Ancient History?

14. If so, where, when and to what level?

15. If you have left secondary education, what are your memories of these subjects?

16. What parts of the course/activities do you remember enjoying most, and why?

17. What parts of the course/activities do you remember NOT enjoying, and why?

18. Can you remember why you chose to take these subjects?

19. Do you have any memories you would like to share of your teachers?

20. Did you find them inspiring or interesting or not, and why?

21. Were you pleased with your results?

22. Has the experience of doing this/these subject(s) at school affected you professionally? If so, how and why?

23. Has your experience of these subjects affected your non-working life, e.g. in recreation, hobbies, social life, holidays, continuation with education in adult life either privately or in university extension classes etc.?

24. Would you encourage young people to choose these subjects today? If so, why?

25. Do you have any memories of how you were assessed, coursework, exams etc.?

26. Did you feel that the teaching and coursework prepared you well for the assessment(s)?

27. Who is your favourite ancient author or topic, and why? (e.g. Homer, or Roman Emperors)

28. An important part of our book will be describing the skills and intellectual competencies which these subjects confer. This is the list that we have developed; please comment on it – supplement, criticise it, if possible, with specific examples from the curriculum you remember.

   1] Cultural literacy: understanding the significance of key figures and events in world history and literature.
   2] Source evaluation: interrogating reliability and authority of evidence and propaganda.
   3] Critical comparison of competing authorities in a complex society.
   4] Articulating arguments: familiarity with great ancient speechmaking and persuasive communication.
   5] Overview of long-term human history: the place of ancient history in human development.
   6] Understanding of competing identities: national, European, cosmopolitan, ethnic, political, religious.
   7] Interdisciplinary skills: thinking about a whole civilisation in the round, both society and art.
   8] Political sophistication: approaching original development of ideas about democracy, republics, empire, citizenship, gender roles.

29. If you are a teacher, are you CURRENTLY teaching these subjects, or would you LIKE to if it were possible?

30. If you are a teacher CURRENTLY teaching these subjects, what do you think of the OCR specifications? (please be honest)

31. Are you happy for us to quote you in our book and if so, are you prepared to be named?

32. If you studied these subjects historically, do you have any photographs, exercise books or any other records which might be of interest to our readership that you would be happy to share with us?

33. Would you be happy to have a phone/online conversation or be visited personally over the next 2 months? If yes, please provide a phone number and a good time for you.

Huge thanks again for taking the time to complete this questionnaire and be involved with our project!

APPENDIX III

Content of OCR qualifications[1] in Ancient History and Classical Civilisation

OCR GCSE Ancient History

Component 01: Greece and Persia

The compulsory Period Study focusses on the Persian Empire under Cyrus the Great, Cambyses II, Darius I and Xerxes I. Students expand their understanding of the unfolding narrative of substantial developments and issues associated with this period.

Students investigate one depth study from the three on offer:

- From tyranny to democracy, 546–483 BC
- Athens in the age of Pericles, 462–429 BC
- Alexander the Great, 356–323 BC

Component 02: Rome and its neighbours

The compulsory longer Period Study focusses on the kings of Rome and the early Roman Republic, with an emphasis on events and characters.

Students investigate one depth study from the three on offer:

- Hannibal and the Second Punic War, 218–201 BC
- Cleopatra: Rome and Egypt, 69–30 BC
- Britannia: from conquest to province, AD 43–c.84

---

[1] OCR uses BC and AD in qualification specifications. The authors prefer to use BCE and CE but have reproduced here the dating system used by the examination body to avoid confusion.

Assessment

Component	Marks	Duration	Weighting
Greece and Persia (01)	100	2 hours	50%
Rome and its neighbours (02)	100	2 hours	50%

A Level Ancient History

Component 01: Greek history

For the compulsory Period Study, students focus on the relations between Greek states, and between Greek states and non-Greek states from 492 to 404 BC, particularly Sparta, Athens and Persia.

For the depth study, students investigate one from:

- The politics and society of Sparta, 478–404 BC
- The politics and culture of Athens, c.460–399 BC
- The rise of Macedon, 359–323 BC

Component 02: Roman history

For the compulsory Period Study, students focus on the reigns of Augustus, Tiberius, Gaius (Caligula), Claudius and Nero.

For the depth study, students study one from:

- The breakdown of the Late Republic, 88–31 BC
- The Flavians, AD 68–96
- Ruling Roman Britain, AD 43–c.128

Assessment

Component	Marks	Duration	Weighting
Greek history (01)	98	2 hours 30 mins	50%
Roman history (02)	98	2 hours 30 mins	50%

GCSE Classical Civilisation

Component group 1: Thematic study

Students study one of the two components listed below. Both components involve a comparative study of ancient Greece and Rome and combine literary and visual/material sources.

The components are:

- Myth and religion
- Women in the ancient world

Component group 2: Literature and culture

Students couple an in-depth cultural study with the study of a related body of literature. They select one from the following three components:

- The Homeric world
- Roman city life
- War and warfare

Assessment

Component	Marks	Duration	Weighting
Component group 1	90	1 hour 30 mins	50%
Component group 2	90	1 hour 30 mins	50%

A Level Classical Civilisation

Component 1: The world of the hero

In this compulsory component, students study either Homer's *Iliad* or *Odyssey* and Vergil's *Aeneid*.

Component group 2: Culture and the arts

The components in this group involve study of visual and material culture and (except for Greek art) literature in translation.

Students study one of:

- Greek theatre
- Imperial image
- Invention of the barbarian
- Greek art

Component group 3: Beliefs and ideas

Components in this group involve study of an area of classical thought along with either literature in translation or visual/material culture.

Students study one of:

- Greek religion
- Love and relationships
- Politics of the Late Republic
- Democracy and the Athenians

Assessment

Component	Marks	Duration	Weighting
Component 1: The world of the hero	100	2 hours 30 mins	40%
Component group 2: Culture and the arts	75	1 hour 45 mins	30%
Component group 3: Beliefs and ideas	75	1 hour 45 mins	30%

APPENDIX IV

Regional Variations

This appendix details eight Classical Studies qualifications which are (or were until recently) offered to secondary phase students in Scotland, Ireland and by international examination boards.

Cambridge International
AS and A Level Classical Studies
A one or two-year course taken by students aged 16–18 in 180 or 360 guided learning hours.

Course Content (from 2022) https://www.cambridgeinternational.org/Images/557256-2022-2024-syllabus.pdf

AS Level
Paper 1 – Greek Civilisation
One topic from:
Alexander the Great
Aristophanes
Themes in Greek Vase Painting

Paper 2 – Roman Civilisation
One topic from:
Augustus
Vergil's *Aeneid*
Architecture of the Roman City (a selection of buildings from Rome, Ostia, Pompeii and Herculaneum)

A Level

Papers 1 and 2 and:

Paper 3 – Classical History
One topic from:
Athens and Sparta
Emperors and Subjects: Claudius, Nero, Domitian and Trajan

Paper 4 – Greek Literature
One topic from:
Greek Tragedy
Homeric Epic

Skills Developed
This course encourages learners to be: **confident** exploring, interpreting and evaluating a wide range of Classical source material; **responsible**, acquiring knowledge and skills through independent reading and study; **reflective**, considering how the Classical world has influenced their own society and reflecting on what they can learn from Classical societies; **innovative**, considering new viewpoints and interpretations of texts, historical sources, artefacts and buildings; **engaged**, developing their understanding of the Classical world and opening up different perspectives and exploring new ideas.

Assessment
AS Level
90 min examination – Greek Civilisation (one essay, one source-based question)
90 min examination – Roman Civilisation (one essay, one source-based question)

A Level
90 min examination – Greek Civilisation (one essay, one source-based question)
90 min examination – Roman Civilisation (one essay, one source-based question)
90 min examination – Classical History (one essay, one source-based question)
90 min examination – Greek Literature (one essay, one source-based question)
A slightly higher weighting is given in Papers 3 and 4 to analysis and evaluation than to knowledge and understanding.

Entry Statistics
N/A

International Baccalaureate https://www.ibo.org/contentassets/b34072a0cb5
54237b8d790c463f1b347/cgrs-ib-examiner-responsible-2018.pdf
Classical Greek and Roman Studies, IB Diploma Programme (offered until 2021)
A two-year course taken by students aged 16–19 at Standard Level in 150 learning hours.

Course Content
Four topics are selected for study, including at least one Greek and one Roman topic.
Two topics must be drawn from the following options:
The *Iliad* or *Odyssey*
Bacchae and *Hippolytus*
The *Aeneid* or *Metamorphoses*
Sources on Roman Religion
A further **two topics** must be chosen from the following options:
Alexander the Great
Athenian Vase Painting
Roman Architecture
Augustan Rome

Skills Developed
Students gain an appreciation of the challenge of reconstructing a coherent and meaningful past. They learn to: **interpret**, and **communicate** about, a range of aspects of Greek and Roman civilisation; **examine** these aspects in social, political and cultural contexts; **understand** that the nature and diversity of sources may lead to **different ways of seeing or experiencing the past**; **develop critical insights** into the structure and impact of diverse forms of cultural, social and political expression; **foster an awareness** of Greek and Roman thought and, in turn, **a deeper awareness** of their own and other histories and cultures.

Assessment
Paper 1 – 90 min examination with essay questions on the first two topics (40%)
Paper 2 – 90 min examination with short-answer questions based on sources (40%)

Internal Assessment – 20 hours' work, 1,500 words (20%)

Entry Statistics
33 entries in 2020, 44 entries in 2019

Ireland – Junior Cycle[1]
Classics (Junior Cycle) https://curriculumonline.ie/junior-cycle/junior-cycle-subjects/classics/
A course taken by students aged 14–15 after three years of post-primary education with approx. 300 hours of teaching.

Course Content
Core Component (100 hours) – Myths and Daily Lives
Classical Studies (100 hours) – The World of Achilles; Rome, Centre of an Empire
Classical Language (100 hours) – Latin or Greek

Skills Developed
Students **explore** ancient Greek and Roman societies through the lens of their texts, literature and language, and through their art, architecture and material culture. Students **discover** what they can learn about **how a society functioned** by interrogating the myriad **structures, behaviours and connections** that they encounter and **relate them to their own experience** and their own world. They **read** narratives, **explore** representations, **analyse** structures, patterns, values and ideologies. Junior Cycle Classics exposes students to activities that encourage **collaboration, creativity, innovation** and **communication**.

Assessment
Assessment comprises two Classroom-Based Assessments, and a final examination. In addition, the second Classroom-Based Assessment will have a written Assessment Task that will be marked, along with the final assessment, by the State Examinations Commission. Students complete a Classroom-Based Assessment for strand 1 (towards the end of second year) and then a second Classroom-Based Assessment for either strand 2 (the classical studies component) or strand 3 (the classical languages component) in term two of third year.

The final examination paper is set and marked by the State Examinations Commission (SEC) and is allocated 90% of the total marks available for the final assessment. The examination lasts two hours and takes place at the end of third year. During this assessment, students are required to engage with, demonstrate comprehension of, and provide written responses to stimulus material. All students answer questions associated with strand 1, the core component, and students then answer questions associated with their chosen strand, either the classical studies strand (strand 2) or the classical language strand (strand 3).

The Junior Cycle Profile of Achievement (JCPA) comprises:
Two Classroom-Based Assessments
A final examination of 120 mins in the third year (90% of the total marks available).

Classical Studies (Senior Cycle) https://www.curriculumonline.ie/getmedia/4f756b6f-29c2-4651-bf1e-06739dee2106/Leaving_Certificate_Specification-Classical_Studies_EN.pdf
A two-year course taken by students aged 16–20 in 180 learning hours – Higher/Ordinary.

Course Content
The World of Heroes
Drama and Spectacle
Power and Identity
Gods and Humans

Skills Developed
Students learn to carefully **read, understand, evaluate and correlate** different types of texts and objects, considering aspects such as bias, genre, style and technique. They learn to **select, organise, analyse and communicate** information clearly and logically and to **evaluate** the reliability of evidence. The course thus supports the development of students' **higher-order thinking** and **inquiry-based learning**, but also areas such as spatial awareness and **visual literacy**. By learning about the diverse and complex values of these societies, students develop the ability to **form and reflect on their own viewpoints**, respect others' viewpoints, and make **informed judgments based on critical thinking**. Students develop information processing skills and critical and **creative thinking** skills by engaging in **independent research** activities where they are required to access a wide variety of primary and secondary sources, **analyse** and **synthesise** these multiple perspectives and use the views of others to help inform their own opinions and conclusions. **Communication** skills will be developed as students engage in **collaborative** work.

Assessment
Written examination (80%)
Section A – Stimulus-driven response (Ordinary Level 60, Higher Level 40)
Section B – Extended answer (Ordinary Level 20, Higher Level 40)
Research study (20%)
Written report (Ordinary Level 20, Higher Level 20)
This report must include a rationale, an extended essay and a reflection in answer to a particular issue or question.

Entry Statistics
492 entries in 2019

Scotland – National 4 https://www.sqa.org.uk/sqa/47440.html?origin=search
Classical Studies

A course taken by students aged 14–16 in 160 hours (directed) + 80 hours (self-directed).

Course Content
Life in Classical Greece (National 4)	6 SCQF credit points
Classical Literature (National 4)	6 SCQF credit points
Life in the Roman World (National 4)	6 SCQF credit points
Added Value Unit: Classical Studies:	
Assignment (National 4)	6 SCQF credit points

Learners choose, research and present their findings on a Classical Studies topic or issue for personal study. Through this activity they further develop and apply the knowledge, understanding and skills acquired in the other three units of the course.

Skills Developed
Classical Studies **fosters an open mind** and **respect** for the values, beliefs and cultures of others; **openness to new thinking** and ideas; **global citizenship**; a framework of religious, political, social, moral and cultural knowledge and understanding; an awareness of how the classical world is **relevant to an understanding of modern society**; a range of **cognitive skills**, the ability to comment on sources of evidence and respond to issues raised by classical literature.

Assessment

Assessment evidence for all of the units can be drawn from a variety of activities and presented in a range of formats including, for example, presentations, posters, brief written responses to questions or participation in group tasks. For the Added Value Unit, work is assessed through controlled assessment by centres and a pass or fail grade is awarded.

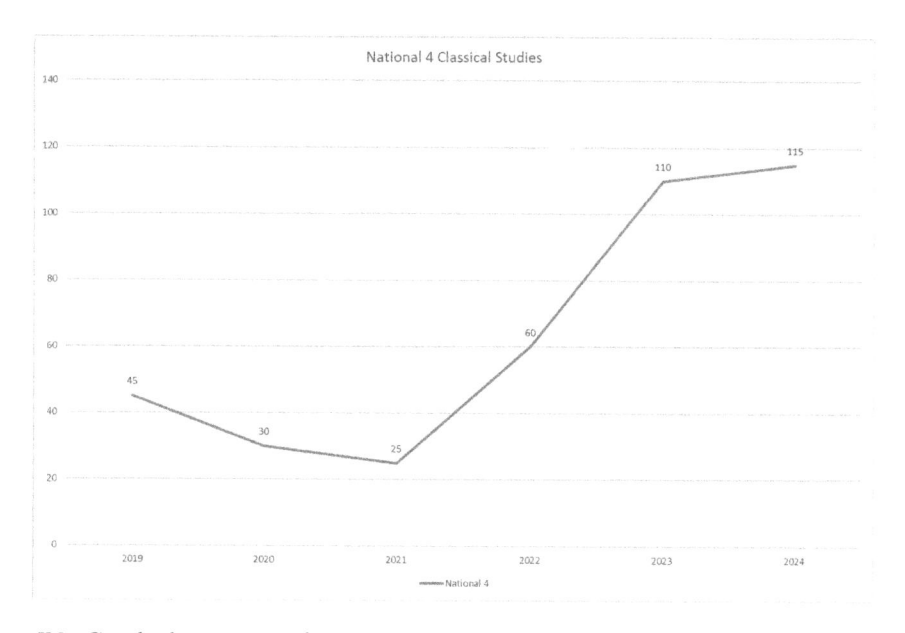

IV.1 Graph showing trend in National 4 Classical Studies uptake (2019–2024).

Scotland – National 5 https://www.sqa.org.uk/sqa/47445.html
Classical Studies
This course should be studied over 160 hours by students aged 14–16 who have achieved the fourth curriculum level or the National 4 Classical Studies course or equivalent qualifications.

Course Content
Section 1: Life in Classical Greece	6 SCQF credit points
Section 2: Classical Literature	6 SCQF credit points
Section 3: Life in the Roman World	6 SCQF credit points
Section 4: Assignment	6 SCQF credit points

Skills Developed
Candidates study the religious, political, social, moral and cultural values and practices of classical Greek and Roman societies. They become more **aware of issues affecting their own society**, and globally, by comparing the classical world with the modern world. Through the focus on **using sources**, candidates **develop knowledge of classical societies**, contributing to citizenship. They develop transferable skills through the emphasis on **investigative and critical-thinking activities**, and throughout the course they progressively **develop literacy skills** and contribute to group work. The course encourages candidates to develop important attitudes, including: an **open mind** and **respect** for the values, beliefs and cultures of others; **openness to new thinking** and ideas; a **sense of responsibility and global citizenship**.

Assessment
The course is assessed by an examination (80 marks) and an assignment (20 marks).

Examination (120 mins):
Section 1 (Life in Classical Greece): 30 marks
Students can be asked to describe an event or aspect of life; analyse an issue and come to a conclusion; compare and contrast aspects of the classical world with the modern world; evaluate the usefulness of a source; explain the meaning of a source or sources.

Section 2 (Classical Literature): 20 marks
Students can be asked to describe a theme as exemplified in a classical text or explain how this theme was viewed more widely in the classical world and compare the classical view of the theme with the way it is viewed in the modern world.

Section 3 (Life in the Roman World): 30 marks
In reference to either Pompeii or Roman Britain, students can be asked to describe an event or aspect of life; analyse an issue and come to a conclusion; compare and contrast aspects of the classical world with the modern world; evaluate the usefulness of a source; explain the meaning of a source or sources.

APPENDIX IV

Assignment: 20 marks

Students choose an appropriate topic or issue which allows them to compare and contrast the classical Greek and/or Roman worlds with the modern world. The research stage is designed to be capable of completion over a notional period of 8 hours and the production of evidence for assessment must be completed within 1 hour and in one sitting. During the research stage, there are no restrictions on the resources to which candidates may have access. During the final production of evidence stage, candidates should only have access to the Classical Studies resource sheet. There is no word count for the assignment; however, the resource sheet must have no more than 200 words on it.

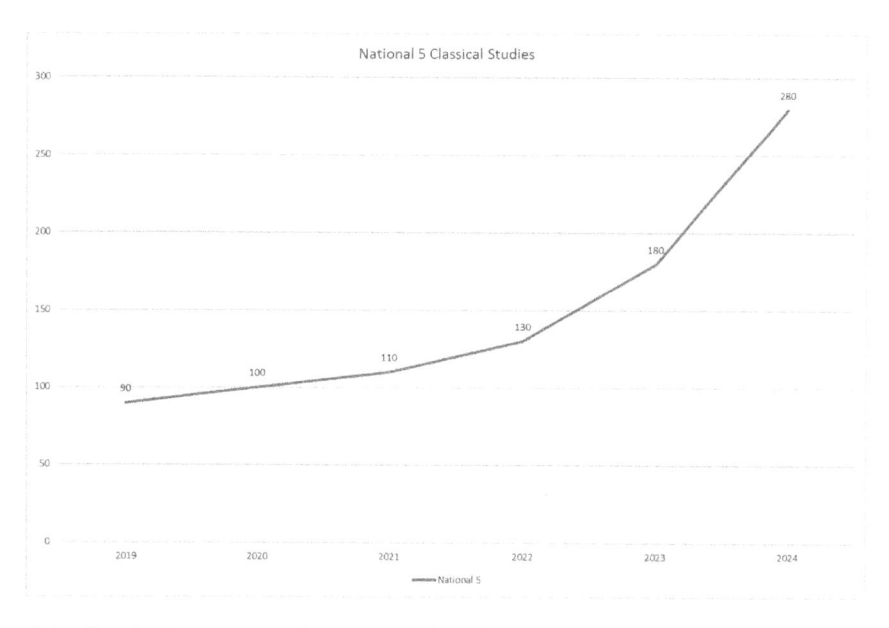

IV.2 Graph showing trend in National 5 Classical Studies uptake (2019–2024).

Scotland – Higher https://www.sqa.org.uk/sqa/47921.html
Classical Studies
A one-year course taken in 160 hours by students aged 15–17.

Course Content
Component 1: Classical Literature
By reading a classical text in translation, students develop knowledge and understanding of universal themes; ideas and values of leadership; fate versus free will; heroism; conflict; and women in society.

Component 2: Classical Society

- Life in Classical Greece (Power and Freedom or Religion and Belief)
- Life in the Roman World (Power and Freedom or Religion and Belief)

Component 3: Assignment

Skills Developed
Students build skills in: **structuring and sustaining lines of reasoned argument** about universal ideas, themes or values revealed by classical literature; **analysing and evaluating** the religious, political, social, moral and cultural values and practices of classical Greek and Roman societies; **comparing** religious, political, social, moral and cultural values and practices of the classical and modern worlds and **drawing reasoned and detailed conclusions; interpreting and understanding** a range of complex sources; **evaluating the reliability and value of a range of complex sources**; **research** and using information collected from a range of sources.

Assessment
70 min examination: Classical Literature (30 marks)
110 min examination: Classical Society (50 marks)
90 min production of evidence: Assignment (30 marks)
(There is no word count for the assignment; a resource sheet of no more than 250 words can be used for support in the final production of evidence stage.)

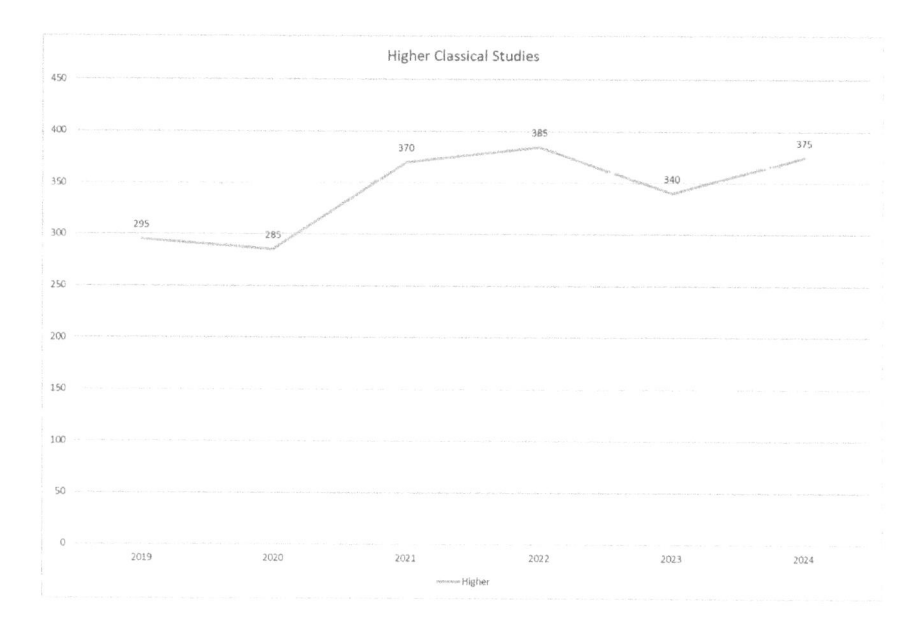

IV.3 Graph showing trend in Higher Classical Studies uptake (2019–2024).

Scotland – Advanced Higher https://www.sqa.org.uk/sqa/48464.html
Classical Studies (C815 77)
A one-year course taken in 160 hours by students aged 16–18 with Higher CS or equivalent.

Course Content
One topic is selected from the following:
History and historiography
Herodotus, Books 1 and 7
Thucydides, Books 1, 4, 7 and 8
Polybius, Book 3
Livy, Praefatio and Book 1
Tacitus, *Annals*, Books 1 and 14
Individual and community
Plato, *Republic*, Books 1–5
Aristotle, *Politics*
Cicero, *De Officiis* (On Duties)
Heroes and heroism

Homer, *Iliad*, Books 1, 6, 22 and 24
Homer, *Odyssey*, Books 1, 5, 6 and 22
Euripides, *Trojan Women*
Vergil, *Aeneid*, Books 1, 2, 4 and 12
Ovid, *Heroides*, 1, 3 and 7
Comedy, satire and society
Aristophanes, *Acharnians, Knights, Clouds, Peace* and *Assembly Women*
Horace, *Satires*, Book 1 (except 7 and 8) and Book 2 (except 1 and 3)
Juvenal, *Satires*, 1, 2, 3, 5, 6, 8, 9, 10 and 11
Additionally, a **dissertation** of 3,000–4,000 words is written on a Classical Studies issue.

Skills Developed
Students **analyse, evaluate and synthesise evidence** from a wide range of sources; **structure and sustain detailed lines of argument**; evaluate some of the religious, political, social, moral or cultural aspects of ancient Greek and Roman civilisation; **compare and contrast** classical Greek and Roman societies with later times; justify appropriate research issues; **plan, research, collect and record information**; explain approaches to organising, presenting and referencing findings; **develop in-depth knowledge** and understanding of universal human themes and values which have a continuing impact on contemporary society.

Assessment
180 min examination (100 marks):
Classical Literature (50 marks)

- one 10-mark question, requiring candidates to analyse a classical source
- one 10-mark question, requiring candidates to evaluate a classical source
- one 15-mark question, requiring candidates to compare two classical sources
- one 15-mark source-based question, comparing the classical and modern worlds

Classical Society (50 marks)

- two 25-mark questions from a choice of four, requiring candidates to analyse, evaluate and synthesise information into a line of argument

Project–dissertation (50 marks)

Entry Statistics

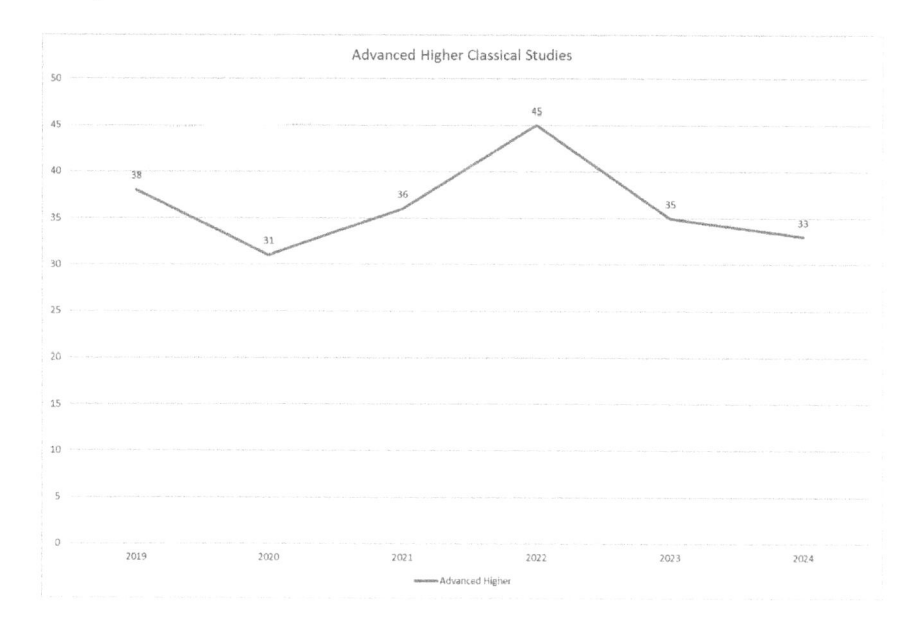

Advanced Higher Classical Studies

Year	Advanced Higher
2019	38
2020	31
2021	36
2022	45
2023	35
2024	33

IV.4 Graph showing trend in Advanced Higher Classical Studies uptake (2019–2024).

Note

[1] For more information about access to Classics Education in Ireland, see Holmes-Henderson et al. (in press).

Consolidated Bibliography

Altick, Richard Daniel (1957) *The English Common Reader: A History of the Mass Reading Public 1800–1900*. Chicago: Chicago University Press.
Anon. (1702, trans.) *Seneca's Morals by Way of Abstract* [8th edition]. London.
Anon. (1704, trans.) *Plutarch's Morals by Way of Abstract: Done from the Greek*. London.
Anon. (1884) 'Obituary: Henry George Bohn', *The Academy* 26, 137. London: J. Murray.
Anon. (1896) *Newsagents' Chronicle*. London: William Dawson & Sons.
Arnold, Matthew (1882) *Irish Essays, and Others*. London: Smith, Elder and Co.
Ashbridge, Jean and R.A. Hubbard (1968) *Classical Studies: Background Reading for Secondary Schools*. London: National Book League.
Azoulay, Vincent (2014) *Pericles of Athens. Translated by Janet Lloyd with a Foreword by Paul Cartledge*. Princeton, New Jersey: Princeton University Press.
Banaji, Marathi (1918) *Companion to Gould's Youth's Noble Path. Selections from Prose and Poetry*. Bombay: Banaji.
Bell, Marvin (2004) *Rampant (Poems)*. Port Townsend, WA: Copper Canyon Press.
Bennett, Scott (1984) 'The Editorial Character and Readership of "the Penny Magazine": An Analysis', *Victorian Periodicals Review* 17, 127–141.
Bérard, Robert (1987) 'Frederick James Gould and the Transformation of Moral Education', *British Journal of Educational Studies* 35, 233–234.
Blok, Rasmus (2002) 'A Sense of Closure: The State of Narration in Digital Literature', in Hans Balling and Anders Klinkby Madsen (eds.) *From Homer to Hypertext: Studies in Narrative, Literature and Media*. Odense: University Press of Southern Denmark, 167–180.
Bloor, Anna, Meghan McCabe and Arlene Holmes-Henderson (2023) 'Using Classical Mythology to Teach English as an Additional Language', in Arlene Holmes-Henderson (ed.) *Expanding Classics: Practitioner Perspectives from Museums and Schools*. London: Routledge, 42–56.

Board of Education (1937) *Handbook of Suggestions for the Consideration of Teachers and Others Concerned in the Work of Public Elementary Schools.* London: His Majesty's Stationery Office.

Brake, Laurel (2012) 'Stead Alone: Journalist, Proprietor, and Publisher 1890–1903', in Brake, King, Luckhurst and Mussell (eds.) *W.T. Stead Newspaper Revolutionary.* London: The British Library, 77–97.

Bridges, Emma (2015) *Imagining Xerxes: Ancient Perspectives on a Persian King.* London: Bloomsbury.

Bristow, Caroline (2021) 'Reforming Qualifications: The How, the Why and the Who', *Journal of Classics Teaching* 22(43): 60–63.

Brosius, Maria (2000, 2023) *The Persian Empire from Cyrus II to Artaxerxes I.* Cambridge: CUP.

Brougham, Henry (1840, trans.) *The Oration of Demosthenes Upon the Crown: Translated into English, with Notes, and the Greek Text.* London: George Knight.

Brougham, Henry (1893) *The Oration of Demosthenes Upon the Crown. Translated into English with Notes by Henry, Lord Brougham.* Revised edition. London: George Routledge and Sons.

Bruce, William (1818) *Literary Essays: The Influence of Political Revolutions on the Progress of Religion and Learning and Advantages of a Classical Education.* Belfast: E. Smyth and Lyons.

Burke, Peter (2001) *Eyewitnessing: The Uses of Images as Historical Evidence.* Ithaca, NY: Cornell University Press.

Camden, William (1610) *Britain, or a Chorographicall Description of the Most Flourishing Kingdomes, England, Scotland, and Ireland, and the Ilands Adjoyning, Out of the Depth of Antiquitie.* Translated by Philemon Holland. London: George Bishop and John Norton.

Carey, John (1992) *The Intellectuals and the Masses.* London and Boston, MA: Faber and Faber.

Cartledge, Paul (1994) 'The Greeks and Anthropology', *Anthropology Today* 10, 3–6.

Cavenagh, F.A. (1929) 'Lord Brougham and the Society for the Diffusion of Useful Knowledge', *The Journal of Adult Education* 4, 3–37.

Chapman, G. (1615) *Homer's Odysses. Translated according to ye Greeke.* London: Nathaniell Butter.

Christoforou, Constantine and Kathryn Tempest (2018) 'Classics After the Classroom', *Bulletin of the Council of University Classical Departments* 47, 1–7.

Clark, William George (1855) 'General Education and Classical Studies', *Cambridge Essays, Contributed by Members of the University.* London: John W. Parker and Son, 282–308.

Clarke, William B. (1831–1832) *Pompeii.* 2 vols. London: Charles Knight.

Classical Association (1962) *Re-Appraisal: Some New Thoughts on the Teaching of Classics.* Oxford: Clarendon Press.

Colman, David Stacy (1962) 'The Classics and History', in *Re-Appraisal: Some New Thoughts on the Teaching of Classics*. Oxford: Clarendon Press, 24–28.

Coney, Thomas (1722) *The Devout Soul: or, an Entertainment for a Penitent*. London: R. Wilkin; W. & J. Innys; W. Taylor.

Couper, William James (1914) *The Millers of Haddington, Dunbar and Dunfermline; a Record of Scottish Bookselling*. London: T.F. Unwin.

Crewe-Milnes, Robert (1921) *Report of the Committee Appointed by the Prime Minister to Inquire into the Position of Classics in the Educational System of the United Kingdom*. London: H. M. Stationery Office.

Cucinotta, Domenico and Maurizio Vanelli (2020) 'World Health Organisation Declares COVID-19 a Pandemic', *Acta Biomedica* 19; 91(1): 157–160.

Cueva, Edmund P., Shannon N. Byrne and Frederick Benda (2009, eds.) *Jesuit Education and the Classics*. Newcastle-Upon-Tyne: Cambridge Scholars Publishing.

Curll, Edmund (1729) *A Young Student's Library or, A Catalogue of Books Belonging to the Late Mr. Lusher*. Tunbridge Wells.

Daly, Nicholas (2012) 'Fiction, Theatre and Early Cinema', in David Glover and Scott McCracken (eds.) *The Cambridge Companion to Popular Fiction*. Cambridge: CUP, 33–49.

Danet, Pierre (1700) *Dictionarium Antiquitatum Romanarum et Graecarum, A Complete Dictionary of the Greek and Roman Antiquities Explaining the Obscure Places in Classic Authors and Ancient Historians*. London.

Davies, Alan (2009) *My Favourite People and Me, 1978–88*. London: Penguin.

Dearing, Ronald (1997) *Higher Education in the Learning Society: Main Report*. London: Her Majesty's Stationery Office. Viewable online at https://education-uk.org/documents/dearing1997/dearing1997.html.

Department for Education (2019) *English Baccalaureate*. https://www.gov.uk/government/publications/english-baccalaureate-ebacc/english-baccalaureate-ebacc

DES (1971) *Classics in the Curriculum* (Education Information Pamphlet). London: Her Majesty's Stationery Office.

DES (1977) *Classics in Comprehensive Schools* (Matters for Discussion no. 2). London: Her Majesty's Stationery Office.

Diaper, William (1722, trans.) *Oppian's Halieuticks of the Nature of Fishes and Fishing of the Ancients in V. Books*. Oxford: at the Theatre.

Dixon, Jessica and Arlene Holmes-Henderson (2024) *Classics in Action*. London: Hodder Education.

d'Orville, Hans (2015) 'New Humanism and Sustainable Development', *Cadmus: Promoting Leadership in Thought that Leads to Action* 2, 90–100.

Draycott, Jane and Kate Cook (2022, eds.) *Women in Classical Video Games*. London: Bloomsbury.

Dryden, John (1903, trans.) *The Works of Virgil*. London: Grant Richards.

Dryden, J. et al. (1680) *Ovid's Epistles Translated by Several Hands*, London.

Easterling, Pat and J.V. Muir (1985, eds.) *Greek Religion and Society*. Cambridge: CUP.

Education for Work (1999) *Classics and Classical Studies and Education for Work—A Guide for Secondary Teachers*. Dundee: Learning and Teaching Scotland.

Elley, Derek (2014) *The Epic Film: Myth and History*. London and New York: Routledge.

Evelyn, John (1656) *An Essay on the First Book of T. Lucretius Carus de Rerum Natura: Interpreted and Made English Verse*. London: Gabriel Bedle and T. Collins.

Feliciano de Oliveira, Dolores (1938) *Frederick James Gould*. Paris: Société positiviste internationale.

Finley, Moses (1965) 'Ancient History in the Senior Forms. Part I', *Didaskalos* 1(3), 75–82.

Finney, Joanne (2023) 'The Books that Shaped Me: Natalie Haynes', *Good Housekeeping*, 12 April 2023. https://www.goodhousekeeping.com/uk/lifestyle/editors-choice-book-reviews/a43577000/the-books-that-shaped-me-natalie-haynes/ [accessed 14 August 2024].

Forrest, Martin (2003) 'The Abolition of Compulsory Latin and Its Consequences', *Greece & Rome* 50 [= *The Classical Association: The First Century 1903–2003* (2003)] 42–66.

Fox, Matthew (2018) 'A Classics Education Can Drive Social Mobility', *TES Magazine*. 19 December 2018. https://www.tes.com/magazine/archive/classics-education-can-drive-social-mobility [accessed 6 April 2025].

Funder, L.M.A., Troels Myrup Kristensen and Vinnie Nørskov (2019) *Classical Heritage and European Identities: The Imagined Geographies of Danish Classicism*. London and New York: Routledge Taylor Francis.

Gilbert, Ann Margaret (1922) *The Work of Lord Brougham for Education in England*. Chambersburg, PA: Franklin Repository.

Godley, Alfred Dennis (1920) *Herodotus, With an English Translation*. Cambridge: Harvard University Press.

Gould, Frederick James (1890) *Stepping-Stones to Agnosticism*. London: Watts and Co.

Gould, Frederick James (1899) *The Children's Book of Moral Lessons*, Vol. 1. London: Watts and Co.

Gould, Frederick James (1903) *The Children's Book of Moral Lessons*, Vol. 2. London: Watts and Co.

Gould, Frederick James (1904) *The Children's Book of Moral Lessons*, Vol. 3. London: Watts and Co.

Gould, Frederick James (1906a) *Life and Manners*. London: Swan Sonnenschein.

Gould, Frederick James (1906b) *The Children's Plutarch*. London: Swan Sonnenschein.

Gould, Frederick James (1907) *The Children's Book of Moral Lessons*, Vol. 4. London: Watts and Co.

Gould, Frederick James (1915) *A Tour in the United States of North America in 1913 & 1914*. London: Moral Education League.

Gould, Frederick James (1916) *Worth While People*. London: Watts and Co.

Gould, Frederick James (1921) *History the Teacher: Education Inspired by Humanity's Story*. London: Methuen.
Gould, Frederick James (1923) *The Life-Story of a Humanist*. London: Watts and Co.
Gould, Frederick James (1924) *300 Stories to Tell; A Book for Parents, Teachers, Public Speakers, and Young Readers*. London: Watts and Co.
Gould, Frederick James (1925) *Britain and Her Commonwealth: Concise View, or Syllabus, of History from Earliest Times to 1914 and After*. London: Watts and Co.
Gould, Frederick James (2012) *The Children's Plutarch: Tales of the Romans*. London: RareBooksClub.
Gould, Frederick James (2017) *Plutarh za Otroke: Zgodbe o Grkih*, trans. Maruša Bračič. Šmarješke Toplice: Stella.
Grant, Michael (1958) *Roman Readings: Translations in Prose and Verse*. London: Pelican.
Green, Arthur George (1974) 'The Teaching of Classics in the Schools of England and Wales in the Twentieth Century', PhD Diss, University of Wales.
Green, Roger Lancelyn (1958) *The Tale of Troy: Retold from the Ancient Authors*, illustrated by Pauline Baynes. London: Puffin.
Hall, Edith (2006) *The Theatrical Cast of Athens*. Oxford: OUP.
Hall, Edith (2008a) 'Ancient Pantomime and the Rise of Ballet', in Edith Hall and Rosie Wyles (eds.) *New Directions in Ancient Pantomime*. Oxford: OUP, 363–377.
Hall, Edith (2008b) 'Navigating the Realms of Gold: Translation as Access Route to the Classics', in A. Lianeri and V. Zajko (eds.) *Translation and the Classic*. Oxford: OUP, 315–341.
Hall, Edith (2008c) *The Return of Ulysses: A Cultural History of Homer's Odyssey*. London: I.B. Tauris.
Hall, Edith (2013a) *Adventures with Iphigenia in Tauris*. New York: OUP.
Hall, Edith (2013b) 'Fast Forward Father', *TLS* 5772, 15 November.
Hall, Edith (2016) 'Intellectual Pleasure and the Woman Translator in 17th- and 18th-c. England', in Rosie Wyles and Edith Hall (eds.) *Women Classical Scholars: Unsealing the Fountain from the Renaissance to Jacqueline de Romilly*. Oxford: OUP, 103–131.
Hall, Edith (2018) 'Classical Epic at the London Fairs: Elkanah Settle's *The Siege of Troy*, 1707–1734', in F. Macintosh, J. McConnell, S. Harrison and C. Kenward (eds.) *Epic Performances*. Oxford: OUP, 439–460.
Hall, Edith (2020) 'Crises of Self & Succession: Herodotus' Cambyses in the English Theatre 1560–1667', in J. Grogan (ed.) *Beyond Greece and Rome: Reading the Ancient Near East in Early Modern Europe*. Oxford: OUP, 282–302.
Hall, Edith (2021) 'Classics Invented: Books, Schools, Universities and Society 1679–1742', in S. Harrison and C. Pelling (eds.) *Classical Scholarship and its History: Festschrift for Christopher Stray*. Berlin: De Gruyter, 35–58.

Hall, Edith (forthcoming a) 'F.J. Gould's Plutarch: Ancient History for Humanist Junior Citizens', in Katarzyna Marciniak (ed.) *Our Mythical History: Children's and Young Adults' Culture in Response to the Heritage of Ancient Greece and Rome*, in the series 'Our Mythical Childhood'. Warsaw: University of Warsaw Press.

Hall, Edith (forthcoming b) 'Brexit, the Roman Empire, and Shakespeare's *Cymbeline*', in B. Holler and A.V. Walser (eds.) *Identitätskonstruktionen. Zur Rolle der Antike für die europäische und aussereuropäische Selbstfindung (Antike nach der Antike)*. Basel and Berlin: Schwabe.

Hall, Edith and Fiona Macintosh (2005) *Greek Tragedy and the British Theatre 1660–1914*. Oxford: OUP.

Hall, Edith and Henry Stead (2020) *A People's History of Classics: Class and Greco-Roman Antiquity in Britain and Ireland 1660–1939*. London: Routledge.

Hansard, *Ancient History A-Level*, House of Commons, Debate, 459, 1004–1014, Wednesday 25 April 2007.

Hansard, *Schools: Ancient History*, House of Lords, Debate, 692, Wednesday 16 May 2007.

Harris, Oliver D. (2015) 'William Camden, Philemon Holland and the 1610 Translation of *Britannia*', *The Antiquaries Journal* 95, 279–303.

Harrison, Thomas (2009) 'The Campaign for Ancient History A Level in Great Britain', in Angelos Chaniotis, Annika Kuhn and Christina Kuhn (eds.), *Applied Classics Comparisons, Constructs, Controversies*. Stuttgart: Franz Steiner Verlag.

Hart, John (1969) 'The JACT Ancient History Project', *Didaskalos* 3(1), 48–59.

Hartwell, Clare and Nikolaus Pevsner (2009) *Lancashire: North*. New Haven, CT: Yale University Press.

Haw, George (1917) *The Life of Story of Will Crooks, MP*. London: Cassell.

Hayward, Frank Herbert and Ebe Minerva White (1942, eds.) *The Last Years of a Great Educationist: A Record of the Work and Thought of F.J. Gould from 1923 to 1938*. Bungay: Richard Clay and Co.

Hill, A. (1709) *A Full and Just Account of the Present State of the Ottoman Empire*. London.

Hobden, Fiona and Amanda Wrigley (2019, eds.) *Ancient Greece on British Television*. Edinburgh: Edinburgh University Press.

Holland, Philemon (1905, trans.) *Hannibal in Italy*, ed. W.H.D. Rouse. London, Glasgow and Dublin: Mackie and Son.

Holland, Philemon (1923, trans.) *Suetonius. History of Twelve Caesars*, ed. J.H. Freese. London: Broadway Translations.

Holmes-Henderson, Arlene (2013) *A Defence of Classical Rhetoric in Scotland's Curriculum for Excellence*. Ed.D thesis, University of Glasgow.

Holmes-Henderson, Arlene, Steven Hunt and Mai Musié (2018, eds.) *Forward with Classics: Classical Languages in Schools and Communities*. London: Bloomsbury.

Holmes-Henderson, A. and B. Watts (2021) 'What Grades are Needed to Study Classical Subjects at UK Universities?', *Journal of Classics Teaching* 22(44), 86–92.

Holmes-Henderson, Arlene (2023a, ed.) *Expanding Classics: Practitioner Perspectives from Museums and Schools.* London: Routledge.

Holmes Henderson, Arlene (2023b) 'The Pioneering Academic Who is Making Classics Cool in Schools', *AHRC blog*, 1 August 2023. https://www.ukri.org/blog/the-pioneering-academic-who-is-making-classics-cool-in-schools/

Holmes-Henderson, Arlene (2023c) 'The Benefits of Improving Children's Access to the Classics', *Museums Journal*, 26 July 2023. https://www.museumsassociation.org/museums-journal/opinion/2023/07/the-benefits-of-improving-childrens-access-to-the-classics/

Holmes-Henderson, Arlene, Steven Hunt and Alex Imrie (2024) 'Ancient Languages in UK Schools: Current Realities and Future Possibilities', in Wendy Ayres-Bennett and Charles Forsdick (eds.) *Languages, Societies and Policy: Languages in Education special issue.* https://www.lspjournal.com/post/ancient-languages-in-uk-schools-current-realities-and-future-possibilities

Holmes-Henderson, Arlene, Bridget Martin and Aryn Penn (in press) 'Classics in Ireland: An Update from Schools', in Emilio Zucchetti, Michele Bellomo, Vittorio Saldutti and Anna Maria Cimino (eds.) *Class and Classics: Subalterns and the Production of Classical Culture.* Berlin: De Gruyter.

Holmes-Henderson, Arlene, Chrissy Partheni and Peter Swallow (forthcoming) 'Digital Resources from Museum Classical Collections: A Case Study of Promoting Access, Diversity and Equality in English High Schools', in Jen Thum, Lisa Haney, Lissette Jiménez and Carl Walsh (eds.) *Teaching About the Ancient World in Museums.* London: Bloomsbury.

Horsley, Gregory (2011) 'One Hundred Years of the Loeb Classical Library', *Buried History* 47, 35–58. https://www.hup.harvard.edu/features/loeb/downloads/buried-history-lcl.pdf

Humanities for the Young School Leaver (1967) *Humanities for the Young School Leaver —An Approach Through Classics.* Schools Council. London: Her Majesty's Stationery Office.

Hunt, Steven (2013) '50 Years of Classical Civilisation', *Fifty Years of the Joint Association of Classical Teachers*, 25–33.

Hunt, Steven (2018a) 'Getting Classics into Secondary Schools: Three Case Studies', *Journal of Classics Teaching* 19(37), 64–70.

Hunt, Steven (2018b) 'Getting Classics into Schools? Classics and the Social Justice Agenda of the UK Coalition Government', in Holmes-Henderson, Arlene, Steven Hunt and Mai Musié (eds.) *Forward with Classics: Classical Languages in Schools and Communities.* London: Bloomsbury, 9–26.

Hunt, Steven and Arlene Holmes-Henderson (2021) 'A Level Classics Poverty: Access, Attainment and Progression', *CUCD Bulletin*, 50. https://cucd.blogs.sas.ac.uk/files/2021/02/Holmes-Henderson-and-Hunt-Classics-Poverty.docx.pdf

Hunt, Steven, Aisha Khan-Evans, Joanne McNamara, Arlene Holmes-Henderson, Jane Ainsworth and Rowlie Darby (2024) 'Initial Teacher Education: A Guide to the Classics PGCEs', CUCD Bulletin, 53, 1–20. https://cucd.blogs.sas.ac.uk/files/2024/10/Classics-PGCEs-guide.pdf

Hutchinson, Horace (1914) *Life of Sir John Lubbock, Lord Avebury*, 2 vols. London: Macmillan.

Hutchinson, W.M.L. (1912, 1914) *The Muses' Pageant: Myths & Legends of Ancient Greece.* 3 vols. London: Dent.

Incorporated Association of Assistant Masters in Secondary Schools (IAAMSS) (1954) *The Teaching of Classics.* Cambridge: CUP.

Irwin, Eleanor (2016) 'An Unconventional Classicist: The Work and Life of Kathleen Freeman', in Rosie Wyles and Edith Hall (eds.) *Women Classical Scholars: Unsealing the Fountain from the Renaissance to Jacqueline de Romilly.* Oxford: OUP, 313–334.

JACT (1964a) *Robbins and the Classics*, ed. Baty, C.W. and J.E. Sharwood Smith [= JACT Pamphlet 2]. London: JACT.

JACT (1964b) *Classics and the Reorganisation of Secondary Schools* [= JACT Pamphlet 2]. London: JACT.

JACT (1986) *GCSE* (Leaflet distributed September). London: JACT.

JACT (2013) *Fifty Years of the Joint Association of Classical Teachers.* https://www.stevenhuntclassics.com/_files/ugd/593fb9_2168fb02cba04858ad-c9b77e7c1d2e25.pdf

Jefferson, Thomas (1784 [1782]) *Notes on the State of Virginia.* Paris: Henry Stevens.

Jones, Joshua (1866) *Classical Studies: Their True Position and Value in Education.* London: Longmans, Green, Reader and Dyer.

Jowett, Benjamin (1881, trans.) *Thucydides: Translated into English.* Oxford: Clarendon Press.

Keats, John (1817) *Poems.* London: Charles and James Ollier.

Kennett, Basil (1695) *Romae Antiquae Notitia: Or The Antiquities of Rome.* London.

LACT (1970a) *Classical Studies in CSE* [LACT Working Paper No. 2]. London: LACT.

LACT (1970b) *Roman Home Life.* London: LACT.

LACT (1971) *Inscriptions of the Roman Empire AD 14–117.* London: LACT.

Lawrence, Caroline (2021) *Amarantus and His Neighbourhood.* London: Independent Publishing Network.

Lawton, Denis (1970) 'Team Teaching', *Didaskalos* 3(4), 322–330.

Leeds Conference (1967) Typescript Minutes of *Didaskalos Conference VII: Classical Civilisation*, BL P905/61.

Leibniz, G.W. (2003) *Sämtliche Schriften und Briefe* I, ed. Heinrich Schepers, Martin Schneider, Philip A. Beeley, Gerhard Biller, Stefan Lorenz, Herma Kliege-Biller. Berlin.

Lewis, Eira (1977) 'Teaching Classics in a Comprehensive School',

Education for Development: Journal of the Faculty of Education, University College, Cardiff, 31–33.
Lewis, Sian (1998–1999) 'Slaves as Viewers and Users of Athenian Pottery', *Hephaistos* 16/17, 71–90.
Liddel, Peter and Tom Harrison (2013) 'Fifty Years and Two Crises: JACT's Ancient History', in *Fifty Years of the Joint Association of Classical Teachers*, 20–24.
Lister, Bob (2007a) 'In Memoriam John Sharwood Smith'. https://arltblog.wordpress.com/2007/10/02/in-memoriam-john-sharwood-smith/
Lister, Bob (2007b) *Changing Classics in Schools*. Cambridge: CUP.
Lister, Bob (2015) 'In Memoriam JACT, 1963–2015', *Greece & Rome* 62(2), 206–217.
Livingston, Richard (1943) 'Concluding Statement' in *Classics and Education for the Professions*. London: John Murray, 17–18.
Lloyd-Jones, Hugh (1991) *Greek in a Cold Climate*. Savage, MD: Barnes and Noble Books.
Lockwood, Tom (2013) 'W.T. Stead's 'Penny Poets': Beyond Baylen', *Interdisciplinary Studies in the Long Nineteenth Century* 19. doi:10.16995/ntn.655
Long, Robert (2017) 'GCSE, AS and A Level', *Briefing Paper* no. 06962, 31 March 2017. London: Commons Library.
Lubbock, John (1887) *The Pleasures of Life*, vol. 1. 2nd edition. London and New York: Macmillan and Co.
Lucas, C.P. (1885) 'The Working Men's College', *Charity Organisation Review* 1, 161–163.
Macaulay, George Campbell (1914) *The History of Herodotus*. London: Macmillan.
Macaulay, Thomas Babington (1842) *Lays of Ancient Rome*. London: Longman, Green, Brown & Longmans.
MacNeice, Louis (1979) *The Collected Poems of Louis MacNeice*. 2nd edition. ed. E.R. Dodds. London: Faber.
Markovich, Slobodan G. (2018) 'Eleftherios Venizelos, British Public Opinion and the Climax of Anglo-Hellenism (1915–1920)', *Balcanica* 45, 125–145.
McOmish, Anna (2023) 'Promoting Inclusivity Through Teaching Ancient History', in Arlene Holmes-Henderson (ed.) *Expanding Classics: Practitioner Perspectives from Museums and Schools*. London: Routledge.
Michelakis, Pantelis and Maria Wyke (2013, eds.) *The Ancient World in Silent Cinema*. Cambridge and New York: CUP.
Morell, John (1814) *Reasons for the Classical Education of Both Sexes*. London: R. Rees.
Moritz, Charles P. (1795) *Travels, Chiefly on Foot, Through Several Parts of England, in 1782*. London: G.G. and J. Robinson.
Morley, Neville (2018) *Classics: Why It Matters*. London: Polity.
Morton, D.J. (1964a) 'The Present Situation', in JACT (1964b), 4–18.
Morton, D.J. (1964b) 'Classical Studies in the Certificate of Secondary Education', in JACT (1964b), 37–42.

Morwood, James (2003) *The Teaching of Classics*. Cambridge: CUP.
Mount, Harry (2020) 'The Decline and Fall of Classics Teaching', *Idler* [online]. https://www.idler.co.uk/article/the-decline-and-fall-of-classics-teaching/.
Murray, Gilbert (1889) *The Place of Greek in Education*: An Inaugural Lecture Delivered in the University of Glasgow November 6th, 1889. Glasgow: James MacLehose and Sons.
Murray, Gilbert (1911, trans.) *Oedipus, King of Thebes*. London: George Allen.
Murray, Oswyn and Penelope Murray (2001) 'Spreading the Word: Teaching Classics in Translation', unpublished paper delivered at a conference in Tokyo.
Murray, Penelope (1989) *Genius: The History of an Idea*. Oxford: Wiley-Blackwell.
Murray, Penelope (1996, ed.) *Plato on Poetry: Ion; Republic 376e–398b9*. Cambridge: CUP.
Murray, Penelope and Peter Wilson (2004, eds.) *Music and the Muses: The Culture of 'Mousikē' in the Classical Athenian City*. Oxford: OUP.
Nicolson, Benedict (1968) *Joseph Wright of Derby: Painter of Light*. Text and Catalogue. London: Paul Mellon Foundation for British Art; Routledge and Kegan Paul.
Norbrook, David (1999) *Writing the English Republic: Poetry, Rhetoric and Politics, 1627–1660*. Cambridge: CUP.
Nowell-Smith, Simon (1958) *The House of Cassell, 1848–1958*. London: Cassell.
OCR (2016) *Moving from Modular to Linear Qualifications*. Cambridge: CUP. https://www.ocr.org.uk/Images/338121-moving-from-modular-to-linear-qualifications-teachers-guide.pdf
Ofsted (2001) *Inspecting Classics 11–16*. London: Office for Standards in Education.
Oldenburg, H. (1975) *The Correspondence of Henry Oldenburg* Vol. X [ed. and trans. A.R. Hall and M.B. Hall]. London: University of Wisconsin Press.
Osborne, Robin and John Claughton (2003) 'Ancient History', in James Morwood (ed.) *The Teaching of Classics*. Cambridge: CUP, 117–123.
O'Sullivan, Carol (2009) 'Translation Within the Margin: The 'Libraries' of Henry Bohn', in J. Milton and P. Bandia (eds.) *Agents of Translation*, vol. 81; Benjamins Translation Library, The European Society for Translation Studies subseries. Amsterdam and Philadelphia: John Benjamins Publishing Company, 107–129.
Pendered, Mary Lucy (1923) *John Martin, Painter. His Life and Times*. London: Hurst and Blackett.
Planning Classical Studies (1967) *Planning Classical Studies in Schools Today: A Working Conference*. London: Institute of Education.
Pomeroy, Arthur J. (2017, ed.) *A Companion to Ancient Greece and Rome on Screen*. Hoboken, NJ: Wiley-Blackwell.
Pope, Alexander (1903, trans.) *The Odyssey of Homer*. London: Grant Richards.

Potter, Amanda and Hunter Gardner (2022, eds.) *Ancient Epic in Film and Television*. Edinburgh: Edinburgh University Press.
Potter, J. (1697) *Archaeologiae Graecae: or, the Antiquities of Greece*. Oxford.
Quarrell, W.H. and W.J.C. Quarrell (1928, eds.) *Oxford in 1710 From the Travels of Zacharias Conrad Von Uffenbach*. Oxford: Basil Blackwell.
Rapple, Brendan A. (2017) *Matthew Arnold and English Education*. Jefferson, NC: MacFarland.
Rauch, Alan (2001) *Useful Knowledge: The Victorians, Morality, and the March of Intellect*. Durham, North Carolina and London: Duke University Press.
Reynard, Anna (2020) 'Classics at Lionheart Trust', *Journal of Classics Teaching* 21(41), 84–85.
Rich, Barnaby (1584, trans.) *The Famous Hystory of Herodotus, Conteyning the Discourse of Dyuers Countreys, the Succession of Theyr Kyngs, etc*. London: Thomas Marshe.
Robbins, Lionel (1963) *Higher Education: Report of the Committee Appointed by the Prime Minister under the Chairmanship of Lord Robbins*. London: Her Majesty's Stationery Office.
Rollinger, Christian (2020, ed.) *Classical Antiquity in Video Games: Playing with the Ancient World*. London: Bloomsbury.
Rolph, C.H. (1980) *London Particulars*. Oxford: OUP.
Rutter, Carol and Tony Howard (2008) 'Professor G.K. Hunter: Shakespeare Scholar and Founding Professor of English Literature at Warwick University', *Independent* obituary, Monday 21 April. https://www.independent.co.uk/news/obituaries/professor-g-k-hunter-shakespeare-scholar-and-founding-professor-of-english-literature-at-warwick-university-812674.html [accessed 6 April 2025].
Sabben-Clare, J.P. and Mark Warman (1978) *The Culture of Athens*. London: LACT.
Sanchez, Olivia and Nicola Felton (2018) 'Developing a Classics Department from Scratch: Two Case Studies' in Arlene Holmes-Henderson, Steven Hunt and Mai Musié (eds.) *Forward with Classics: Classical Languages in Schools and Communities*. London: Bloomsbury, 161–170.
Searle, Emma, Lucy Jackson and Michael Scott (2018) 'Widening Access to Classics in the UK: How the Impact, Public Engagement, Outreach and Knowledge Exchange Agenda Have Helped', in Arlene Holmes-Henderson, Steven Hunt and Mai Musié (eds.) *Forward with Classics: Classical Languages in Schools and Communities*. London: Bloomsbury, 27–47.
Seith, Emma (2018) 'Call to Reverse Near-Extinction of Classics in Scottish Schools', *TES*, 29 March 2018. https://aceclassics.org.uk/images/downloads/call-to-reverse-near-extinction-of-classics-in-scottish-schools.pdf
Shelford, April G. (2007) *Transforming the Republic of Letters: Pierre-Daniel Huet and European Intellectual Life, 1650–1720*. Rochester, NY: University of Rochester Press.

Sidgwick, Arthur Hugh (1920) *The Oxford Magazine*, vol. 38 (5 March): 259–260. Oxford: Horace Hart.

Soudien, Crain (2017) 'The Significance of New Humanism for Education and Development', *Prospects* 47, 309–320.

Sparrow, F.H. (1965) 'History at the Advanced Level', *Didaskalos* 3.1, 23–30.

St Clair, William (1998) *Lord Elgin and the Marbles*. 4th edition. Oxford: OUP.

Stamper, Joseph (1960) *So Long Ago*. London: Hutchinson.

Stead, W.T. (1901) 'The World's Classics; or Bound Books for the Million: The Last Word in Cheap Literature', in W.T. Stead (ed.) *Wake Up! John Bull. An Illustrated Supplement to The Review of Reviews*, no. 5.24 (15 November). London: Stead, 544–545.

Stray, Christopher (1977) *The Changing Forms and Current Decline of Classics as Exemplary Curricular Knowledge, with Special Reference to the Experience of Classics Teachers in South Wales*. MSc thesis, University of Wales.

Stray, Christopher (1998) *Classics Transformed: Schools, Universities, and Society in England, 1830–1960*. Oxford: OUP.

Stray, Christopher (2006) 'Sonnenschein, Edward Adolf', in David Cannadine et al. (eds.) *Oxford Dictionary of National Biography*, Oxford: OUP. https://doi.org/10.1093/ref:odnb/36194

Swallow, Peter and Edith Hall (2020, eds.) *Aristophanic Humour*. London: Bloomsbury.

Swallow, Peter (2023) *Aristophanes in Britain: Old Comedy in the Nineteenth Century*. Oxford: Oxford University Press.

Sydenham, Floyer (1761, trans.) *The Banquet, A Dialogue of Plato Concerning Love*. London: H. Woodfall.

Taylor, Thomas and Floyer Sydenham (1804) *The Works of Plato*. London: T. Taylor.

Taylor, Amber, Arlene Holmes-Henderson and Sharon Jones (2022) 'Classics Education in Northern Irish Primary Schools: Curriculum Policy and Classroom Practice', *Journal of Classics Teaching*, 1–7.

Telford, Muriel (1971) 'Presidential Address at JACT AGM 1981', BL typescript X0981/111.

Theodorakopoulos, Elena (2010) *Ancient Rome at the Cinema: Story and Spectacle in Hollywood and Rome*. Exeter: Bristol Phoenix.

Thompson, Dorothy J. (2016) 'Finley and the Teaching of Ancient History', in Daniel Jew, Robin Osborne and Michael Scott (eds.) *M.I. Finley: An Ancient Historian and His Impact*. Cambridge: CUP, 26–50.

Turner, Susanne (2023) 'Whose Museum is it Anyway? Connecting with Communities at the Museum of Classical Archaeology', in Arlene Holmes-Henderson (ed.) *Expanding Classics: Practitioner Perspectives from Museums and Schools*. London: Routledge, 90–109.

University of Wisconsin (1913) *Character Building in Our Schools*. Madison, WI: The University of Wisconsin, University Extension Division.
Vonledebur, Catherine (2019) 'Top Historians and Authors to Speak at Free Warwick University Ancient Worlds Study Day', *Coventry Observer*, 19 November 2019. https://coventryobserver.co.uk/news/brush-up-on-your-knowledge-of-ancient-worlds-at-free-warwick-university-study-day-with-top-historians-and-authors-16039/
Waterfield, Giles (2015) *The People's Galleries: Art Museums and Exhibitions in Britain, 1800–1914*. New Haven, Connecticut and London: Yale University Press.
Weale, Sally (2025) 'Classicists take 'ancient philosophical wisdom' into English jails', *The Guardian*, 12 April 2025. https://www.theguardian.com/society/2025/apr/12/classics-philosophy-england-jails-prison-education-durham
Webster, T.B.L. (1964) 'Robbins and the Classics', in JACT (1964a), 5–9.
Whitehead, Catherine S. (1989) *The Third Programme: A Literary History*. Oxford: OUP.
Whyte, Frederic (1925) *The Life and Letters of W.T. Stead*, 2 vols. London: Johnathan Cape.
Wilson, Andrew (2019) *Investigating Civilisations: The Persians*. Haverhill: Hands Up Education.
Wilson, David M. (2002) *British Museum: A History*. London: British Museum.
Wilson, Penelope (2012) 'The Place of Classics in Education and Publishing', in David Hopkins and Charles Martindale (eds.) *The Oxford History of Classical Reception in English Literature* (vol. 3.). Oxford: OUP, 29–52.
Woolcock, Nicola (2019) 'Poorer Pupils Learn to Benefit from Classics', *The Times*, 9 November 2019. https://www.thetimes.com/uk/article/poorer-pupils-learn-to-benefit-from-classics-oqb6sohb3
Wrigley, Amanda (2015) *Greece on Air*. Oxford: OUP.
Wyles, Rosie (2016) 'Ménage's Learned Ladies: Anne Dacier (1647–1720) and Anna Maria van Schurman (1607–1678)', in Rosie Wyles and Edith Hall (eds.) *Women Classical Scholars: Unsealing the Fountain from the Renaissance to Jacqueline de Romilly*. Oxford: OUP, 61–77.
Wyles, Rosie and Edith Hall (2016, eds.) *Women Classical Scholars: Unsealing the Fountain from the Renaissance to Jacqueline de Romilly*. Oxford: OUP.
Yeats, William Butler (1919) *The Wild Swans at Coole*. 2nd edition. New York: The MacMillan Co.

Index

A Levels 33–34, 38, 44, 61, 71,
  155–156, 163, 169, 175
  Ancient History 33–34, 38, 48, 50,
    61, 62–78, 81, 97–99, 177
  Classical Civilisation 34, 49, 50–51,
    55–56, 81, 83, 85, 88, 89, 94, 96,
    99, 114, 119, 140, 143, 146, 164,
    165, 171, 177
  Greek 40, 55, 102, 177
  Latin 40, 55, 82, 102, 177
Achilles 11, 23, 48, 145, 170
Actium, battle of 99
Adams, Ellen 143
Adams, Gemma 85
Adonis, Andrew 70
Advocating Classics Education (ACE)
  93, 95, 109–158, 162, 164, 173, 176
  events 119–134
  impact 154–156
  patrons 115–118
Aelian 3
Aesop 3, 11, 13, 20, 23
after-school clubs 162
Agbamu, Samuel 112
Alcibiades 11, 48, 84, 86
Alexander the Great 11, 23, 26, 61,
  75, 91
All-Party Parliamentary Groups
  (APPGs) 69, 111, 158
Allen, George 14
Allen, Lindsay 144
Almond, David 153

Amarantus Project 74–75
Andrew, Charlie 132
Andrews, Ben 82
Angel, Lucy 134
Antigonus 11
antiquarianism 12
AQA (examination board) 73
archaeology 2, 12, 17, 20, 36, 66, 67,
  73, 75, 83, 97, 106, 118, 120, 126,
  137, 142, 164
Archimedes 23, 61
Aristophanes 15, 20, 42, 48, 63, 76,
  84, 86, 111, 126, 130, 165
Aristotle 4, 18, 20, 23, 27, 111, 119
Arnold, Matthew 28
Artemidorus of Daldis 5
Arts and Humanities Research
  Council (AHRC) 109, 111, 138, 142,
  146, 147, 154, 174
Ashbridge, Jean 47
Association for the Reform of Latin
  Teaching (ARLT) 41
Athens, ancient 12, 23, 26, 47, 48, 66,
  89, 91, 127, 131, 163, 164, 165
Augustus, emperor 3, 4, 23, 24, 66,
  88, 89, 91, 99
Australia 62
Avlamis, Pavlos 145

Baddiel, David 99
'Balfour' Education Act (1902) 37
Ball, Caroline 120

Barker, Andrew 104
Barker, Pat 167
Barlow, Shirley 99–102, 105
Barratt, Pamela 86
Bath, Somerset 121–122, 137
Baty, C.W. 43
BBC 10, 55, 69, 81, 101, 124
Beasley, Simon 110
Bell, Edward 12
Bell, Marcus 112, **123**, 135
Beloe, Robert 43
Bill of Rights 6
Billinge, Mike 83
Birrell, Augustine 24
Bohn, Henry 12, 14
Bothwell, Cathy 153
Bowden, Hugh 137, 145
Bower, Ben 128
Brabazon, James 81
Bragg, Ed 110
Braidley, Lindsey 122
Brazil 27
Brexit 92
Bridges, Emma 93–97, 117, **133**
Bristow, Caroline 72, **110**
British Museum 17, 114, 140–142, 167
Brosius, Maria 65
Brougham, Henry 16, 20–21
Browes, Nicole 123
Brown, A.F.J. 49
Brunt, Peter 62, 64
Bulwer-Lytton, Edward 16, 20
Burden-Stevens, Christopher 120
Burns, Robert 10
'Butler' Education Act (1944) 1, 38

Cambridge School Classics Project (CSCP) 48, 51, 70, 74, 170
Camden, William 3, **4**
Campbell-Thow, Gillian 126
CANI (Classical Association of Northern Ireland) 124, 142, 178
Cannon, Charlotte 145
Caractacus 35
Carberry, Neil 72

Carrington, Jo 122
Cartledge, Paul 76, **115**
Casati, Costanza 167
Cassell, John 12, 13, 35
Cawkwell, George 64
Caxton, William 3
Chambers, Robert 11–12
Chambers, William 11
Chapman, George 8–9
Chaucer, Geoffrey 3
China 89
Choricius 5
Christie, Agatha 54
Christie, Andrew 150
Cicero 4, 15, 20, 70, 73, 83, 89, 91, 97, 98, 117
Cincinnatus 23
cinema *see* film
'Circular 10/65' 49–50
citizenship 24, 27, 37, 42, 69, 88
Civil War, English 4
Classical Archaeology, Museum of (Cambridge) (MoCA) 142, 146, 147–148, 167
Classical Association 25, 33, 39, 41, 62, 74, 75–76, 117, 135, 136, 138, 143, 145, 146, 150, 151, 152, 156, 162, 165, 167, 168–169, 170, 176
Classical Association of Scotland (CAS) 126, 133, 134, 142, 177
Classical Collections Network (CCN) 142
Classics, definition of 2
Classics for All (CfA) 120, 134, 152, 165, 166, 168–169
Clive of India 27
coinage 3, 24, 91, 114, 123, 130, 135, 152
competitions 121, 123, 128, 169, 170
comprehensive schools 1, 2, 41, 42, 43, 46–47, 49–50, 52, 81, 82, 83, 87, 94, 120, 140, 143, 152
Cooke, Kitty **114**
Corke-Webster, James 145
Cosgrave, Elinor 120

course-work assessment 44
Covid-19 133, 167
Coyle, Do 126
CPD (Continuing Professional Development) 140
Cranc, Walter 25
Crewe-Milnes, Robert Offley Ashburton, marquess of Crewe 35–36, 37
'cribs' 7, 53
Crooks, Will 10
Crosland, Anthony 50
CSE (Certificate of School Education) 42–48, 51, 56, 81, 99
Cunningham, Ann 126
Curran, John 124
Czechoslovakia 27

D'Alconzo, Nicolò 122
Dacier, Madame (Anne Le Fèvre) 6–7
Danet, Pierre 8
Davies, Alan 101
Davis, H.W.C. 74
Dearing, Ronald 67
Dearnaley, Will 145
Delphin editions 6–7, 9
democracy 15, 36, 41, 55, 70, 88, 143, 153, 165, 166
Demosthenes 3, 15, 20, 21, 23
Denmark 34, 43
Dent, Joseph Malaby 14
Department of Education and Science (DES) 46, 49, 50
Descartes, René 6
Devlin, Nicola 144
DfE (Department for Education) 72, 174, 176–177, 178
Dhindsa, Hardeep 150
digital learning 76, 138
  sourcebooks, digital 146, 148–150
dioramas 16
Direct Grant schools 38, 49, 84, 100
Dixon, Jessica 164
Dobson, Stephen 110, 132
Dodds, E.R. 43

Doherty, Edda-Jane 145
Downes, Caron 90, 92, 93
Drakeford, Mark 101
drama, ancient 7, 15, 21, 47, 86, 91, 101, 114, 119, 124, 128, 132, 141, 146, 157
Draper, Jenny 145
Dryden, John 6, 9, 14

EAL (English as an Additional Language) 162
Easterling, Pat 49, 102
Easton, Esther 10
EBacc (English Baccalaureate) 72, 74, 163, 174–175
Education Acts see 'Balfour' Education Act (1902); 'Butler' Education Act (1944); Education Act (1918); Education Act (1921); Education Act (Scotland); Elementary Education Act (1870); Elementary Education Act (1880)
Education Act (1918) 37, 38
Education Act (1921) 37
Education Act (Scotland) 38
Eduqas (exam board) 145
Edwards, Terry 68
Egypt, ancient 2, 36, 65, 74, 89, 168
Elementary Education Act (1870) 22, 33
Elementary Education Act (1880) 15, 33
Eleven-Plus examination (11-plus) 38
Elgin, Lord 17
Eliot, T.S. 84
elitism 103, 175
Empire, British 27
English and Media Centre (EMC) 137–138
English Heritage 151, 152
Ennew, Christine 130
epic 4, 45, 52, 96, 104, 128, 165
Epictetus 3, 20, 23
Euripides 15, 18, 20, 46, 90, 91, 101, 103, 112, 122, 165

Eutropius 6
Evelyn, John 4
exemplars, moral 22, 23–24, 26
extra-curricular activities 93, 122, 162–163, 171

Fallon, Michael 69
fee-paying schools 35, 38, 43–44, 46, 50, 61, 76, 95, 102, 142, 177
FIEC (International Federation of Associations of Classical Studies) 139–140
film 15, 16, 52, 54, 119, 139, 145–146, 153–154, 169
Finley, Moses 41, 62–64, 67, 68
Fisher, Nick 105
Flitton, Rob 121
Florus 7
Forrest, Martin 48, 49
Found, Paul 110, **119**
Fox, Matthew 126, 127
France 16, 27, 28
Freeman, Kathleen 105
Freud, Sigmund 5
Froebel, Friedrich 102

Gandhara 89
GCSEs 51–52, 72, 76, 95, 162, 163, 165, 175
  Ancient History 71, 77, 130, 136, 155
  Classical Civilisation 44, 51, 52, 89, 90, 91, 92, 130, 136, 141–142, 143, 145, 146, 148, 155, 156, 164, 177
  Greek 177
  Latin 93, 177
Gee, Martin 92
General Teaching Council for Scotland (GTCS) 134, 177
Gibbon, Edward 11, 15, 20
Gibbon, Jenny 52, 69, 70
Gidlow, Tom 129
Gladstone, William Ewart 53
Goff, Barbara 129
Goh, Ian 150

Goodwin, Laurence 145
Gooptu, Christina 92
Gould, Frederick James 21–27
Gove, Michael 71
Gower, John 3
Graeco-Turkish War 35
Graham, Emma-Jayne 132
grammar schools 1, 17, 38, 40, 44, 46, 49, 61, 82, 84, 86, 90, 100, 119
Gransden, Ken 104
Greenstock, Mark 64
Grigsby, Paul **131**, **139**
Grilli, Francesca 87, 93
Gunpowder Plot 5

Hadrian's Wall 94, 143, 151, 152, **153**
Haley, Maria 110, 120
Hall, Edith **34**, 38, 55, 90, 96, **100**, **110**, 111, 125, **127**, 128, 129, **130**, 132, 133, 134, 135–136, 139, 140, 141, 144–145, 147, 151, 152, 153, **154**, 156, 157
Hamer, Chandler 145
Hamilton, William 17
Hancock-Jones, Rob 145
Harper, Elodie 167
Harrap, George 39
Harris, Edmund 17
Harris, Robert 70
Harrison, Tony 93, 145, 153
Hart, John 67
Hauser, Emily 167
Haynes, Natalie 116, 119, 124, 126, 145, 167
Haywood, Jan 132
Herculaneum, Italy 12, 16, 129
Herodian 3
Herodotus 3, 20, 26, 48, 53–54, 61, 66, 98
Hesiod 20
Hibbert, James 17
Higgins, Charlotte 117, 120, 123
Hill, Aaron 9
Historical Association 135–136
HMI (Her Majesty's Inspectors) 28, 50

Hobbs, Jo 89
Hodgson, Cecily 46
Hodgson, Hilary 120
Hoggart, Richard 15
Holland, Philemon 3
Holland, Tom 69, 70
Holmes-Henderson, Arlene 75, **110**, 111, 112, 123, 125, 126, 128, 129, **130**, **131**, 132, 134, 135–136, 137–138, 139, 140, 142, 145, 146, 147, 150, 151, **154**, 156, 157, 158, 164
Homer 8–10, 13, 15, 18, 20, 53, 73, 91, 96–97, 104, 105, 117, 137, 143, 144, 165
Hope, Laura 151, 152
Horace 41, 48, 63, 143
Hughes, Jessica **132**
humanism, new 28
Hunt, Steven 72, 150
Hunter, George 103–104
Hutchinson, Winifred Margaret Lambart 15

Iakovou, Pantelis 145
Imrie Alex 126, 134
independent schools *see* fee-paying schools
India 26, 27, 113
Initial Teacher Training (ITT) 97, 176–177
interdisciplinarity 88, 89, 91, 101
Italy 16, 27

JACT (Joint Association of Classical Teachers) 41, 42, 44, 47, 48–49, 50, 51–52, 55, 81
James I, king of England 4
Japan 27
Jefferson, Thomas 27
Jenkins, Susan 145
Jenkinson, Laura 85, 122
Jenner, Greg 167
Jesuits 5, 8
Johnson, Boris 69, 70, **71**
Johnson, Jo 145

Jones, Thomas 35
Jonson, Ben 4
Josephus 15
Jowett, Benjamin 21
Juckes, Cheryl 90, 92, 93
Julius Caesar 3, 11, 23, 61, 97
Juvenal 90

Keats, John 8
Kennedy, Steven 76
Kennett, Basil 8
Kerridge, Richard 136
Key Stages 137
Khan-Evans, Aisha 137
Kingsley, Charles 46
Klemm, Helen 152
Knight, Charles 16
Kruschwitz, Peter 129
KS3 (Key Stage 3) 74, 75, 122, 137, 162, 163, 175
Kuhivchak, Lidia 141, 145

Ladosz, Justyna 147
languages, ancient 5, 8, 9, 33, 36, 37, 38, 43, 47, 50, 56, 62, 72, 81, 85, 95, 96, 101, 120, 142, 164, 171, 177
Lashly, Jo 110, 145
Latham, Caroline 114
Lawrence, Caroline 75
Lawrence, D.H. 52
Laws, David 72
League of Nations 26
LEAs (Local Education Authorities) 25, 44, 49, 56, 126, 134, 177
Leibniz, Gottfried Wilhelm 6
Lewis, Eira 1–2
Lewis, Sian 15
Libanius 5
Lieu, Sam 104
Lister, Bob 41
literacy, cultural 87, 106
literacy, emotional 90, 96, 106
literacy, financial 174
literature 10, 11, 12, 13, 18, 21, 25, 27, 33, 36, 39, 43, 44, 45, 46, 47, 49,

52, 55, 56, 63, 73, 84, 86, 87, 89, 90, 91–93, 95, 97, 99, 101, 102, 103–104, 105, 106, 118, 120, 122, 142, 153, 165, 166, 167, 171
Livy 3, 13, 15, 20, 47, 48
Lloyd George, David 12, 34, 35
Lloyd-Jones, Hugh 54
London Association of Classical Teachers (LACT) 47
LACTOR (London Association of Classical Teachers – Original Records) 49, 55, 64–65
Loughton, Tim 105
Louis XIV, king of France 6
Louis de France (Dauphin) 6
Lubbock, John 20
Lucian 5
Pseudo-Lucian 89
Lucretius 4
Lynch, Mike 134

McCarthyism 62
Macaulay, Thomas Babington 13, 84
McFarlane Nigel 83
McInnes-Gibbons, Rory 111, 151, 152, 153, **154**
McKellar, Andy 126
MacNeice, Louis 56
McOmish, Anna 162
McVeigh, Helen 124, 171
Maidwell, Lewis 6
Marcus Aurelius 15, 18, 20, 23
Mars, Helen 92
Marshall, Sharon 122
Martial 9
Martin, John 16
Mason, Adam 92, 93
Mastin, Steve 119, 125, 136
Masuda, Neil 105
Melluish, Tommy 39
Melmoth, William 15
Mercury, Freddie 127
Merivale, Charles 15
Midgley, David 114
military history 46, 62, 64, 66, 128
Miller, George 11

Miller, Hugh 10
Miller, Madeline 167
Miller, Maria 68
Montausier, duke of 6
Moore, Nancy 91, 93
Mortimer, Lottie 145
Morton, D.J. 44
Mullins, Edwin Roscoe 18
Multi-Academy Trusts (MATs) 121, 145
Murray, Gilbert 2, 21, 26
Murray, Oswyn 65, **67**, 73, 76
Murray, Penny 102–105
Murrell, John 68
museums 16–17, 19, 27, 36, 83, 87, 92, 93, 99, 109, 114, 119, 121, 122, 124, 126, 128, 140–141, 142, 146, 147–149, 151, 152, 153–155, 156, 158, 163, 167, 168
Mycenaeans 143
myths 5, 6, 15, 16, 22, 23, 44, 45, 46, 51, 81, 84, 85, 86, 91, 92, 96, 101, 116, 122, 127, 143, 145, 148, 150, 163, 167, 168, 170, 171

NEC (National Extension College) 165, 171
Network for Working-Class Classicists (NWCC) 82
New Zealand 43
Nicholson, John 7
Noble, Matt 123
Norgate, Stephanie 105
North, Thomas 3
Northern Ireland 26, 34, 124, 142, 168, 178
Norway 27
novels 2, 84, 167, 171
numismatics *see* coinage

O Levels 38, 40, 44, 51, 104
O'Toole, Robert 131
OCR (examination board) 56, 65, 67, 68, 69, 71, 72, 73, 76, 88, 136, 143, 146, 149, 165, 176
Ofqual 71, 176

Ofsted 162
Oikonomou, Maria 150
Oldenburg, Henry 6
Oliver, Jack 145
Olympic Games 145, 170
Oppian 5
Orbilian Society 41
Orgee, Alex 136
Orpheus 45
Osborne, Robin 68, 69
Ovid 3, 9, 11, 48, 105, 137, 170
Oxbridge entry requirements for 35–36, 40, 95

papyrology 36, 55
paraphrases 5, 9
parents, attitudes of 167–168
Parham, Ken 94–95
Parker, Judith 145
Partheni, Chrissy 142, 148
Parthenon Friezes 17, 18, 19, 27, 141
Parthia 89
Patel, Nimisha 113
Pearce, John 137, 144
Pelling, Christopher 127
Pericles 18, 21, 23, 48
Persian Empire 3, 5, 48, 65–66, 89, 96, 117, 144
Petronius 90
PGCE (Postgraduate Certificate in Education) 97, 137, 145, 151, 176, 177
PGDE (Postgraduate Diploma in Education) 176, 177
Pheidias 18, 19
philosophy 3, 5, 6, 12, 15, 18, 22, 33, 45, 89, 101, 104, 105, 117, 120, 157, 163, 164, 171
Pickering, Ken 110
Pillinger, Emily 137, 144
Pindar 11, 174
Plastow, Christine 132
Plato 5, 11, 20, 21, 22, 23, 48, 103, 145
Playmobil 86
Pliny the Younger 13, 15, 44, 48, 89
Plutarch 3, 7, 15, 20, 22, 23–26, 45, 48, 61, 78, 86

Poland 27
Polybius 3
Pomey, François 8
Pompeii, Italy 12, 16, 27, 75, 129, 152, 163, 171
Pompey 11, 23, 73, 97
Pope, Alexander 9–10, 14
Potter, John 7–8
Powell, J. Enoch 53, 127
Poynder, Sarah 115
Pratt, Lynne 134
prisons 109, 135, 157–158
private schools *see* fee-paying schools
public schools *see* fee-paying schools
Pym, Dora 39–40
Pythagoras 23, 26

QAA (Quality Assurance Agency for Higher Education) 176

radio 15, 55, 69, 70, 105, 116, 124, 167
Rathbone, Dominic 144
Rawlinson, George 53
Rees, B.R. 43
Reid, George 19
Renault, Mary 84
Renshaw, James 76
Restoration, the 4, 5
Rhodes, Peter 96
Rich, Barnaby 5
Richards, Grant 13–14
Rieu, E.V. 52–53
'Robbins Report' 42
Rollin, Charles 13–14
Rooke, Alexandria 86, 145
Rowe, Kenneth R. 46

Saint, Jennifer 167
Salem, Saara 145
Sandys, George 11
Sappho 18, 91, 144
Schofield Malcolm 117
School Certificate 38
science 6, 18, 20, 23, 28, 33, 36, 44, 63, 72, 111

Scotland 11, 26, 34, 126–127, 134, 142, 168, 177, 178
Scott, Michael 131, 140
Scottish Qualifications Authority (SQA) 134
secondary modern schools 1, 38, 39–40, 81
secularism 21, 22–23, 27
Sélincourt, Aubrey de 53
Seneca 7
Settle, Elkanah 4
Sewell, Seb 133
sexuality 74, 90, 105, 106, 112, 148
Shakespeare, William 3, 93, 136, 137
Shaw, Frances 92
Shearer, Jennifer 134
Sidgwick, Arthur 21
Silk, Michael 103
Siwicki, Chris 122
Sixth Form Colleges 50, 51, 73, 78, 82, 84, 87, 91, 92, 97, 99, 106, 118, 143, 146, 150, 163, 175
slavery 24, 55, 62, 74, 101
Smith, Francis Kinchin 39
Smith, John Sharwood 41, 43, 46, 47, 49, **50**, 62, 64, 81
Socrates 11, 23, 48, 61, 122
Sonnenschein, William Swan 24–25
Sophocles 15, 18, 20, 21, 44, 83, 119, 137, 157, 165
source evaluation 87, 88
Spain 27
Sparrow, F.H. 63–64
Spooner, Adrian 85
Squire Sian 91, 93
Sri Lanka 27
Stafford Emma 110, 120
Stamper, Joseph 13
Stead, Henry 132, **133**, 145, 153
Stead, W.T. 13
Stevenson, Frances 35
Stewart, Peter 89
Stoicism 3, 18, 117
Stone, Vicky 119

Stray, Christopher 1, 33, **34**
Suetonius 3, 88
suffrage, women's 26
summer schools 93, 95, 143–145, 164, 169, 171
Swallow, Peter 111, 149, 151, 158
Sydenham, Floyer 5

Tacitus 4, 7, 15, 20, 35, 63, 83, 88
Taylor, Michael 146
Taylor, Thomas 5
television 15, 16, 52, 55, 69, 97, 101, 105, 163
Telford, Muriel 50
theatre Greek *see* drama ancient
Thirtle Robert 105
Thompson, William 46
Thoresby, Ralph 17
Thucydides 18, 20, 21, 48, 63
trainee teachers 129, 137, 177
translations 3, 4, 6–7, 9, 10, 11, 12, 15, 20, 21, 27, 34, 36, 48, 65, 114, 146–147
Trapp, Mike 145
Trevelyan, Charles 26
Trojan War 42, 48, 61, 96, 116, 140, 170
Turner, Helen 145
Turner, Susanne 142, 147

UCAS (Universities and Colleges Admissions Service) 95, 113
Uffenbach, Zacharias Conrad von 17
UNESCO 28
United States of America 26, 62, 100, 135
universities 41, 42, 43, 50, 53, 56, 72, 74, 112, 113, 158, 171, 176
Ann Arbor 100
Aston 137
Birmingham 25
Bristol 39, 95, 111, 121
Cambridge 40, 41, 49, 115, 117, 147, 166

Cardiff 43, 105
Chichester 105
Durham 96, 111, 117, 150–153, 156, 157, 174
Edinburgh 126, 134
Exeter 111, 122
Glasgow 111, 126
Goldsmiths University of London 112
Kent 111, 119–120
King's College London (KCL) 111
Lancaster 97
Leeds 45, 46, 111, 120
Leicester 177
Liverpool 150
London 20, 39, 45, 63, 117
New York 116
Newcastle 65
Nottingham 44, 67, 111
Open 83, 87, 93, 111, 114, 117, 132–133, 164, 166
Oxford 40, 67
Queen Mary University of London (QML) 114
Queen's University Belfast 111, 124
Reading 33, 111, 112, 128–129
Roehampton 111, 129
St Andrews 111, 133–134
Sheffield 35
Staffordshire 118
Sussex 82, 145
Swansea 111, 127
Sydney 62
University College London (UCL) 93
Warwick 102, 103, 104, 130–131, 139

vases 16, 24, 45, 91, 92, 144
Vergil 3, 9, 10, 13, 14, 15, 20, 96, 99, 104, 140, 165
virtual reality 131
Vitruvius 122

Wales 26, 34, 37, 43, 44, 46, 47, 52, 56, 101, 127, 178
Wallace-Hadrill, Andrew 129, **130**
Walmsley, Joan 70
Walsh, Hannah 121
Watts, Bella 112, **113**
Webster, Lucy 138
Webster, T.B.L. 42, 43
Westerley, Lucy 69
Whitworth, Penny 90, 92, 93
Wilkinson, Ross 152
Williams, Gemma 120, **139**, 140, 150
Williams, Paulette 135
Williams, William Emrys 53
Winnifrith, Tom 104
Women's Classical Committee (WCC) 135
Wood, Ella 128
Woolf, Greg 95, **118**
Workers' Educational Association 33, 37
Working Classicists 82, 99
World War I 26, 35, 54
Wright, Joseph 12, 16
Wright, Peter 73–74, 76, 97–99, 150, 175
Wyles, Rosie 76, 119

Xenophon 3, 20
Xerxes 75, 96, 117

Yeats, W.B. 102

The manufacturer's authorised representative in the EU for product safety is:
Easy Access System Europe, Mustamäe tee 50, 10621 Tallinn, Estonia
https://easproject.com (gpsr.requests@easproject.com)